The Voluntary Environmentalists

Can businesses voluntarily adopt progressive environmental policies? Most environmental regulations are based on the assumption that the pursuit of profit leads firms to pollute the environment, and therefore governments must impose mandatory regulations. However, new instruments such as voluntary programs are increasingly important. Drawing on the economic theory of club goods, this book offers a theoretical account of voluntary environmental programs by identifying the institutional features that influence conditions under which programs can be effective. By linking program efficacy to club design, it focuses attention on collective-action challenges faced by green clubs. Several analytic techniques are used to investigate the adoption and efficacy of ISO 14001, the most widely recognized voluntary environmental program in the world. These analyses show that, while the value of ISO 14001's brand reputation varies across policy and economic contexts, on average ISO 14001 members pollute less and comply better with governmental regulations.

ASEEM PRAKASH is an Associate Professor in the Department of Political Science, University of Washington, Seattle.

MATTHEW POTOSKI is an Associate Professor in the Department of Political Science, Iowa State University.

The Voluntary Environmentalists

Green Clubs, ISO 14001, and Voluntary Regulations

ASEEM PRAKASH

and

MATTHEW POTOSKI

CAMBRIDGE
UNIVERSITY PRESS

CAMBRIDGE UNIVERSITY PRESS
Cambridge, New York, Melbourne, Madrid, Cape Town, Singapore, São Paulo

Cambridge University Press
The Edinburgh Building, Cambridge CB2 2RU, UK

Published in the United States of America by Cambridge University Press, New York

www.cambridge.org
Information on this title: www.cambridge.org/9780521677721

© Aseem Prakash and Matthew Potoski 2006

First published 2006

Printed in the United Kingdom at the University Press, Cambridge

A catalogue record for this publication is available from the British Library

ISBN-13 978-0-521-86041-3 hardback
ISBN-10 0-521-86041-5 hardback
ISBN-13 978-0-521-67772-1 paperback
ISBN-10 0-521-67772-6 paperback

To Alexander and Nives – Aseem
To Ben and Alicia – Matt

Contents

Figures

Tables

Preface

This book examines how voluntary regulatory programs can mitigate collective-action problems. Drawing on club theory, we present a theoretical perspective to help scholars and policy-makers to think systematically about the challenges and opportunities of voluntary regulation. While the book focuses on voluntary environmental regulation, our approach is sufficiently general to be applicable to voluntary regulatory programs in other issue areas.

The assumption underlying most environmental regulation in the world today is that the pursuit of profit leads firms to pollute the environment. The standard prescription for mitigating pollution's harms has been for governments to enact regulations that *command* firms to meet specific pollution targets and *control* how firms do it, such as by prescribing specific pollution-control technologies for firms' production processes. While command and control regulations have had undeniable successes in reducing pollution, they have been criticized for being inefficient because they do not discriminate between costly and cheap pollution control. Budgetary pressures have curtailed governments' monitoring and enforcement programs and thereby undermined their efficacy. In light of such criticisms, several new policy instruments have been offered to complement command and control regulations. We firmly believe that the command and control system should continue to serve as the backbone of environmental governance. The challenge is to find new policy tools that can preserve its virtues and yet mitigate its negatives. One such tool, voluntary environmental programs, or "green clubs" as we term them, looks to improve firms' environmental performance by having firms voluntarily adopt an environmentally progressive code of conduct.

At first glance, voluntary programs may seem hopelessly naïve, if the assumption that profit maximization inevitably leads firms to externalize costs has any merit. While many voluntary programs are in operation around the world today, research provides no clear answer about the overall efficacy of these programs. Some studies suggest that one particular voluntary program improves participating firms' environmental behavior beyond what they would have done in the absence of the program, while studies of other programs have failed to find evidence of improved environmental performance among participants. We believe that the core theoretical challenge in voluntary program research is to identify what distinguishes the effective voluntary programs from the ineffective.

The book takes up the challenge of developing a theoretical account of voluntary environmental programs by identifying the core institutional features that distinguish effective programs from failures. Our theoretical framework draws on the economic theory of club goods (Buchanan, 1965; Cornes and Sandler, 1996). A club provides members with shared, group benefits from which non-members are excluded. Voluntary programs are like clubs in that they offer an excludable benefit that firms receive from their stakeholders because participation in the program signals that the firm is taking progressive environmental action. Because club membership creates benefits for firms by enhancing their standing with stakeholders, clubs can require member firms to incur the costs that stem from taking progressive environmental action. While command and control regulations seek to persuade firms to adopt such policies via the stick of mandatory enforcement, green clubs seek to do so via the carrot of enhancing firms' reputation through their membership in the club.

However, participating firms may have incentives to free-ride and enjoy the goodwill benefits of affiliating with the club's brand without paying the costs of adhering to its club requirements. That is, once they have joined the club, members may shirk their responsibilities and not perform according to the club's code of conduct. Effective clubs therefore need mechanisms to monitor and enforce their rules.

If voluntary programs function as clubs in the sense we described, two central questions emerge for studying these programs:

- Why do some firms join green clubs and not others? What enhances a club's brand reputation and how does this reputation induce firms to join the club?
- Does joining the club change participating firms' environmental and regulatory performances? After all, green clubs are useful tools to

the extent they can induce firms to reduce their harm to the environment and show better compliance with public law.

We empirically examine our theoretical ideas about voluntary programs by analyzing ISO 14001, the most widely recognized voluntary environmental program in the world today. Our analyses show that the value of ISO 14001's brand reputation, and therefore its attractiveness to firms, varies across the policy and economic contexts in which firms operate. Our analyses also indicate that, at least in the US, joining ISO 14001 reduces the amount of time member firms spend out of compliance with government regulations and reduces the amount of toxic pollutants they release into the atmosphere. In other words, ISO 14001 induces firms to pollute less and better comply with governmental regulations.

The book makes three key contributions:

- It outlines an accessible yet robust theoretical framework for studying voluntary programs. We present a new theory, firmly grounded in the rational behavior of firms and their stakeholders, which can help account for the different research findings on the efficacy of voluntary environmental programs. This is an important contribution because the study of voluntary programs, while still in its infancy, is growing rapidly in many disciplines, including management, public policy, economics, political science, law, and sociology. Indeed, while we focus on environmental programs, our theory is sufficiently generalizable to apply to many other policy areas in which voluntary programs have been emerging.

- This book employs sophisticated quantitative tools to examine fundamental questions about voluntary programs. We supplement our quantitative analyses with short case studies of ISO 14001 adoption in the US and UK, and evidence from interviews with government regulatory officials and industrial managers.

- Most social science disciplines have become increasingly divided between scholars studying "domestic" issues and those studying "international" issues. This is one of the few texts that bridge the domestic–international divide by examining both the international and domestic (US) dimensions of ISO 14001's diffusion and efficacy.

Acknowledgements

We began working on this project in August 2001. We initially worked on papers that helped us to think carefully about important issues in voluntary programs and focus our thoughts into a more coherent research program. In 2004, we embarked on a book project that would pull together our work, refine our theoretical approach to studying voluntary programs, and therefore present a theoretically compelling statement on voluntary program research.

This project has received valuable support, input, and feedback from several individuals. These include Werner Antweiler, Ken Bickers, Patrick Brandt, John Bolis, Trevor Brown, Chuck Corell, Michael Craft, Tom Eggert, Jeff Fiagle, Dan Fiorino, William Glasser, Reiner Grundmann, Jay Hamilton, Kathryn Harrison, Virginia Haufler, Ronnie Garcia-Johnson, Bob Kagan, Kelly Kollman, David Levy, Barbara Lither, Robert Lowry, Mark Lubell, Erik Lundsgaarde, Peter May, John Meyer, Mark McDermid, Frank Montabon, Tom Rice, David Ronald, Susan Roothan, Erika Sasser, Doug Smith, Mark Smith, Jeffrey Smoller, Theresa Squatrito, Abhishek Srivastava, Mark Stephan, Alex Tuckness, Michael Ward, and John Wilkerson. Parts of the book were presented at the annual conferences of the American Political Science Association, the Midwest Political Science Association, Association of Public Policy Analysis and Management, and the International Studies Association, and at seminars hosted by Iowa State University and Indiana University. We are grateful to Chris Harrison, the commissioning editor, for his support for this project. Sarah Edrington, Joseph Haley, Melissa Homrig, Dan Murray, and Jason Stonerook provided excellent research assistance.

This book draws on the following published papers:

1. Green Clubs and Voluntary Governance: ISO 14001 and Firms' Regulatory Compliance. *American Journal of Political Science*, 2005, 49(2): 235–248; with permission from Blackwell Publishing.

2. Covenant with Weak Swords: ISO 14001 and Firms' Environmental Performance. _Journal of Policy Analysis and Management_, 2005, 24(4); with permission from Wiley Interscience.
3. Regulatory Convergence in Non-Governmental Regimes? An Empirical Examination of Cross-National Adoption of ISO 14001. _Journal of Politics_, 2004, 66(3): 885–905; with permission from Blackwell Publishing.
4. The Regulation Dilemma: Cooperation and Conflict in Environmental Governance. _Public Administration Review_, 2004, 64(2): 137–148; with permission from Blackwell Publishing.
5. Policy Modes, Business, and the Natural Environment. _Business Strategy and the Environment_, 2004, 13(2): 107–128; with permission from Wiley Interscience.
6. EMS-Based Environmental Regimes as Club Goods: Examining Variations in Firm-level Adoption of ISO 14001 and EMAS in UK, US, and Germany. _Policy Sciences_, 2002, 35(1): 43–67; with permission from Springer.

Our respective universities provided generous financial support. Matthew Potoski received financial support from the Iowa State University Institute of Science and Society and the Iowa State University College of Liberal Arts and Sciences. Aseem Prakash received support from University of Washington's Royalty Research Fund.

Finally, we would like to acknowledge the support and encouragement from our wives and families. While they have tolerated our devotion to this project for several years, their support during summers of 2004 and 2005 was very helpful in seeing this project to completion. We dedicate this book to them.

1 | *Introduction*

THIS book studies collective action via non-governmental institutions to address environmental problems. Individually rational behavior can sometimes produce outcomes that are harmful to society as a whole. While people can seek to design institutions to structure collective action in more desirable ways, there is no guarantee that these institutions will always succeed in harmonizing individual goals with social outcomes. This challenge is particularly severe in the environmental policy area. Looking to increase profits, a firm may emit toxic pollutants into the atmosphere, causing harm to its neighbors. While the firm's profits may increase, from a broader perspective, the harm to the society caused by its emissions all too often outweighs the higher profits the firm enjoys. How can the firm be persuaded to take into account the costs it has imposed on others and reduce its pollution emissions? During the twentieth century, governments have sought to mitigate pollution's harms through command and control regulations that set standards for firms' environmental performance, prescribe pollution-control technologies firms must adopt, monitor whether firms are adhering to governmental prescriptions, and sanction those that do not. The assumption is that without detailed orders from the government, backed by coercive enforcement, firms are likely to sacrifice a cleaner environment for their own profits.

Many question whether such government regulation is a panacea for solving pollution problems (Coase, 1960; Ostrom, 1990). After all, governments themselves are sometimes apt to fail (Wolf, 1979), clearing the way for unscrupulous firms to pollute at the public's expense. There is no assurance that politicians or bureaucrats will craft the perfect law that serves a broader social good. And there is the question of whether governments have the resources to enforce complicated and detailed laws. For those who see government regulation as an imperfect solution to ameliorate environmental problems, voluntary programs are a way to encourage firms to serve broader public interests in ways that counter government regulation's weaknesses. By and large, voluntary programs are most often viewed as complements to public regulation, building on the foundation of government standards and laws, a perspective we adopt here. In some ways, voluntary regulatory programs have become a political desideratum of our times, a centrist, "Third Way" formula for achieving the goals of the left (promoting the general welfare by encouraging firms to produce public goods) through the means of the right (using mechanisms that harness private interests for public ends).

While voluntary regulatory systems for businesses and industry have existed for several centuries (Webb, 2004), over the last twenty years or so, governments, industry associations and even environmental groups have launched a wide array of voluntary environmental programs. By joining a voluntary environmental program, a firm pledges to take progressive environmental action beyond what its government regulations mandate. Such programs challenge the assumption that if left to their own devices, firms always choose higher pollution over more socially responsible environmental stewardship. But voluntary programs vary in their effectiveness; some have even been shown to be mere public relations exercises that do little to improve their members' environmental behavior. Recent accounting scandals pose serious questions about whether businesses can voluntarily regulate themselves.

In this book, we submit voluntary environmental programs to theoretical and empirical scrutiny. Our theoretical inquiry analyzes voluntary programs as clubs, in an economic sense of the term (Buchanan, 1965). A club provides members with a shared group benefit from which non-members are excluded. Effective voluntary programs, or "green clubs" as we refer to them, are like clubs in that they offer an excludable benefit to their members in the form of goodwill that firms receive from stakeholders because the firms have taken the progressive environmental action codified in the club's membership rules. In other words, in return for taking on the costs of joining the club and thereby producing public goods such as a cleaner environment, members enjoy the rewards of affiliating with the club's brand reputation. Firms decide whether or not to join the club based on their perceptions of the club's benefits and costs. Firms' perceptions are likely to be contingent on the economic and policy contexts in which they operate, as well as their firm-level character-istics. Once they join a program, firms also decide whether to adhere to club rules or shirk their membership responsibilities. This decision is likely to be influenced by whether the club has a monitoring and enforcement program in place.

To empirically test our theoretical ideas about voluntary programs, we examine ISO 14001, the most widely adopted voluntary environ-mental program in the world today. Although launched only in 1996, nearly 50,000 facilities in 118 countries have joined this green club. Our analyses focus on two questions:

- What factors shape firms' perceptions about ISO 14001's reputa-tional value, and therefore their decisions about joining the program?
- Do ISO 14001's members improve their environmental and regula-tory performance beyond what they would have achieved had they not joined the program?

To investigate these questions, we employ several techniques, in-cluding cross-national case studies, large-sample analyses of ISO 14001 adoption rates across countries, a large-sample facility-level study of US industrial facilities, and analytical interviews with US government regulators and facility environmental managers. Our re-sults show that the value of ISO 14001's reputation varies across policy and economic contexts (local, national, and international) and is an important factor in inducing firms to join the program. Our analyses also indicate that, at least in the US, joining ISO 14001 reduces the amount of time members spend out of compliance with government regulations and reduces the amount of toxic pollutants they release into the atmosphere. While this does not mean that every ISO 14001 certified facility improved its environmental and regula-tory performance, our analyses suggest that, on average, ISO 14001 improves the alignment of firms' private motives with societal benefits. Furthermore, the appeal of ISO 14001 (the reputational value of join-ing this club) is highest for firms that, have mid-range environmental and regulatory performance. Neither the environmental leaders nor the environmental laggards are as excited about joining ISO 14001 as mid-range firms, which typically constitute the largest proportion of a population. As a result, ISO 14001 is potentially a policy tool with a wide appeal rather than appealing only to a small niche.

These empirical inquiries, coupled with our theoretical analysis, suggest conditions under which voluntary programs can serve as effective policy tools. First, clubs must require behavior from their members that, at least in the eyes of members' stakeholders (such as their regulators, suppliers, and customers), leads to desirable environmental outcomes. Only then will stakeholders offer the goodwill benefits that serve as the reward members receive for joining a club. The size and scope of these rewards are likely to vary with the credibility of the sponsoring organization, the stringency of the requirements the club imposes on its members, the level of stakeholders' involvement in developing the club standards, and the firms' location in policy and economic contexts. Second, clubs need credible monitoring and enforcement mechanisms to ensure that members do not shirk and instead adhere to club standards after they join the program. These mechanisms might include third-party auditing, mandatory information disclosures of audit findings, and sanctioning of those who shirk. By mitigating shirking, effective monitoring and enforcement leads to improved environmental performance and strengthens the club's brand reputation among firms' stakeholders. In the next section of this chapter, we briefly survey the recent history of environmental governance, focusing mostly on the US. We then describe new tools of environmental governance and how green clubs are important components of the emerging environmental governance paradigm.

Can businesses be trusted? Regulating for environmental protection

Horror visited the US Steel company-town of Donora on Halloween night, 1948, when a temperature inversion descended on the town. Fumes from US Steel's smelting plants blanketed the town for four days, and crept murderously into the citizens' homes. If the smog had lasted another evening "the casualty list would have been 1,000 instead of 20," said local doctor William Rongaus at the time . . . The "Donora Death Fog," as it became known, spawned numerous angry lawsuits and the first calls for national legislation to protect the public from industrial air pollution.

A PHS report released in 1949 reported that "no single substance" was responsible for the Donora deaths and laid major blame for the tragedy on the temperature inversion. But according to industry consultant Philip

Sadtler, in an interview taped shortly before his 1996 death, that report was a whitewash. "It was murder," said Sadtler about Donora. "The directors of US Steel should have gone to jail for killing people." . . . For giant fluoride emitters such as US Steel and the Aluminum Company of America (Alcoa), the cost of a national fluoride clean-up "would certainly have been in the billions," said Sadtler. So concealing the true cause of the Donora accident was vital. "It would have complicated things enormously for them if the public had been alerted to [the dangers of] fluoride. (Bryson, 1998)

The "Donora Death Fog" became a rallying cry for members of the fledgling US environmental movement in the 1950s. In 1962, Rachel Carson (1962), a former marine biologist with the US Fish and Wild-life Service, published her book *Silent Spring*, further exposing the hazards of the pesticide DDT.[1] In the face of such drastic examples of corporate environmental malfeasance, strong government regulation seemed to be the only way to prevent businesses from causing large-scale environmental harm and human suffering. Public concern for the environment mounted through the 1960s, leading President Nixon in 1970 to sign the National Environmental Policy Act, establish the Environmental Protection Agency, and thereby lay the foundation for federal government's approach to environmental regulation that continues today. The wave of 1970s environmental laws that fol-lowed – the Clean Air Act,[2] the Clean Water Act and the Resources Conservation and Recovery Act – targeted the largest and most visible pollution problems, the "big fish" of industrial pollution. These laws codified the command and control regulatory approach: com-prehensive government regulations to govern firms' environmental practices and pollution releases, strict government-run monitoring programs to detect firms' violations, and sufficiently severe penalties

---

[1] Carlson's critics tried to smear the book and its author. An executive of the American Cyanamid Company noted: "if man were to faithfully follow the teachings of Miss Carson, we would return to the Dark Ages, and the insects and diseases and vermin would once again inherit the earth." Monsanto pub-lished and distributed a brochure parodying *Silent Spring*. This brochure, *The Desolate Year*, invoked the horrors of famine and disease because chemical pesticides had been banned (NRDC, 1997).

[2] Though the Clean Air Act was originally passed in 1963, the command and control thrust of a national air-pollution program emerged in 1970. This Clean Air Act underwent significant revisions, first in 1977 and then in 1990.

for non-compliance to compel firms' compliance with regulatory standards.[3] Underlying the command and control approach was the assumption that businesses would protect the environment only when laws compelled them to do so.

Command and control was a strong initial policy response to the big environmental problems of the 1970s. It successfully harvested the low-hanging fruit – the large, concentrated and visible pollution problems that were relatively easy to identify and ameliorate, if not clean up. Detailed regulations governing pollution-control technologies and emissions made explicit what businesses were required to do. Expansive state and federal monitoring and enforcement programs were established to ensure firms complied with all the new environmental standards. All in all, few would contest that command and control laws have dramatically reduced industrial pollution and improved the quality of the natural environment (Cole and Grossman, 1999). The environment is generally, although perhaps unevenly, cleaner, thanks in large part to command and control regulations. In the US, for example, states with stronger command and control regulatory regimes saw greater pollution reductions between 1973–1975 and 1985–1987 (Ringquist, 1993). Indeed, "Cleveland's Cuyahoga river, which once caught fire, now features cruise boats" (Kettl, 2002: vii).

Yet by the 1980s and 1990s, command and control regulation had started to come under critical scrutiny in the US and abroad. Businesses complained that the requirements of command and control, such as obtaining complex permits and maintaining paper-trails to document their environmental operations, created high compliance costs that hurt productivity and profits (Jaffe *et al.*, 1995; Walley and Whitehead, 1994). Because different agencies administer different permit programs, a large US facility might need 100 different government permits to comply with different federal and state regulatory statutes (Rabe, 2002). According to the US Office of Management and Budget (2002), complying with environmental regulations cost US

[3] Under the 1990 amendments to the Clean Air Act, the US Congress required the EPA to establish national ambient air-quality standards for specified hazardous pollutants. The states are required to develop state-level implementation plans and have them approved by the EPA. Facilities are subjected to some version of the best available technology requirement, depending on factors including whether they are in an "attainment area."

businesses $144 billion in 1997 (in 1996 dollars). By prescribing the technology firms must use to control pollution during production, command and control constrains firms' operational flexibility and thereby undermines efficiency, creating both static and dynamic ineffi-ciencies in terms of impeding industry innovation (Jaffe *et al.*, 1995; Kettl, 2002; Eisner, 2004).[4] Command and control also focuses atten-tion on end-of-pipe pollution reductions rather than on preventing pollution in the first place. In addition, some have argued that command and control regulations are particularly prone to policy "capture." Complex environmental regulations may become eligibility standards that protect incumbent firms from new competitors (Zywicki, 1999).[5] Finally, command and control's media-focused laws may encourage firms to substitute pollutants across media (GAO, 1994).

Command and control's limitations are also apparent to govern-ment regulators (Fiorino, 1999). Because command and control regulations are enforcement-intensive, declining agency budgets (espe-cially in the US) relative to regulatory mandates have undermined enforcement frequency and efficacy.[6] The EPA's enforcement staff fell 13 per cent from 2001 to 2002 and was projected to fall an additional

[4] Porter and Van der Linde (1995) suggest that stringent but properly designed command and control policies can create incentives for firms to innovate. Because firms are often unaware of profitable opportunities flowing from pro-gressive environmental policies, the authors believe that stringent command and control regulations can focus firms' attention on such opportunities. For a critique, see Rugman and Verbeke (1998).

[5] Some command and control laws have led to litigation and created "rents" for lawyers. An often-mentioned example is the Superfund created under the Com-prehensive Environmental Response, Compensation, and Liability Act of 1980. Some estimate that almost one-third of the Superfund expenditures incurred by companies are towards litigation and legal fees, and the EPA has incurred similar levels of legal costs (Sablatura, 1995).

[6] In accordance with deterrence-based regulation (Becker, 1968; Stigler, 1970), Regen *et al.* (1997) report that the EPA's enforcement budget critically influences the manufacturing industry's expenditures on pollution-control equipment. If declining enforcement budgets dilute the efficacy of the command and control approach, why would Congress make complex laws but undermine them by not providing enforcement budgets? Plausibly, enacting stringent laws allows politi-cians to claim that they are tough on polluters, while the political return on enforcement budgets (which compete with their other spending priorities) may be limited. Partisan control of Congress may influence enforcement budgets as well: slashing the EPA's budget has been an important item on the Republican agenda. In the glory days of the "Contract with America," (then) Majority Whip Tom DeLay (R-TX) noted that:

6 per cent in 2003 (Baltimore, 2002).[7] Even three decades after the enactment of the Clean Water Act, regulators have been able to assess water quality for only 4 per cent of the ocean shorelines and 23 per cent of river miles (Metzenbaum, 2002). Between 1996 and 1998, less than 1 per cent of the 122,226 large regulated facilities in the US were inspected for air, water and hazardous waste pollution (Hale, 1998).[8]

Finally, command and control has been criticized for contributing to the costly adversarial regulatory culture among business, regulators, and citizens (Vogel, 1986; Kagan, 1991; Kollman and Prakash, 2001). Command and control pits regulators and firms in a contentious stance, resulting in more lawsuits and larger societal costs (Reilly, 1999; but see Coglianese, 1996).[9] Rigidly enforcing regulations and "going by the book" (Bardach and Kagan, 1982) increases firms' compliance costs, and creates incentives for firms to evade regulations. In a vicious cycle, regulators may respond with more monitoring, stricter enforcement, and harsher penalties.[10] More promising is an enforcement approach where firms voluntarily improve their environmental performance and governments redirect enforcement resources

---

> The critical promise we made to the American people was to get the government off their backs, *and the EPA, the gestapo of government,* pure and simple has been one of the major "clawhose" that the government has maintained on the backs of our constituents.   (Michels, 1995; italics not in the original)

[7] For most command and control environmental regulations in the US, the federal government delegates enforcement and even some policy standard responsibility to state governments. If states do not meet the minimum federal standards, the EPA can preempt the state policy and conduct enforcement or issue standards itself. State environmental protection agencies conduct the bulk of the monitoring and enforcement activities (Brown, 2001), although the EPA conducts some as well. While some states have developed regulatory standards more stringent than those that the federal standards require (Potoski, 2001) and preemption is uncommon, competition among states coupled with the threat of preemption constrains the degree of variation among states' environmental programs.

[8] In Teubner's (1983) conception of reflexive law, this represents the crisis of the "interventist state" while green clubs are a manifestations of reflexive law.

[9] Citizen lawsuits are explicitly permitted under some statutes, for example, Section 304 of the Clean Air Act. Fearing the capture of the environmental bureaucracy by the industry, Congress created the provision of "private attorney generals" where citizens can sue the government to enforce the law and recoup some of the legal costs.

[10] This point is developed in chapter 2. We term it the "regulation dilemma," and examine how green clubs may help in overcoming it.

to more valuable tasks (Majumdar and Marcus, 2001). Some even blame command and control laws (though incorrectly in all likelihood) for the job losses in the manufacturing sector in the 1980s and the 1990s (Palmer *et al.*, 1995; for a recent review of the trade–environment debate, see Frankel, 2003).

With command and control having focused on the large, concentrated and stationary pollution sources (Gunningham and Sinclair, 2002), the next generation of environmental problem centers on the dispersed and often invisible sources that add up to large problems (Fiorino, 1999). Such problems exacerbate command and control's weaknesses: writing regulations finely nuanced for pollution problems that are highly variable, technical and diffuse is quite burdensome and monitoring and inspecting these dispersed sources is yet more expensive and onerous. Command and control regulations *alone* may be ill-equipped to take the steps to address the next generation of environmental challenges.

On a more general level the diminishing returns to command and control regulations are indicative of "government failures" (Wolf, 1979). Solving environmental problems would be simpler if government officials had perfect information, there were no "agency conflicts" (Berle and Means, 1932), and there were no transaction costs associated with developing, monitoring, and enforcing policy decisions. Unfortunately, real-world policy complexities and uncertainties in social interaction exceed the government's ability to perfectly predict future events, specify policies for all circumstances, and devise low-cost mechanisms to ensure that the policy outcomes match specified objectives. Like any organization, governments and policymakers are "boundedly rational" (Simon, 1957; Jones, 2001) and constrained by limited resources such as time, information, expertise, and finances. Governments, especially in developing countries, often lack information and expertise to correctly design policies. Monitoring and enforcement is expensive and more complex regulations carry higher monitoring and enforcement costs. Governments can be "captured" by the very industries they were designed to regulate (Stigler, 1971) and bureaucratic infighting might impede policy development (Allison, 1971).

By highlighting the governmental failures that can plague command and control regulation we are not advocating dismantling government and rolling back command and control regulations. Our intention is to show that every policy approach has vulnerabilities, including voluntary regulations. Both scholars and analysts should be aware of the costs and benefits of different policy approaches and look for ways to balance one's weaknesses against others' strengths. Like command and control, voluntary governance approaches are neither a curse nor a panacea. Our approach is to view command and control as a baseline and think of new approaches that would complement command and control in ways that enhance its positives and ameliorate its deficiencies.

New tools for environmental governance

While command and control regulation is more effective than no regulation,[11] its high costs and limitations suggest the opportunity for a new breed of regulatory tools.[12] Through the 1980s and 1990s, environmental scholars, analysts and regulators began to propose several new approaches to addressing environmental problems. These approaches promise to safeguard better the natural environment by complementing command and control and addressing its weaknesses. The assumption underlying these tools is that, contrary to the command and control's assumed hostility, businesses, governments and perhaps moderate environmental groups can work cooperatively to improve environmental conditions. Some commentators (somewhat skeptically) term this policy shift as "weak ecological modernization" (Hajer, 1995; Mol and Sonnenfeld, 2000) where economic growth and environmental sustainability are viewed as mutually supportive. Thus, a central theme underlying the new environmental governance tools is

---

[11] Arguably, a complete absence of federal regulations may spur firms and citizens to use courts to settle environmental disputes. For example, in common-law countries, a tort-based approach to environmental governance may provide an alternative to federal regulation-based environmental governance system. Because in contemporary times such examples cannot be found, it is difficult to comment on the relative efficacy of a tort-based approach in relation to command and control.

[12] Fiorino (2001) highlights the need to foster "social learning" in the environmental governance system. Although existing and future environmental challenges require regulatory institutions to adopt a "social learning" approach (of which flexible regulation is an important element), their policies and their regulatory cultures remain rooted in the "technical learning" (command and control regulation) mode. On reflexive law, see Teubner (1983).

a shift from *exclusive reliance* on centralized rule design, technology specification, and strict enforcement of complex laws, to finding incentives to induce firms voluntarily to undertake environmentally progressive action – such as superior compliance with government regulations and perhaps even to take actions beyond the regulations' requirements. Where governmental failures such as monitoring problems, information asymmetries, and agency conflict undermine command and control regulation, the new policy tools look to reduce governments' burdens and mitigate government failures by channeling firms' interests in higher profits and greater legitimacy towards broader public goals for a cleaner environment. Among the various new policy experiments in practice today, three innovations stand out: market-based permits, mandatory information disclosures, and voluntary programs.[13]

Below we briefly discuss each of these three new environmental policy tools. As the "reinventing government" (Osborne and Gaebler, 1992) controversies remind us, new need not be better and may even be worse. The new environmental policy tools have fueled important debates about whether firms can be motivated to safeguard the environment without the compelling stick of command and control regulations, about whether the policy tools can achieve results beyond what would happen in their absence, and about what conditions are necessary for them to be effective.

Market-based policies

A market is a system of rules, norms and practices that allow for the voluntary exchange of goods and services among actors. Markets can be effective means for harmonizing individual action with broader societal objectives (Tietenberg, 1974; Anderson and Leal, 1991), dynamics that Adam Smith (1776) described so clearly:

Every individual necessarily labours to render the annual revenue of the society as great as he can. He generally, indeed, neither intends to promote the publick interest, nor knows how much he is promoting it . . .

---

[13] Private agreements via direct bargaining between the polluters and the pollutees are another innovative policy mode (Borkey *et al.*, 1998). But for Japan, this instrument has not been widely used by policy-makers, and therefore is not discussed here.

He intends only his own gain, and he is in this, as in many other cases, led by an invisible hand to promote an end which was no part of his intention.

Well-functioning markets require some fairly strict conditions. Markets need large numbers of buyers and sellers,[14] participants need to be well informed about products and each other's preferences, and actors must be able to enter and exit the market and exchange resources at low costs. Markets can fail when these conditions do not hold, leading to conditions where private incentives are not in sync with the collective good. For many scholars and policy analysts, correcting market failures is the fundamental rationale for government intervention in human interactions (Pigou, 1960).

Market failures imply that the invisible hand does not compel firms to internalize the external costs of their actions. Externalities are the negative or positive effects of actions experienced by those not involved in a market transaction. Externalities mean that the social costs and benefits of a transaction differ from its private costs and benefits. Pollution is a negative externality because its social cost, the harm people experience from pollution, is not reflected in the private costs of those producing products that lead to the pollution. Because firms typically respond to private costs in making their environmental choices, they underestimate the total costs of their activities to society at large. As a result, firms tend to overproduce "social bads," Externalities constitute the reason why policy-makers employ command and control regulations to compel firms to take into account *all* the costs of their action, some of which they would otherwise have externalized.[15]

One alternative (and sometimes complementary) strategy to command and control is for governments to establish new rule systems

---

[14] Research suggests that contested markets with a limited number of participants but fierce levels of competition can achieve welfare outcomes comparable to a perfectly competitive model with unlimited buyers and sellers (Coursey et al., 1984).

[15] Some attribute externalities to incomplete delineation of property rights (Anderson and Leal, 2001). If the government were to specify property rights, there would be no externalities. Alternatively, pollution emitters and pollution victims could bargain and arrive at optimum pollution levels (Coase, 1960). Thus, externalities do not automatically require government intervention.

to facilitate mutually beneficial market exchanges that internalize pollution externalities by harnessing firms' profit motives. In the area of environmental policy, examples of market-based policies include pollution taxes, emission fees, and tradable emissions permits (OECD, 1989). In these "market" approaches, governments create property rights that grant firms legal authority to emit specified quantities of pollution, thereby putting economic value to every unit of pollution. For example, firms may pay a discharge fee for every unit of pollution they emit or discharge. Firms can then compare their marginal costs of pollution abatement (reflected in the fee amount) against the marginal costs of pollution emission, and then decide their optimal pollution levels. To reduce aggregate pollution emissions, governments can hike up the pollution tax or the emission fee. In tradable permits, governments allocate specified quantities of pollutants to firms, and establish a market in which firms can buy and sell their pollution rights. If a firm believes that its marginal costs of pollution abatement for a unit of pollution are less than the market price, it can sell a unit of the right to pollute to another firm for whom abating pollution emissions is more costly. Thus, price signals and firms' individual cost structures replace legal and administrative fiats as inducements for firms to reduce pollution. To reduce overall pollution levels, governments can lower the aggregate amount of pollution rights granted to firms, perhaps even by buying back pollution permits from the market. Of course, market-based approaches do not obviate the need for some monitoring and enforcement since firms may still have incentives to emit more pollution than their permit allows.

Like any policy approach, market-based approaches have drawbacks. Markets require a well-functioning property rights system so that excessive resources are not expended in monitoring, enforcement, and litigation. The implicit norms that often constitute the foundations of efficient markets tend to require time to evolve. As complex social institutions (North, 1990), governments often cannot establish markets in a single coup. Developing property rights that unitize environmental resources, transforming them from open access resources to tradable commodities, can be very difficult and is an inherently political enterprise (Dolsak and Ostrom, 2002). Establishing markets creates "winners" and "losers" often without a clear mechanism for compensating the losers, creating important distributional consequences that raise a range of important ethical questions.[16] Efficient solutions may not be equitable. Markets may create incentives for firms to relocate to less expensive jurisdictions which are often inhabited by disadvantaged groups. Another ethical issue is that markets may destigmatize and perhaps even legitimize pollution (Bullard, 1990).

Empirical evidence suggests market-based approaches have had varying success: while tradable permits for air-pollution control have been thriving in the US (such as the sulfur-dioxide emission markets established under the Clean Air Act), market-based instruments have failed in Poland, Germany, and the United Kingdom (Tietenberg, 2002). Recent experience with US energy deregulation suggests that establishing and running market-based instruments can be tragically vulnerable to manipulation.

Mandatory information-based approaches

Firms may be more inclined to take environmentally progressive action if their key stakeholders who want to clean the environment know of the good they are doing. Without such information, stakeholders cannot differentiate between environmentally progressive firms and laggards and therefore cannot reward or punish them accordingly, even if the stakeholders are strongly inclined to do so. Mandatory information-based policies do not specify the production technologies or emission levels that firms must achieve (as in command and control policies). Nor do they put cost on units of pollution generated by firms (as in market-based instruments). Rather, they seek to lower stakeholders' transaction costs for influencing firms' environmental behavior by requiring firms systematically to disclose information about their environmental operations, programs, and behavior. Armed with this information, stakeholders can influence firms to improve performance by discriminating among which products to buy, which firms to pressure, and so on (Hamilton, 1995;

---

[16] While this book does not examine distributional issues, we recognize that Coase (1960) notes the presence of multiple efficient equilibriums that correspond to different initial allocation of property rights. Thus, it is difficult to defend on efficiency grounds why a certain property right allocation is superior to another. But governments have to decide on one – and this is an inherently political task.

Arora and Cason, 1996; Khanna and Damon, 1999).[17] As Justice Brandeis (1914)[18] so clearly noted, law alone does not solve social problems, "Publicity is justly commended as a remedy for social and industrial diseases. Sunlight is said to be the best of disinfectants."[19]

Examples of mandatory information-disclosure programs in environmental policy include emission registers and product labels that codify product information. In 1990, the European Union mandated (via Directive 313, *Freedom to Access Information on the Environment*) that its member countries enact legislation that would provide public information on environmental issues.[20] In 2000, the European

---

[17] A recent survey of 140 US firms representing $2.5 trillion in combined revenues suggests that 75 per cent of these firms have adopted some sustainable business activities. Importantly, 90 per cent of them attribute "enhanced reputation" as the reason for adopting such practices (PricewaterhouseCoopers, 2002).

[18] Justice Brandeis was arguing in the context of banking monopolies. His book, *Other People's Money*, is a compilation of articles he wrote in the *Harper's Weekly*. These articles supported the New Freedom campaign of President Woodrow Wilson which provided a manifesto for the Progressive movement.

[19] Sand (2002) points out that industrialized countries differ regarding mandatory disclosure of information reported to the government. While Britain, France, and Germany have had a tradition of maintaining secrecy, Scandinavian countries and the US do not. As early as 1776, Swedish citizens had the right to access public data. Starting with the federal Administrative Procedures Act of 1944 and California's "Brown Act" in 1952, the US has also been in the forefront of empowering its citizens by providing public access to information reported to the governments. Thus, policies that mandate public disclosures of environmental information should be viewed as a continuation of a broader quest for an open society.

[20] The directive notes that:

> Disparities between the laws in force in the Member States concerning access to environmental information held by public authorities can create inequality within the Community as regards access to information and/or as regards conditions of competition. "Information relating to the environment" means any available information in written, visual, aural or database form on the state of water, air, soil, fauna, flora, land and natural sites, and on activities or measures adversely affecting or likely so to affect these, and on activities or measures designed to protect these (including administrative measures and environmental management programmes). Public authorities are required to make available information relating to the environment to any natural or legal person at his request and without his having to prove an interest. The Member States must define the practical arrangements under which such information is effectively made available. Requests for information must be answered as soon as possible, and at the latest within two months. (Europa, 2003)

Union, under the aegis of the European Environment Agency, established the European Pollution Emission Register which provides "access to information on the annual emissions of 9387 industrial facilities in the 15 Member States of the EU as well as Norway and Hungary – mostly from the year 2001" (EPER, 2003). The register allows for grouping information by pollutant, activity, medium, and country. In 1992, Canada established the National Pollutant Release Inventory that provides details of industrial facilities' emissions, releases and transfers of many pollutant chemicals (Environment Canada, 2003; Antweiler and Harrison, 2003). In the US, the Toxics Release Inventory Program (TRI) was established in 1987 under Section 313 of the Emergency Planning and Community Right to Know Act. The TRI covers facilities that have ten or more full-time employees, are included in Standard Industrial Classification codes 20 through 39, and manufacture or process more than 25,000 or 10,000 pounds respectively of specific chemicals during the calendar year.[21] The creation of the TRI has had important policy consequences. Hamilton (1995) reports that firms with higher levels of pollution emissions were more likely to receive negative coverage in the print media soon after the TRI data were first released. Financial markets responded to the negative information: firms receiving negative press coverage of their environmental performance lost about $4.1 million in valuations on the day TRI figures were released.[22]

Mandatory information disclosures may not work well if the relevant information is difficult to collect, disseminate, interpret, and apply. A key reason for the popularity of the TRI Program is that its information can be easily accessed over the Internet. Effective mandatory disclosure policies may also require well-functioning stock markets, free press, high literacy levels, and a well-organized civil society that enable stakeholders to use the information to translate

---

[21] In 1986, California enacted the Safe Drinking Water and Toxic Enforcement Act (Proposition 65) that required mandatory disclosures regarding specified toxic chemicals in drinking water (Sand, 2002).

[22] In some ways, TRI information has a shock value. One would expect that the largest declines in stock prices will take place not for the largest polluters but for firms whose pollution levels were not well known. Khanna *et al.* (1998) examine this in the context of the US chemical industry and find that repeated provision of the TRI information caused investors to focus on the changes in pollution levels and negative stock-market returns for even known polluters.

their preferences into pressures on firms. Because information is not knowledge, the average citizen may not have the expertise or resources to understand complex information. They often rely on "experts" and interest groups to do so. Mandatory disclosure policies may empower actors whose private objectives may not necessarily align with societal goals.[23] Further, "experts" often seek to differentiate themselves by providing their own spin on the information. Debates often become politicized and the ensuing epistemic confusion could distract from the policy objective of protecting the environment.

Voluntary environmental programs: green clubs

A third category of environmental policy instruments, voluntary environmental programs, or green clubs as we call them, are codified programs and practices that firms pledge to adopt and follow. Reading through the academic environmental policy literature one comes across different theoretical approaches to studying voluntary programs. Among these approaches are non-state market-driven systems (Cashore *et al.*, 2004), certification codes (Gereffi *et al.*, 2001), private authority regimes (Cutler *et al.*, 1999; Hall and Biersteker, 2002), and voluntary programs (Haufler, 2001). While these approaches provide valuable insights for voluntary governance, our club theory approach offers three distinctive features. First, we are most interested in identifying effective programs and linking them to institutional design features. Our approach is to focus on the institutional bases of collective action dilemmas that can potentially undermine program efficacy. Second, our conceptualization is broad enough to apply to a broad variety of voluntary programs, allowing us, for example, to compare government-sponsored programs with those sponsored by non-governmental actors. Third, we seek to explain the attractiveness of a voluntary club to firms in terms of goodwill members may receive from stakeholders in their market and non-market environments. Thus, in our approach, depending on the specific context in which the club operates, regulators, NGOs, customers,

---

[23] Product labels have had varying levels of success as tools for marketing "green products." The reasons are manifold including collective action dilemma at the consumer level where consumers want environmental benefits of green products but do not want to pay for them (Prakash, 2002).

insurers, or creditors may have different assessments of how to reward (or ignore) firms' participation in a voluntary program.

Green clubs may specify standards for participating firms' environmental management systems, procedures for reducing their pollution emissions, programs for their recycling and resource usage programs, and so on. By adhering to the club rules, members provide a broader public good, such as a cleaner environment or better compliance with environmental regulations, beyond what they would otherwise have unilaterally produced.[24] Clubs provide stakeholders with a low-cost tool to differentiate environmentally progressive firms from laggards so that they can shower goodwill on the leaders, and heap scorn and punishment on the laggards.

Those advocating green clubs view them as improving participants' performance, and therefore creating a win-all scenario. Regulators win because the environment is cleaner and their enforcement burdens are lower, or at least they can concentrate resources more efficiently on monitoring non-club members. Consumers and other stakeholders win because they can better identify environmentally friendly firms and more accurately target their purchases, investments, or protests. Citizens win because they enjoy a cleaner environment without additional taxes. And firms win by enjoying more goodwill from their stakeholders.

Green club supporters also claim that clubs can reverse regulatory inflation in terms of the increased scope, number, and complexity of regulations. We alluded earlier to the institutional and capacity constraints faced by governments in designing market-based and mandatory information-based policies. Arguably, green clubs may face fewer such problems because they can be established and implemented by non-governmental actors that may not face similar budget constraints. Market-based permits may allow for efficient allocations of quotas. But governments still need to monitor to ensure that firms are not exceeding their quotas. In voluntary clubs, club sponsors can delegate this task to private agents. If effective enforcement is the key to improved members' environmental performance, and therefore to

---

[24] But participating firms may not provide public goods at the optimal level, especially compared to the situation when the provision level is stipulated by command and control regulations. On welfare implications of voluntary regulatory approaches, see Lyon and Maxwell (2004).

the club's reputation, club sponsors may have incentives to devise credible monitoring and enforcement mechanisms.[25]

In the public policy lexicon, a voluntary program's "brand image" is a club good, in an economic sense of the term. Clubs are institutions whose benefits are non-rival but excludable (Buchanan, 1965).[26] Viewed this way, club goods are jointly usable by club members while non-members can be prevented from enjoying clubs' benefits, usually through a set of exclusionary membership rules. For voluntary environmental programs, the club's excludable benefit is the positive image, goodwill, legitimacy, and reputation for environmental stewardship that comes from association with the voluntary program. To employ Gunningham *et al.*'s (2003) terminology, green clubs can bestow on participating firms a "social license" to operate. Each club member contributes to the club's reputation by adhering to the club standards (the rules and programs regarding members' environmental practices) and by publicizing the club's brand image through their deeds. The marginal cost of producing the club benefit declines with each new member because increased membership spreads the club's brand name more broadly. Such "network effects" increase the club's visibility and perhaps its value to new members. As we demonstrate in chapter 4,

---

[25] Are, then, voluntary programs tools for "weak governments" that want to but cannot develop and implement stringent regulations? Arguably, voluntary programs can mitigate institutional and resource constraints that governments face. Would we then expect to find voluntary programs proliferating in developing countries as opposed to developed countries? Though it is difficult to generalize, it may be that regulatory innovations, of which voluntary programs are an important component, are undertaken more aggressively in developed countries than in developing countries. Thus, the ability and incentives for "weak governments" to supply such innovations is questionable. Voluntary programs also need to be demanded by citizens and other stakeholders and such demands are likely to be higher in developed countries. As an empirical fact, most of the ISO 14001 participants are in developed countries (with strong governments and stringent environmental regulation). As we demonstrate in chapter 4, firms in developing countries also have incentives to join this program, if their trading partners (typically in developed countries) support this green club.

[26] By focusing on incentives as drivers of firm behavior, our approach to voluntary regulation adopts the tools of rational-choice institutionalism. Much of the "environmental management" literature also employs an institutional approach that is grounded in organization theory and sociological institutionalism (Keohane, 1989; Ostrom, 1991). Unlike our focus on incentives, sociological approaches do not view the rational calculus of costs and benefits as driving firm behavior; rather, they posit that firms join green clubs primarily for cognitive and normative reasons (Hoffman 1997; Hoffman and Ventresca, 2002).

past levels of ISO 14001 adoption serve as a positive inducement for new firms to join the club.[27]

It is important to emphasize that what matters for our theoretical analysis is not so much whether the club benefit is "material" or "psychological" but rather that these benefits are "excludable" in the sense that non-club members can be prevented from enjoying them. Well-established public policy and political economy literatures examine clubs that create non-tangible benefits. Scholars use the club concept to examine issues pertaining to national security, military alliances, democracy, and financial standards, to name a few (Cornes and Sandler, 1996). Whether clubs are more often physical or psychological is not central to our argument. As long as excludability can be enforced, whether by building fences or by establishing a branding mechanism that allows stakeholders to differentiate members from non-members (as the consumer marketing literature demonstrates), one can create a club good.

Some firms have successfully built their own company or product-brand images for environmental stewardship; for example, few would question the ice-cream company Ben and Jerry's progressive environmental credentials. For a firm working alone, building such a green reputation generally requires substantial upfront investment.[28] A larger group of firms coming together in a club can capture scale economies to build a progressive environmental reputation at a lower cost. The positive reputation one member creates constitutes a positive externality that spills over to other club members, as members share advertising and promotion costs. Importantly, being part of a larger brand system, an effect akin to a network effect (Farrell and Shapiro, 1985), can provide the brand with a degree of legitimacy that one firm alone may find difficult to acquire.

---

[27] There could be diminishing returns to membership expansion; at some point, membership growth could reach its limits and crowding offsets the advantages of new members. In such scenarios, a club with universal membership would do little to distinguish members from non-members. To date, no (universal) green club has achieved a membership level sufficient for diminishing returns to set in – certainly not ISO 14001. Virtually, every club we know of seeks to expand its membership base. We discuss this issue in chapter 2.

[28] As we demonstrate in chapter 4, firms having products with well-developed (commercial) brand names are less likely to seek another (environmental) brand name by joining a green club.

Like markets and governments, clubs are also vulnerable to institutional failures. Two categories of club failures are theoretically salient and the focus here. The first, what we call the *Olsonian dilemma*, occurs when clubs are unable to attract many members. Whatever their other virtues, clubs with few members can hardly be considered successful. Low membership risks a vicious cycle because without a critical membership mass, efficient production of reputational value and goodwill benefits becomes more difficult, making the club less attractive to new members. Effective clubs must therefore develop strategies to attract a sufficient number of members. Clubs can solve this problem by offering potential members the chance to affiliate with a substantial and valuable club reputation for environmental stewardship.[29]

The second club failure pertains to *shirking*. Shirking means that some firms formally adopt the program's environmental standards, but do not actually implement and practice them, while nevertheless continuing to claim to be environmentally progressive by virtue of their club membership. The benefit of club membership continues to accrue to all members, including shirkers. As the word spreads about large-scale shirking, a program's reputation diminishes. Shirkers impose negative externalities on other members by tarnishing the club's reputation. In the language of clubs, shirking is akin to enjoying the reputational value of program participation without paying the costs of producing that reputation.

Shirking stems from information asymmetries among firms, their stakeholders, and club sponsors. Some green clubs do not require members to provide sponsors or stakeholders access to adequate and unvarnished information about their environmental operations or adherence to club standards. Clubs may not be effective without mechanisms for monitoring and enforcing members' adherence to club standards. Stakeholders rely on the club sponsors to enforce club

---

[29] Much of the club literature examines membership size from the perspective of optimal club size (Cornes and Sandler, 1996). We are not aware of any voluntary environmental program that has overcrowding issues. For the club studied here – ISO 14001 – membership levels are small in relation to total number of facilities. To illustrate, in the US, only 2,620 facilities joined ISO 14001 by 2002, eight years after its launch (ISO, 2003), whereas over 30,000 industrial facilities are listed in the EPA's TRI program, arguably a key target audience for ISO 14001.

standards but, unlike public regulation (such as command and control regulations and mandatory disclosure policies) where stakeholders have more access to observing the rule-making, monitoring and enforcement, clubs often operate behind closed doors. This exacerbates stakeholders' difficulties in learning about the club and how well its members adhere to club standards. The lack of public scrutiny has led several environmentalists to call into question green clubs' accountability. Indeed, many environmental groups believe that lax enforcement will cause rampant shirking and transform even well-intentioned green clubs into greenwashes. More broadly, environmental groups question whether firms have incentives to credibly self-govern. The recent Enron meltdown, problems at the New York Stock Exchange and the resistance of the accounting/consulting industry to meaningful reforms provide little confidence about firms' trustworthiness. More broadly, in academic circles some have questioned the efficacy of audits as instruments for social control (Power, 1994, 1997; Ball *et al.*, 2000).

Effective clubs combat shirking which may stem either from adverse selection in which environmental laggards join the club or from moral hazard in which firms become laggards under the guise of club membership. The remedy for adverse selection is stringent club standards that require firms to take effective progressive environmental action in order to become members. The remedy for moral hazard is for the club to establish credible monitoring and enforcement mechanisms to ensure members are living up to their club obligations.

To combat shirking, clubs can develop credible monitoring and enforcement systems to ensure that members comply with club rules. After all, at least some club sponsors can be expected to want their clubs to succeed. Oversight or certification processes can be first-party (self-certification), second-party (certified from a manager from a different unit of the same company or a different firm within the same industry), third-party (certification by an external auditor but paid for by the company), and fourth-party (certification by an external auditor who is not paid for by the company) (Gereffi *et al.*, 2001). First-party is the least credible while fourth-party is the most credible because the auditor is more independent and institutionalized. In reality, very few clubs have fourth-party oversight; third-party is generally considered to be the "best practice" today. This is based on the assumption that external auditors will provide an accurate picture of firms' environmental practices. Although third-party auditing has several merits, it may not be perfect because the firm hires the auditor, which can give auditors incentives to provide favorable reviews.[30]

In sum, this discussion has highlighted some of the strengths and weaknesses of several environmental governance approaches.[31] Each approach has its strengths, though none is a panacea. In the remainder of the book, we focus on voluntary programs, specifically ISO 14001. We examine why firms have joined this club and whether it has improved firms' environmental and regulatory performance. We view voluntary programs such as ISO 14001 as complements to command and control that create incentives for firms to comply better with government regulations and even go beyond what the regulations require. Command and control has served a useful historic purpose and will continue to be the main pillar of environmental governance. However, it has shortfalls and the policy challenge is to devise new instruments that overcome such shortfalls without dismantling the system. We examine conditions under which voluntary programs can serve as such useful policy instruments.

Our theoretical analysis of green clubs, presented in chapter 2, suggests that to be effective, clubs must overcome two collective action problems. First, they must attract members to join the club and pay the costs of meeting the club's conduct standards. In other

---

[30] Clubs have varying strategies to combat the Olsonian and the Shirking collective action dilemmas, as we will discuss throughout. For example, industry-level clubs, such as the chemical industry's Responsible Care program or the forestry industry's Sustainable Forestry Initiative, have mitigated the Olsonian dilemma by bundling club membership with association membership. That is, the industry association requires member firms to adhere to the principles of Responsible Care/Sustainable Forestry Initiative if they wish to retain membership of the industry association (the American Chemistry Council in the case of the chemical industry and the American Forest and Paper Association in the case of the forestry industry). Because of this bundling strategy, firms sign on to the club when they join the industry association. For such clubs, the crucial challenge is the mitigation of shirking. While there could be a situation where firms refuse to join an industry or trade association because of tough requirements imposed by the green club that comes along with it, we are not aware of any such case.

[31] Systems of environmental governance typically employ a multitude of policy instruments. This raises the issue of instrument mix: how do different combinations of instruments fare in varying policy contexts? While our empirical analyses in chapters 4 and 5 that examine ISO 14001's efficacy control for the policy and institutional contexts in which firms operate, a systematic study of the issue of instrument mix is beyond the purview of this book.

words, a club must solve the Olsonian dilemma. Second, a club must prevent its members from shirking their club responsibilities after they have joined. To investigate how green clubs address these dilemmas, we categorize programs along two institutional dimensions. *Club standards* define the actions that members must undertake to join the club. *Enforcement rules* are the monitoring and enforcement mechanisms that look to ensure members continue to adhere to club standards once they have joined the club. We examine how variations in these rules influence green clubs' success in mitigating the two collective action dilemmas.

Based on the two key institutional attributes, we introduce a typology of green clubs in chapter 2. We identify four ideal club types: stringent club standards with enforcement rules (Type 1: Mandarins), stringent club standards without enforcement rules (Type 2: Country Clubs), lenient club standards with enforcement rules (Type 3: Bootcamps), and lenient club standards without credible enforcement rules (Type 4: Greenwashes).

We suggest that from a policy perspective, Bootcamps and Mandarins have the most merit. We show that our typology has some potential in explaining why some clubs are effective in that they induce significant environmental improvement across a broad membership roster, why other programs have attracted members but have not induced any significant improvement in them, and yet others have failed to attract a large membership roster, leaving them with a small cadre of high-performing firms.

Finally, it is worth making a clarification here about how we view green clubs in the broader public policy context. We take an expansive view of public policy; instead of focusing on government promulgated policies alone, we believe that any instrument with a broader public impact should be considered a policy instrument. Public policy in this sense centers on governance, rather than only on government. The important point for this book is that we study how new instruments cohere with traditional governmental ones. While government agencies have established their own green clubs, sometimes even as formal policy instruments, these are non-traditional policies that look to have a broader impact on the public. Indeed, part of the design challenge for governmental agencies establishing their own green clubs is to assess how they will fit both with extant governmental policies and with non-governmental policies, including non-governmental green clubs. We examine the coherence of green clubs with traditional policy instruments in terms of the clubs' impact on firms' regulatory and environmental performance.

Green clubs and ISO 14001

Since the late 1980s, there has been a steadily growing interest in voluntary environmental regulations among businesses, trade associations, regulators and even some environmental groups (Gibson, 1999; Haufler, 2001).[32] Today there are many green clubs in operation around the world. The US EPA has launched over 40 voluntary programs, including 33/50, Green Lights, Common Sense, and Energy Star. The American Chemistry Council (formerly, The Chemical Manufacturers Association) launched its own program, Responsible Care, in the late 1980s and mandated that all its members join. Several other national-level chemical industry associations have also launched their own versions of Responsible Care (Garcia-Johnson, 2000). The American Forest & Paper Association established the Sustainable Forestry Initiative in 1992 and required that its members join it. Greenpeace, along with other NGOs, established the Forest Stewardship Council (FSC) in 1993 (Cashore *et al.*, 2004). The FSC registration is offered in several countries around the world.

We focus on ISO 14001, the most widely accepted green club in the world today. By December 2002, 49,462 facilities across 118 countries had received certification as members of ISO 14001 (ISO, 2003). The Geneva-based International Organization for Standardization (ISO), a non-governmental organization, launched ISO 14001 in 1996. Founded in 1947, the ISO is made up of (non-governmental) national standards institutions from around the world, such as the British Standards Institution, the Deutsche Institut Normen and the American National Standards Institute. ISO's central mission is to facilitate international trade and commerce by developing international standards and codes; to date, ISO 14001 has produced about 14,000 standards. In developing these standards, the ISO consults key

---

[32] Broadly, non-governmental regimes have proliferated across issue areas. Recent important works include Cutler *et al.* (1999), Mattli (2001), Kollman and Prakash (2001), Hall and Biersteker (2002), Cashore *et al.* (2004), and Web (2004).

participants including firms, regulators, and other stakeholders through technical committees comprising members from around the world.

In the late 1980s, scholars began to argue, perhaps somewhat optimistically, that because pollution represents wasted resources (Hunt and Auster, 1990; Porter, 1991; Bringer and Benforado, 1994; Fischer and Schot 1993), pollution control should fall under the aegis of quality assurance. Pollution reduction should therefore raise profits, and businesses should be treated as partners in environmental governance. Thus, pollution reduction was seen as a simple way to align private incentives to achieve public goals.

In October 1996, ISO launched the ISO 14000 series of standards, based on principles similar to those inscribed in ISO 9000.[33] ISO 14000 consists of a certification standard (ISO 14001), and eighteen guideline standards governing environmental labeling (14020 and 14021), environmental performance evaluations (14031), and life-cycle assessment (14040–43, 14048–49). For our purpose, only ISO 14001 is relevant because it is the only standard for which firms can receive certification. ISO 14001 requires members to establish policies, systems, and structures – commonly known as an environmental management system or EMS – which together look to ensure that firms comply with the law while encouraging them to exceed the law's requirements. ISO 14001 is a process-based or management systems-based standard, rather than an outcome or technology-based standard, predicated on the belief that if appropriate processes and internal systems are in place, the desired outcomes will follow. To join ISO 14001, the ISO requires facilities to subject their EMS to external third-party audits that verify facilities have met the ISO 14001 standards. Once certified, ISO 14001 does not require members to demonstrate improvements in regulatory compliance to maintain membership; it only seeks their commitment to do so and views the establishment of EMS as evidence of such commitment. However, the ISO does require annual recertification audits. The cost of ISO 14001

---

[33] In the language of marketing, ISO 14001 was a brand extension strategy on the part of the ISO. Combining corporate branding (ISO) with product branding (14001) enables companies to enjoy economies of scale in branding and yet distinguish individual products. The automobile industry is a good example of such a strategy on a large scale.

certification can range from $25,000 to $100,000 *per facility* (Kolk, 2000), and some cost estimates range higher. To illustrate, for a firm with twenty facilities, these costs could add up to $2 million. Furthermore, there can be substantial indirect costs of maintaining paper-trails and documenting management processes. Because firms are under tremendous pressure to rein in costs and environmental programs are under close scrutiny – what Arthur D. Little terms the "Green Wall" – the benefits and costs of any voluntary program are closely scrutinized (Prakash, 2000a).

Among EMS-based green clubs, many consider ISO 14001 to be the gold standard because ISO 14001 is well known around the world and regulators have a solid understanding of how it works. ISO 14001 reduces regulators' workload in terms of identifying paper-trails and elements of management systems within firms. This is not to say that regulators give ISO 14001 firms an "auto pass" on regulations, although the government regulators we spoke with recognized that an EMS can signal firms' intentions to pursue environmental objectives in a disciplined manner. Externally verified EMS programs such as ISO 14001 may indicate that this objective is pursued more rigorously.

Research methods and design

A command and control regulatory approach is based on the assumption that if left to their own devices businesses will not adopt environmentally sound policies. Effective green clubs seek to strengthen command and control regulations and perhaps even encourage firms to go beyond the law's requirements. To assess the empirical claims about green clubs in a theoretically rigorous way, this book focuses on two questions:[34]

- Does the reputational value of affiliating with ISO 14001 induce firms to join the club?
- Does joining ISO 14001 induce members to take progressive environmental action beyond what they would otherwise take unilaterally?

---

[34] Future research should also examine how the economic benefit (typically examined in terms of market capitalization) of joining a club varies across clubs.

We address these questions empirically. We demonstrate that ISO 14001 can successfully overcome shirking and align firms' incentives with public objectives. We explain how firm characteristics and the economic and political contexts in which firms are located influence their perceptions of ISO 14001's reputational value, and therefore their propensities to join the program. In other words, we examine the influence of both the micro and the macro factors on mitigating the Olsonian and shirking dilemmas.

Analytic approach

To address our two key questions, we employ several analytic approaches. First, we examine ISO 14001's adoption across countries and within the US. In studying cross-national diffusion, we first present a comparative case study of ISO 14001's reception in the US and the UK. We focus on these countries because while they share common attributes such as a common-law legal system and Anglo-Saxon capitalist institutions that crucially shape ISO 14001's reputational benefits, the former is a laggard in ISO 14001 adoption while the latter is a leader. Through these case studies, we highlight the influence of policy contexts and regulatory cultures on firms' perceptions of the value of joining ISO 14001. Building on the comparative case studies, we then examine cross-national ISO 14001 adoption rates in 59 countries. Subsequently, we examine ISO 14001 adoption among US facilities.

There is an established literature that suggests that national-level institutions influence adoption of organizational practices across issue areas (Cole, 1989; Baron *et al.*, 1988; Guillen, 1994). Our objective is to understand how institutions and policy contexts across countries (which are highly variable) and within the US (which are less variable because local institutions are nested within national institutions) explain firms' perceptions of ISO 14001's reputational value and therefore their decisions about the program. While the cross-national analyses enables us to examine important structural factors in the economic and policy contexts in which firms operate, the domestic analysis enables us to focus on firm- and facility-level variables, the data for which are not available for cross-national studies.

Finally, to better assess the value of ISO 14001's reputation for its members, we supplement our statistical analysis with interviews with nine US government regulators and two dozen US facility managers.[35] These interviews are not intended as formal case studies in a strictly analytic sense. Rather, they serve as illustrative examples of how regulators and facility managers perceive ISO 14001 and its members. We conducted these interviews in person, over the phone, and via email. Our objective was to assess how regulators and managers view ISO 14001 and assess the standing of its reputation among firms' stakeholders. For most in-person and phone interviews, within 24 hours of the interview, we emailed a summary of the interview to the respondent for further explanation and to confirm the accuracy of our understanding of the interview highlights.

This multi-method analytic approach offers several advantages. Comparative case studies are very helpful in delving deep into key explanatory variables and understanding how they influence national-level processes. Our case studies focus on domestic institutions, the regulatory environment created by governments, and firms' reactions to government regulations, as the key explanatory variables for ISO 14001 adoption. We explore how business–governmental relations play an important role in influencing firms' perceptions of ISO 14001's reputational value, and hence its adoption. We find that along with non-adversarial business–government relations, the UK also has a sponsoring organization that vigorously promotes ISO 14001. Such institutions do not exist in the US, leading to lower ISO 14001 adoption rates.

Business–government relations and sponsoring organizations are not the only factors that can affect the benefits firms receive for joining ISO 14001. Large-scale empirical studies are helpful in assessing the contributions of a longer slate of variables that can influence whether firms adopt ISO 14001. We show that firms are more likely to join ISO 14001 in countries where consumers are better able to use the ISO 14001 brand to discriminate among firms, and where they have more resources and inclinations to reward firms for taking progressive environmental action.

To examine how ISO 14001 affects members' environmental and regulatory performance, our large-sample analysis compares ISO

---

[35] Regulators work for the EPA-Washington DC, EPA Region 10, Texas, Wisconsin, Iowa, and Arizona. In his book, *Greening the Firm*, Aseem Prakash interviewed more than twenty managers working for Baxter International and Eli Lilly regarding ISO 14001 and related environmental issues.

14001 adopters and non-adopters, controlling for a host of potential confounding variables. We control for factors such as the past environmental performance and regulatory compliance that may induce facilities to join ISO 14001 and also to improve their environmental and regulatory performance. Because the data demands for such an analysis are quite high, we limit our study to a sample of over 3,000 facilities regulated under the US Clean Air Act for which we were able to obtain suitable data. In examining environmental performance we adjust the pollutants for their toxicity levels. The results from these analyses imply that as a group, ISO 14001 certified facilities have better regulatory compliance records and lower pollution emissions than if they had not joined the program. This result persists even while controlling for facilities' compliance histories as well as potential endogeneity between facilities' environmental performance and their decisions to join ISO 14001. In these analyses we have operationalized efficacy very precisely: changes in environmental performance (emissions of toxic pollutants adjusted for their toxicity) and regulatory performance (proportion of time out of compliance with public law). The book neither makes any claims about ISO 14001's impact on national-level environmental indicators nor whether ISO 14001 is ameliorating any specific environmental problem.[36] We also do not suggest that voluntary programs are the panacea for environmental problems. However, we do demonstrate that under certain conditions, voluntary programs can create incentives for participating firms to reduce pollution and to improve their compliance with public law.

The contribution of this book

This book makes important theoretical and empirical contributions to the growing literature on the new tools for environmental governance. It contributes to debates about voluntary environmental programs'

---

[36] As we note in the concluding chapter, the issue of program efficacy needs to be studied further; specifically various dimensions of environmental performance need to be examined. For example, future research could examine issues such as whether firms participating in voluntary programs tend to focus on reducing local and visible sources of pollution as opposed to protecting the global commons or reducing pollution in some medium (say water) as opposed to others (say air).

efficacy and about how the political and economic contexts influence firms' incentives to join these programs.

Novel theoretical approach

Our key theoretical contribution is the novel application of club theory to voluntary environmental programs. Club theory offers powerful insights for studying voluntary environmental programs by showing the causal mechanisms for how effective programs induce members to take progressive environmental action beyond what they would take unilaterally. Club theory allows us to understand better and predict conditions under which green clubs are effective and when firms are more likely to join them. We do so by identifying two salient institutional dimensions – club standards which specify the systems and programs firms need to put in place to join a club and retain its membership, and monitoring rules which specify monitoring and enforcement mechanisms established by program sponsors to ensure that members adhere to club rules. Our theoretical approach leads us to examine how club standards and monitoring rules might resolve the fundamental sources of club failure: the Olsonian dilemma and the Shirking dilemma. Applying club theory to voluntary programs may suggest conditions for when these programs might be effective and when they might fail.

Understanding the efficacy of voluntary environmental programs

An emerging literature has examined the efficacy of green clubs in terms of firms' environmental and regulatory performance. The evidence on environmental performance is mixed; while some studies show that voluntary environmental programs improve members' performance beyond what they would otherwise achieve, others suggest that these programs have no effect on members' performance. To illustrate, Khanna and Damon (1999) find that the release of the chemicals targeted by the US EPA's 33/50 program declined significantly post-adoption; hence, this voluntary program was effective. However, King and Lenox (2000) report that releases of toxic chemicals did not decline faster for firms that participated in the chemical industry's Responsible Care program compared to those that did not.

Welch *et al.* (2000) likewise find that participating electric utilities in
the US EPA's Climate Change program did not reduce their CO_2
emissions more than non-participants. Regarding regulatory performance, Dasgupta *et al.* (2000) report that adopting environmental
management practices along the lines prescribed by ISO 14001 improved Mexican facilities' self-reported compliance with public law.
Complicating matters is the absence of a theory laying out the key
analytic dimensions to facilitate comparisons across programs.

We contribute to the literature by first presenting a theoretically
rigorous framework for studying voluntary programs that accounts
for the differences in the efficacy of these programs. We do this by
identifying the institutional design features that influence why firms
join voluntary programs and whether joining the program improves
their performance.

Why firms join voluntary environmental programs

Our inquiry also contributes to the literature on why firms join
voluntary environmental programs. Empirical studies report that
firms are more inclined to join voluntary programs when they are in
closer contact with the final consumer, are concerned about their
company or corporate image (Arora and Cason, 1996; Khanna and
Damon, 1999; King and Lenox, 2000), experience competitive pressure (Arora and Cason, 1996), show high dependence on the stock
market, are subjected to stakeholder pressure (Henriques and Sadorsky,
1996 but see Dasgupta *et al.*, 2000), experience greater regulatory
pressures (Khanna and Damon, 1999; Videras and Alberini, 2000),
and have poor environmental records (Arora and Cason, 1996). These
studies have tended to focus almost exclusively on the US. Cross-
national studies are rare, triangulated studies are rarer still, and this
book will fill in the important gap by studying ISO 14001 adoption
both in the US and around the world, using both large- and small-sample
research designs.

Outline

The book proceeds as follows. Chapter 2 presents our theoretical
analysis of voluntary environmental programs. We examine voluntary
programs via the lens of club theory, locate club goods in the broader

institutionalist tradition, and develop a typology of voluntary environmental programs. From our green club theory, we draw empirical conjectures for how these programs operate in different contexts. Chapter 3 presents a brief history of international standardization, an overview of ISO 14001, and explains how ISO 14001's analytical dimensions can be examined through the lenses of club theory. Chapter 4 examines ISO 14001's diffusion across countries and within the US. The first part presents a comparative case study of ISO diffusion in the US and the UK. In the second part, building on the insights generated by the comparative case study, we present an empirical analysis of ISO diffusion rates across 59 countries. In the third part, we present an empirical analysis of ISO 14001 diffusion within the US. Chapter 5 examines ISO 14001's efficacy in terms of the impact of ISO 14001 membership on firms' regulatory performance (whether ISO 14001 participants better comply with public law compared to non-participants) and on their environmental performance (whether ISO 14001 participants pollute less than non-participants). It is important to point out that while our empirical analyses provide important support for some implications of our theoretical framework, and our review of the literature suggests our framework can help resolve the conflicting research on voluntary environmental programs, we do not provide a comprehensive test of all aspects of our framework (specifically, the club typology). Our theoretical framework lays the groundwork for future work in this area. Chapter 6 presents conclusions; we also identify theoretical and policy implications of the study and provide suggestions for further research.

2 | *Green clubs: an institutionalist perspective*

T HE Queen Elizabeth Way, a four-lane highway outside of Toronto, Canada, is home to industrial facilities belonging to several major automotive companies and their suppliers. Among the factories, restaurants, and gas stations in this extended industrial park, one can sometimes spot signs next to factories that proclaim "ISO 14001 Certified." ISO 14001 has been well received throughout the automobile industry and several companies have been advertising their participation in this program. Honda's corporate website provides the following information under the heading "Green Factories":

All major Honda plants worldwide already meet the toughest international environmental management standards (ISO 14001), covering a host of environmental areas, such as waste disposal, water treatment and energy use.

Judging by the signs along the Queen Elizabeth Way, ISO 14001 certification is not confined to facilities belonging to the major auto companies; many of their suppliers have received certification as well. Indeed, green clubs can be found in many industries outside of heavy manufacturing, such as forestry and paper production. Weyerhaeuser, the timber giant, proudly proclaims on its website:

- 100 per cent of timberlands owned or managed by Weyerhaeuser were operated under environmental management systems registered to the ISO 14001 standard.
- 100 per cent of North American timberlands owned or managed by Weyerhaeuser were third-party certified to the forest management standards of either the Sustainable Forestry Initiative (SFI); or the Canadian Standards Association (CSA). (Weyerhauser, 2005)

And of course, ISO 14001 is not the only green club. Several makers of consumer goods have opted to join a "fair trade coffee" club sponsored by a non-governmental organization, Global Exchange. Along with appealing to consumers' egalitarian sense, the club also looks to appeal to their desires to protect the environment and improve their health. Procter & Gamble, a major coffee marketer in the US, explains these goals clearly on its website:

But Fair Trade java is good for you too: More than 80 per cent of it is certified organic. Another bonus: Most of it is shade-grown, meaning no forests were clear-cut to make room for planting . . . Starbucks and Seattle's Best have been selling Fair Trade coffee since 2000 and 2001, respectively . Also, Sara Lee Coffee & Tea has been supplying Fair Trade coffee to restaurants and cafeterias across the country for more than two years . . . Last fall, Procter & Gamble introduced Millstone Mountain Moonlight Fair Trade Certified coffee, which is sold by mail order or online (800-729-5282 or www.millstone.com). And Dunkin' Donuts became one of the movement's largest supporters this spring, when it rolled out a new line of espresso-based beverages using only Fair Trade Certified coffee.

(Millstone, 2005)

As these examples suggest, green clubs are well established around the world, across issue areas and across product categories. Furthermore, companies promote their membership in these clubs in their corporate publicity campaigns. Yet despite considerable scrutiny, there is no consensus among scholars, government regulators or businesses about how or when green clubs improve participants' performance. In this chapter, we draw on club theory to outline a perspective and green club typology for understanding how voluntary programs function and the conditions under which they improve participating firms' environmental performance. We then place ISO 14001 in this typology and explore this program's strengths and limitations. Our goal is to identify green clubs' key analytic features, both for studying a single program and for making cross-program comparisons.

For some time, command and control regulations have been the foundation for environmental governance across most of the world. Despite some current frustrations with this policy approach, we would not want to understate its efficacy and importance, particularly given the historical context in which it emerged. Cities are no longer routinely engulfed in smog, rivers do not catch fire, and companies do not recklessly dump industrial waste into landfills. Without doubt, command and control regulations have significantly reduced pollution

(Ringquist, 1993) to the point where environmental governance now faces different challenges, which require exploring new instruments that capture the benefits of command and control while mitigating its costs. To be clear, we do not advocate dismantling command and control. Rather, the objective is to harness its potential better, create incentives for firms to comply with its requirements, and hopefully even go beyond compliance to create a policy environment where regulators, businesses, and environmental groups work cooperatively towards the shared goal of protecting the environment (Ayres and Braithwaite, 1992; Fiorino, 2001; NAPA, 2001).

As discussed in chapter 1, green clubs are an important category of new environmental policy tools. Effective green clubs induce participating firms to incur the private costs of undertaking progressive environmental action beyond what they would take unilaterally. By adopting the program's standards, participating firms produce a public good, such as reduced pollution emissions or better compliance with governmental regulations. Simply put, by offering excludable club benefits, green clubs can potentially induce firms to produce public benefits at their own expense.

While much can be said about the promise of green clubs, they carry important risks, if not drawbacks. Many environmental groups are skeptical that voluntary programs compel firms to adopt expensive environmental programs beyond what is legally required of them (Steinzor, 1998), especially if the membership benefits are non-monetary and accrue over the long term. When it comes to progressive, socially responsible action, such as protecting the environment, the harsh discipline of the stock market may prevent firms from going beyond empty publicity gestures. Some green clubs may have been intentionally designed to serve as empty gestures or green-washes. Thus, one should be careful of making sweeping generalizations about the efficacy or inefficacy of green clubs as a policy instrument.

The standard for judging the efficacy of a green club should not be simply whether its members are "cleaner" than non-members. Rather, the standard should be whether a green club induces participants to take voluntary progressive environmental action beyond what they would have taken without the program. In other words, are members "cleaner" than they would be without the program? This begs another question: from a potential participant's perspective, what are the advantages of progressive environmental action taken via green club membership compared to the same action taken unilaterally? Why join a club and subject yourself to the scrutiny of its monitoring mechanisms when you could instead simply copy the club's standards and perform according to its requirements? In our view, what compels firms to join a club is not some excuse to take the environmental action that the club requires of its members, but rather to garner the club's reputational value for environmental stewardship. Our contention is that firms can earn such reputational value more effectively via club membership than through their own unilateral action.

Given the debates surrounding green clubs, one might be tempted to simplify the controversy to empirical questions about their efficacy. Instead of endless theoretical debates about whether voluntary programs are effective, why not simply investigate whether voluntary programs change participants' behaviors in desirable ways? Does evidence suggest that green club participants pollute less, or comply better with public law? While perhaps useful in some narrow sense, we believe such an "atheoretical" approach is limited because it does not help us to identify the key analytical features that distinguish effective green clubs from their ineffective counterparts. A theoretical account is important because empirical studies of programs' effectiveness have produced uneven results, suggesting that some broader analytic framework is required to explain why some programs are effective and others are not. Consider a few prominent examples. Aside from the question of whether these programs change participants' environmental performance, some voluntary programs have had trouble attracting large rosters of participants – even the EPA's 33/50 program attracted only 13 per cent of the facilities contacted by the EPA (Prakash, 2000a). A program with a small membership roster is bound to have a limited policy impact.

Generalizing from empirical studies is difficult because voluntary programs vary in many ways. To facilitate cross-program comparisons that might resolve these disparate findings, some scholars have looked to typologies based on programs' descriptive characteristics. Programs differ in their eligibility criteria (who can join the program), the standards of behavior and action they impose on members, and the procedures for monitoring and ensuring compliance with those standards. Along these lines, some scholars attribute program efficacy to the characteristics of program sponsors (Carmin *et al.*, 2003), such as whether sponsorship is local or international, or sponsored by government, an NGO, or an industrial association. Other explanations might focus on whether the programs' requirements are process-based, such as adopting an environmental management system (EMS), or outcome-based, such as achieving specified levels of pollution reduction. These typologies offer some plausible explanations, and to be fair, they have not been formally tested empirically through cross-program comparisons. Notwithstanding several excellent empirical studies on voluntary program efficacy, a generalizable theoretical framework that accounts for varying efficacy *across* programs is lacking.

From a policy perspective, the uneven efficacy of voluntary programs is a bit unsettling. Ideally, we would like to know, *ex ante*, whether a voluntary program has the potential to induce members to take progressive action beyond what they would achieve unilaterally. This would enable the policy-makers to design and support credible voluntary programs that can yield desired policy outcomes.

As we noted in chapter 1, voluntary programs are institutions – bundles of rules that shape actors' behavior. We view them as a specific type of institution: clubs. Indeed, here we term voluntary environmental programs "green clubs" to emphasize their club features. Via club rules, effective voluntary programs must impose some significant new obligations on firms that are beyond the requirements of governmental law. These obligations, which we call club standards, require participating firms to produce some broader public good, such as a cleaner environment through lower pollution emissions. One convenient way of assessing the stringency of these requirements is to examine the costs firms bear to adopt and adhere to them. In effective programs, the participants' membership costs – activities such as the adoption of new internal policies and/or institution of new management systems – lead them to produce public goods.

The broad collective action literature suggests that actors are un-likely to incur private costs to produce a public good (Olson, 1965). How do green clubs attempt to solve this dilemma? Effective green clubs offer an excludable benefit, something of value given to participants and withheld from non-participants, to induce firms to take on the non-trivial costs of club membership voluntarily. In our view, the most salient excludable benefit for green clubs is the goodwill members receive from their external stakeholders as a consequence of their club membership. Participating in a green club with a strong positive reputation can improve members' relations with government regulators, consumers, and environmental groups. This can lead to monetary and non-monetary benefits as these external stakeholders interact more favorably with the green club's participants.

Club membership matters because environmentally progressive action taken collectively under the aegis of the green club's brand identity is more valuable to the potential club member than the same action undertaken unilaterally. This is because progressive action stemming from club membership provides a more institutionalized and therefore more credible signal of firms' environmental performance, and is likely to become better known to external stakeholders. Because green clubs (as voluntary programs) are institutionalized collectives, their policies are more stable and enduring, and their members' progressive action is more credible. Collective action taken via green clubs generates scale economies in producing clubs' reputation, because larger membership rosters generate more network effects that in turn enhance the program's visibility to external stakeholders.

As scholars working within the institutionalist tradition, we explore how different green club rule configurations mitigate collective action problems. We are interested in how voluntary programs, conceived as green clubs, can effectively tackle collective action problems by aligning individual interests with the general good of society. To realize their promise, green clubs must solve two collective action problems. First, they must solve the Olsonian dilemma by attracting members who are willing to pay the costs of club participation. Second, they must mitigate the incentives of members to shirk, thereby ensuring that members continue to adhere to club standards after they have joined the club. To investigate how green clubs address these dilemmas, we categorize programs along two institutional dimensions. *Club standards* are the rules governing what members must do to join the club. *Enforcement rules* are the monitoring regimes that ensure members continue to adhere to club standards. We examine how variations in these rules influence green clubs' success in mitigating collective action dilemmas. Based on these two key institutional attributes, we introduced a typology of green clubs briefly in chapter 1. We identified four ideal club types – stringent club standards with enforcement rules (Type 1: Mandarins); stringent club standards without enforcement rules (Type 2: Country Clubs); lenient club standards with enforcement rules (Type 3: Bootcamps); and lenient club standards without credible enforcement rules (Type 4: Greenwashes). We also suggested that from a policy perspective, Bootcamps and Mandarins have the most merit.

Although we focus on the voluntary programs in the environmental policy area, our theoretical framework is sufficiently general to apply to voluntary programs in other areas as well. Our goal in this chapter is to present our theory and identify key variables that influence clubs' efficacy and diffusion. In the second section of this chapter, we identify three types of benefits that green clubs create – public, private, and club – and we show how only club benefits provide the rationale for firms to join green clubs and take "beyond compliance" environmental actions that that membership entails. In the third section, we describe the Olsonian and shirking collective action dilemmas that impede club efficacy. We then investigate how club standards and enforcement rules can mitigate these dilemmas. We examine how, within the context of a given green club, firms respond to different club standards. We sketch green clubs' potential role in fostering cooperation between firms and regulators, and how this could generate important public policy dividends. The fourth section proposes a typology of clubs and examines which club types can be expected to serve policy goals best. We place ISO 14001 in this typology and examine key issues that could influence its efficacy and diffusion. Finally, in the concluding section, we summarize our key arguments and identify issues we will go on to investigate. In the remainder of the book, we examine ISO 14001 through the lenses of our theoretical framework. In chapters 4 and 5, drawing on the insights developed in this chapter, we test hypotheses about ISO 14001's efficacy and diffusion.

An institutional approach to policy design

Perhaps the fundamental challenge in structuring human interaction involves solving problems where individually beneficial actions are incompatible with the welfare of the larger group. One way to solve these social dilemmas is to devise institutions that align individual incentives so they make decisions that are compatible with group outcomes.[1] Institutions thus potentially solve, or perhaps mitigate, collective action problems, depending on how their rules fit with exogenous circumstances.[2] Of course, institutions might also create new social dilemmas or exacerbate existing ones. After all, institutions are an intervening variable between individual action and collective outcomes. The policy challenge is to "get them right" so that individual rationality coheres with the collective well-being.

While there are several strands of institutionalist approaches (DiMaggio and Powell, 1983; Granovetter, 1985; Keohane, 1989; Ostrom, 1991), two are most salient for our purposes: rational-choice institutionalism and sociological institutionalism. Both focus on the rules governing human interaction. However, a key difference between the two is their model of human behavior. The rational-choice version views actors as making choices that increase their net benefits (benefits minus costs). The sociological version views actors responding to the logic of appropriateness, that is, choosing the course of action that seems most normatively appropriate (March and Olsen, 1989). Thus, the rational-choice version argues that institutions alter the incentives actors face while the sociological version views institutions as signals of normatively appropriate behaviors.

We draw on both versions of institutionalism. We view clubs as institutions that alter the cost–benefit calculus of taking progressive environmental action. They do so by offering excludable benefits such as the goodwill and legitimacy members receive from various stakeholders. While these may translate into tangible rewards, clubs may also bestow important but non-quantifiable benefits. In chapter 4, while examining the diffusion of ISO 14001 across countries, we test both rational and normative variables as drivers of ISO 14001 adoption.

---

[1] Although institutions may be devised to solve collective action problems, they may malfunction or have unintended consequences. Some institutions may be devised to accentuate, not solve, collective action problems. Colonial rulers are known to have established institutions that created incentives for their colonial subjects to fight with each other, and not unite to fight against the colonizing country.

[2] Institutions are often nested in other overarching institutions: subnational institutions are nested in national-level institutions. Thus, encompassing institutions may set parameters that influence institutional functioning, change, and efficacy.

Notwithstanding the differences in these institutionalisms, scholars adopting an institutionalist approach typically focus on one or more of the following questions:

- how do institutions emerge and change[3]
- how do institutions function[4]
- how do institutions influence individual behaviors and collective outcomes?

Unlike organizations that are physical entities, institutions are bundles of rules that permit, prescribe, or prohibit specific behaviors (North, 1990; Ostrom, 1990). Our theoretical approach to studying voluntary environmental programs is institutionalist in that we investigate how to structure rules for non-governmental governance – voluntary environmental programs – to induce firms to produce a public good in the form of a cleaner environment.[5] Institutions established by sovereign governments can carry the force of law. As

---

[3] Historical institutionalists and sociological institutionalists are less concerned with this issue because they tend to focus on durable, pre-existing institutions (Commons, 1961; P. Hall, 1986). On the other hand, new-institutionalists focus on institutional emergence because they believe that most institutions are human artifacts (North, 1990; Ostrom, 1990). This is not to say new-institutionalists treat institutions as a dependent variable only. Institutions are not created in a vacuum. Nor do newly minted institutions function in an institution-free context. New-institutionalists recognize this. For them, institutions can serve both as the independent and the dependent variable depending on the research question. As we demonstrate in chapter 4, the diffusion of ISO 14001 crucially depends on the institutional context in which firms operate.

[4] Sociological institutionalists pay a lot of attention to institutional diffusion issues, both at the micro, organizational level (Di Maggio and Powell, 1983) as well as at the macro, country level. Instead of viewing efficiency, or the "logic of consequentiality," as the key diffusion driver, they focus on the role of norms, or the "logic of appropriateness" (March and Olsen, 1989).

[5] Consider, for example, the well-established literature on organizing collective action through another set of non-governance institutions: common-pool resource regimes (Ostrom, 1990). This literature has typically examined how communities have established institutions to manage natural resources such as forests, fisheries, and water, that are rival but not excludable: specifically, how these communities have mitigated the "tragedy of commons" through self-organized institutions. These communities often depend on the resources for their livelihood. Although sharing several similarities, the research on voluntary environmental programs is not concerned with mitigating the tragedy of commons. It is concerned with the conditions under which firms are willing to adopt policies beyond the requirements of the law and how this translates into firms' environmental and regulatory performance.

sovereigns, governments can write laws prescribing behavioral standards and compelling compliance among target populations by monitoring their behavior and sanctioning non-compliance.[6]

Non-governmental institutions sponsored by interest groups, citizen associations and the like are different from governmental institutions because the sovereign (sponsor) cannot formally mandate adoption among the targeted population.[7] Not surprisingly, then, non-governmental institutions tend to combat collective-action problems with carrots rather than sticks. Rather than focusing on compliance with mandatory law, studying voluntary institutions centers on two questions: how much of the targeted population cooperates or joins the institution, and does the participation change behavior in the desired ways?

Whether through coercive sticks, softer carrots, or perhaps by changing actors' preferences, institutions carry considerable potential in solving the collective action problems that plague human interactions. Indeed, this is the promise of markets: the "invisible hand" of well-functioning markets harmonizes individual decisions with collective outcomes. Of course, markets often fail. Market failures rooted in natural monopolies, externalities, and information asymmetries suggest that the divergence between individual and group rationality cannot always be resolved via extant market-based institutions. Either existing market rules need to be revised or new non-market institutions created, and of course there is no guarantee that the new institution will fare any better.[8] This is where a good theory can be helpful: by focusing our attention on key issues to improve the chances of

---

[6] In response to a new rule, actors may alter their behavior in unexpected and perhaps even undesirable ways. Rules prohibiting under-age smoking may lead young people to believe that smoking is "cool" and increase the incidence of under-age smoking. Hence, a mere change in behavior is not sufficient to assess institutional efficacy; actors' behaviors must change in desired ways.

[7] Government-sponsored voluntary programs also have club characteristics. To keep our narrative simple, we simply term all such programs, governmental as well as non-governmental, voluntary clubs.

[8] Prior to Coase (1960), economists typically recommended government intervention to correct market failures. Coase argued that this need not be so. Both governments and markets fail because of transaction costs. The policy task is to undertake comparative institutionalist analysis rather than assume that governments do not fail. In his Nobel Prize Lecture, Coase (1991) noted:

> Pigou's conclusion and that of most economists using standard economic theory was, and perhaps still is, that some kind of government action (usually the

designing an institution that harmonizes individual and collective rationalities.

At a more fundamental level, collective action dilemmas can be traced to the physical nature of goods and the context in which actors seek to produce, exchange, and consume goods and services. Two attributes are especially important: excludability and rivalry. Excludability means that it is technologically feasible and economical for one person to exclude another from appropriating the benefits of a good once it has been produced. An absence of excludability creates incentives for actors to "free-ride," that is, to enjoy the benefits without contributing to the good's production (Olson, 1965). Why would a person incur costs if he/she cannot be prevented from appropriating a good's benefits?

Rivalry implies that if one person consumes a particular unit of a good, it is no longer available for another person to consume. Rivalry in consumption can create incentives for actors to over-consume resources – the logic being, if I do not consume it, then someone else will, and therefore deny me the benefits from future consumption. Over-consumption can lead to resource degradation. If rivalrous resources are excludable, their scarcity may lead to higher prices, thereby lowering consumption. Problems arise when goods are non-excludable, because in such cases scarcity does not translate into higher prices that curb consumption. Thus, non-excludability becomes a root cause of market failures.

Based on these physical characteristics, products can be classified into four stylized categories: private goods (rival, excludable), public

imposition of taxes) was required to restrain those whose actions had harmful effects on others, often termed negative externalities. What I showed in that article, as I thought, was that in a regime of zero transaction costs, an assumption of standard economic theory, negotiations between the parties would lead to those arrangements being made which would maximise wealth and this irrespective of the initial assignment of rights . . . The significance to me of the Coase Theorem is that it undermines the Pigovian system. Since standard economic theory assumes transaction costs to be zero, the Coase Theorem demonstrates that the Pigovian solutions are unnecessary in these circumstances. Of course, it does not imply, when transaction costs are positive, that government actions (such as government operation, regulation or taxation, including subsidies) could not produce a better result than relying on negotiations between individuals in the market. Whether this would be so could be discovered not by studying imaginary governments but what real governments actually do. My conclusion: let us study the world of positive transaction costs.

Table 2.1. The nature of goods and services

	Excludable	*Not excludable*
Rival	Private	Common-pool resources
Non-rival	Club	Public

goods (non-rival, non-excludable), common-pool resources or CPRs (rival, non-excludable),[9] and impure public goods (non-rival, excludable) (Ostrom and Ostrom, 1977).

Private goods can be produced and exchanged through markets without significant collective action problems. In other words, when individuals produce, buy and sell private goods, they not only make themselves better off, they also improve the lots of those with whom they are exchanging resources. Adam Smith's invisible hand raises the tide and the boats in it. Such rosy win–win scenarios do not occur for public goods, clubs goods, and common-pool resources. For public goods and common-pool resources, non-excludability is an obvious source of collective action problems. A cleaner environment is an example of a non-excludable good: after all, everyone breathes outdoor air. Not surprisingly then, the production of environmental benefits creates collective action problems: individuals are not willing to incur private costs to produce a non-excludable environmental benefit. This provides the rationale for government intervention via command and control regulations. Realizing that individual actors are likely to harm the environment in pursuit of their own welfare, the government promulgates regulations that compel them to protect the environment. We examine another instrument – green clubs – that look to induce actors to incur private costs to produce non-excludable environmental benefits. We explain how clubs can potentially mitigate their collective action dilemmas and therefore potentially induce

---

[9] Ostrom (1990), the leading authority on CPRs, models the CPR dilemma as a prisoner's dilemma game. To mitigate a CPR dilemma, institutions need to mitigate incentives for actors to "defect" and increase incentives to "cooperate." This is sought to be achieved by generating trust among actors, creating a long shadow of the future, providing credible monitoring and sanctioning mechanisms. Ostrom identifies "design principles" that are likely to support viable regimes to manage CPRs, especially those related to natural resources such as water, forests, and grasslands.

participating firms to incur private costs to produce non-excludable environmental benefits.

Voluntary programs as clubs

Clubs are institutions that supply impure public goods. While the literature on "impure public goods" has an impressive lineage (Pigou, 1960; Knight, 1924; Tiebout, 1956; and Wiseman, 1957), James Buchanan (1965) is generally credited with introducing the theoretical concept of clubs in an economic sense. Building on Samuelson's (1954) dichotomous classification of goods as either public or private, Buchanan identified clubs as institutions for producing and allocating goods that are neither fully private (rivalrous and excludable), nor fully public (non-rivalrous, non-excludable). Club theory has been applied to examine policy issues pertaining to zoning, busing, road congestion, city size, and military alliances.[10]

Unlike pure public goods where the benefits one recipient receives are made available to all (that is, benefits are non-excludable), club goods provide excludable benefits that can be targeted to select individuals while being withheld (partially or completely) from other individuals.[11] Since benefits are excludable, club sponsors can compel club beneficiaries to defray the goods' production costs. For example, club sponsors can assess tolls (per use of the club) or membership fees (for extended use) to finance the club. Club goods are non-rivalrous in that what one individual consumes is still available for others to consume as well. Consequently, the average per recipient cost of producing the benefit declines with additional recipients until at some point crowding, or over-consumption, sets in and thereafter additional recipients diminish the quality of the club good.[12] A good example of

---

[10] For an excellent review of club theory and its applications, see Cornes and Sandler (1996).

[11] Schelling (1969) points out that the taste for association can induce members to join a club. Here the associational benefit is attributed to internal audiences. I may join a book club because I like to associate with others who attend it. This theoretical point certainly applies to some clubs. However, it is not relevant for our analysis of voluntary programs as clubs because our analytic focus is on the external public goods the clubs generate rather than the feeling of solidarity among members.

[12] With crowding, club benefits become partially rival. Not all clubs are equally susceptible to crowding. To some extent, this depends on the boundary

a club in this sense is a country club: the excludable benefit club members receive is access to the club's swimming, golfing, and other facilities. From a broader welfare perspective, club goods can generally be produced and allocated efficiently. Club memberships can be allocated efficiently because once tee times become scarce and the swimming pool is too crowded, the club can hike its membership fees to bring membership to optimal levels, while an entrepreneurial farmer can turn his cow pasture into golf courses to meet the demand for country club memberships.

Where green clubs differ from such traditional clubs is that their purpose is not just to produce the club good, but also to produce a broader public good.[13] Green clubs produce environmental public goods by requiring members to incur private costs, as codified in the club's membership standards and mechanisms for ensuring compliance with those standards. The costs of club membership must be nontrivial because producing a public good is not free. For green clubs, the main costs of joining the club are generally not direct payments to club sponsors. Rather, they are the monetary and non-monetary costs of adopting and adhering to the club's requirements. We can identify two categories of costs to club membership: an initiation fee and ongoing membership dues. For green clubs, initiation fees are reflected in the costs of receiving initial certification as bona fide members. Membership dues are the ongoing costs of adhering to those membership standards over time.

From the perspective of (potential) members, green clubs generate three kinds of benefits:

- *public* benefits that accrue to society;
- *private* benefits that accrue to a single member firm only;
- *club* benefits that accrue to club members only.

Public benefits are the public goods that clubs produce, and as such are the ultimate welfare gain to society. Such benefits accrue to every-

conditions or the entry conditions set for joining the club. See Olson's (1965) distinction between inclusive and exclusive clubs on this count. From our perspective, increased membership, instead of leading to overcrowding and erosion of club benefits, should create positive "network effects" for the club's name recognition.

[13] Clubs may also produce public goods such as social capital as happy byproducts of their existence (Putnam, 1995).

body, including non-club members. Potential public benefits of a green club includes a cleaner environment, lower polluting production processes, better wildlife habitat protection, or any other environmentally beneficial practice.

In some cases, a green club's behavior standards may produce significant private benefits for members.[14] Private benefits accrue only to individual club members, not to other club members, and certainly not to non-members. The actions required to join a green club may generate private benefits, such as if the club requires actions that help members uncover waste and therefore reduce costs and improve profits. Several environmental management scholars suggest that there are substantial profits to be garnered if firms were to clean up their polluting ways, perhaps because managers have not been trained to look for them, perhaps because of search costs, or perhaps because of institutional norms/assumptions that environmental compliance is always a cost to be minimized (Bringer and Benforado, 1994; Fischer and Schot, 1993; Hunt and Auster, 1990). In other words, there is no dearth of win–win opportunities, if only managers knew how to spot them. Porter and Linde (1995) suggest that strict government regulations can focus managerial attention on such opportunities, compelling firms to realize profits they would otherwise have missed. Leaving aside debates about the size of such "green dividends" (Porter and Linde, 1995; but also Walley and Whitehead, 1994) in terms of our rational actor model, such private benefits have limited utility for evaluating voluntary programs because a profit-oriented firm is likely to take these actions unilaterally, without joining the club, in order to enjoy the private benefits such actions produce. If the private gain from unilaterally adopting progressive environmental policies were sufficient (that is, pollution reduction would generate private benefits on a large scale), then green clubs or any other regulation would not be necessary to produce the public goods we desire.[15] Clearly, this is

---

[14] Some firms invest in expensive policies that are "beyond compliance" with government regulations simply because they believe morally it is the "right thing to do" (Hoffman, 1997; Prakash, 2000a; Gunningham *et al.*, 2003). Not enough firms, however, are likely to provide public benefits emanating without compensation or coercion, a key rationale behind command and control policies.

[15] Unlike Porter and Linde (1995), we do not believe that the presumption of green dividends can form the basis of public policy. While win–win opportunities may persist, stringent command and control regulations, and the

not the case, as witnessed by the widespread demand among citizens in the US and around the world for a healthier planet. Polluters need to be either coerced through command and control regulations or induced through the promise of some other benefit to achieve the clean environment people want.

The central feature of green clubs is the benefits they offer to their members. Club benefits are something valuable that club sponsors can bestow upon members and withhold from non-members. In the case of green clubs, excludable club benefits generally stem from the goodwill that members receive from external stakeholders in return for affiliating with the club. Green club members often receive a certification that enables them to advertise that they are different from non-members by virtue of their club participation. Affiliating with a green club's positive brand reputation can benefit club members in several ways (Overdevest, 2005). In its broadest sense, membership reduces transaction costs for stakeholders to distinguish members from non-members. Credible clubs provide information about members' progressive environmental activities, potentially valuable information because so much of firms' environmental activities are unobservable to most external stakeholders (though different stakeholders may have different information about firms' performance).[16] Affiliation with a club and its reputation is thus akin to building organizational reputations: the value is in how they shape stakeholders' interactions with the organization (Carpenter, 2001). The extent to which members benefit from their club's reputation is influenced in turn by how much various stakeholders such as consumers, regulators, investors, and suppliers can identify club members and reward them. How the stakeholders reward club members is contingent partly on stakeholders' volition – whether stakeholders hold salient environmental preferences – and partly on ability – whether

stock-market pressures to improve profitability, have led managers to harvest the low-hanging fruit. We believe that firms are now in the trade-off zone where firms can be induced voluntarily to take on additional costs only with promise of new benefits, not the ones Porter and Linde (1995) suggest.

[16] Some scholars incorrectly view club benefits as a common-pool resource and label it as a "reputational common" (King and Lenox, 2000). The analytic distinction between a club good and a common-pool resource is not a matter of semantics because it bears upon how we visualize core functions of a voluntary program and conditions under which a program can succeed in attracting members.

stakeholders have the information, resources, and the disposition to translate their preferences into action affecting firms.

Freeman (1984: 46) defines stakeholders as "any group or individual who can affect or is affected by the achievement of [an] organization's objectives." For our analyses of green clubs, we use the term "stakeholders" to refer to individuals and groups that might reward (or sanction) firms for taking pro-environmental action. Stakeholders include regulators, consumers, stockholders, residents of neighborhoods surrounding the firm, and environmental groups. Rewards may be monetary, such as consumers buying products because they were produced in an environmentally progressive way, or nonmonetary, or not directly monetary, such as avoiding negative publicity from an environmental group protesting a firm's unsatisfactory environmental record (Gunningham *et al.*, 2003).

In the case of regulators, firms' club membership can generate goodwill that induces regulators to offer club members tangible benefits such as flexibility in meeting pollution regulations, quicker inspections, fast tracking permit applications, etc. Consumers who care about the environment may reward club members for taking environmentally progressive action by paying a price premium for their products (Charter and Polonsky, 1999; but see Harrison and Werner, 2002). In the US auto industry, it has become standard practice for the major manufacturers to boost their environmental reputation by requiring vendors to receive ISO 14001.

In addition to goodwill benefits, there could also be some gains for club members in terms of learning about how to find and implement "win–win" opportunities such as premium prices for green branded goods, cost savings on energy and waste disposal, and lower insurance and compliance costs. While sociological institutionalists might call this mimetic behavior, we view them as reduced search and information costs by virtue of club membership. Thus, these benefits have the characteristics of club goods, not of private goods. Firms cannot corner them by unilateral action, but only through joining the club.

In important ways, the size of a club's membership roster influences the value of its club benefits. More members create more opportunities to capture economies of scale in building reputations (McGuire, 1972), a dynamic akin to network effects (Bessen and Saloner, 1988). Network effects pertain to changes in the benefit that an actor derives from a good when the number of other actors consuming the same good changes. Network effects create increasing returns to scale: with every additional unit, the marginal cost of production decreases.[17] Having more members helps advertise a club broadly among stakeholders as one member's progressive environmental activities generate positive reputational and goodwill externalities for other members.[18] This club "branding" reduces transaction costs for stakeholders to distinguish the environmental performance of members from non-members.[19] The benefits a member derives from joining a club depends also on how many others have joined the club. Language groups can be thought of as clubs amenable to network effects: the more people speak a given language, the higher are the benefits from learning it.

The benefits of club membership are non-rival (or partially rival) because positive reputational benefits garnered by one member can be simultaneously enjoyed by other members. At some point, crowding would set in. A club with universal membership would do little to

[17] This potentially creates path dependencies where past choices regarding a specific network (which influence the costs and benefits of joining it relative to other networks) influence subsequent choices. Although not necessary, an "inferior" network with first-mover advantages may out-compete "superior" networks because of its lower costs, the QWERTY typewriter being a classic example (David, 1985).

[18] Network effects should not be confused with network externalities if network participants internalize these effects. In our case, the network effects are external to an individual firm and yet internal to the club. In many ways, what is internal and what is external depends on where we draw the boundary. In our case, club membership defines the boundary. For a detailed discussion, see Liebowitz and Margolis (1995b).

[19] New members create externalities, positive and negative, for existing members. Some potential members may be so desirable that clubs may waive fees and preconditions to entice them to join. Country clubs are known to compete to get trophy celebrities because their presence enhances the club's reputation. Likewise, Rotary clubs have been known to induct locally eminent people as honorary members. While recognizing that heterogeneity in members' attributes influences any club's reputation, we treat this within the purview of club standards, not in terms of club strategies directed to recruit specific actors. We do not find cases where voluntary programs pursue specific firms with incentives that were unavailable to other members. On the contrary, some NGO-sponsored clubs have pursued big industry players with negative incentives (threats of campaigns and boycotts) if they do not join the NGO club. In the forestry sector, the strategies of NGOs to persuade large firms to join the Forest Stewardship Council Club illustrate this point (Bartley, 2003; Cashore et al., 2004).

distinguish environmentally progressive firms. Much of the club literature examines membership size from the perspective of optimal club size (Cornes and Sandler, 1996). We are not aware of any voluntary environmental program, including ISO 14001, that has overcrowding issues.

While a green club with universal membership would do little to identify environmentally progressive firms,[20] universal membership is sometimes a desired objective, though universal in this sense means members of a particular industry association or group. In industry-sponsored clubs such as the chemical industry's Responsible Care Program and the forestry industry's Sustainable Forestry Initiative, the industry associations require all of its members to subscribe to the club. These green clubs represent an industry's response to its own collective reputation problem. Members of the industry collectively sought to build an image of responsibility and environmental steward-ship. To do so, the industry club requires members to adopt specific standards for their environmental operations. If some members do not join the club, and thereby do not adopt its new progressive environ-mental practices, their relative slack in environmental performance creates negative externalities for other industry members because stakeholders, already having negative perceptions about the industry, may believe that weak environmental performance is an industry-wide phenomenon. A few bad apples can tarnish the image of the good ones, especially if stakeholders have few incentives or opportunities to distinguish among industry members.[21] Mandatory membership is not uncommon for green clubs sponsored by industry associations.

Some firms unilaterally take progressive environmental action to boost their reputation with stakeholders. Indeed, it is not hard to think

---

[20] There is some question about how to assess clubs' welfare implications: should it be from the perspective of club members (Buchanan, 1965) or the whole economy (Ng, 1973)? In other words, should voluntary programs devise rules so as to maximize reputational benefits for club members or devise rules to maximize the production of public goods? In our view, the focus needs to be balanced: green clubs need to supply positive reputational benefits, which then induce members to join the club and take on the costs of producing its public good.

[21] In a media-saturated society where agendas are driven by sound bites, long and complex explanations may not work well. Media may portray a bad apple as the industry mascot. A good strategy is to be proactive and ensure that all firms join the industry club.

of specific companies that have well-earned reputations for being environmental leaders. If some firms can take such unilateral action, what is the advantage of green clubs? Green club membership offers several advantages over unilateral action for enhancing firms' reputations among stakeholders. Unilateral commitments to environmental stewardship may be less credible because they are less institutionalized (also, see Gunningham and Sinclair, 2002). When individual firms make their own rules, they can more easily change them. Being part of larger brand system is likely to provide the club with a degree of legitimacy that a firm alone may find difficult to acquire. Because green clubs can also capture economies of scale and network externalities, progressive environmental action taken as part of a club can do more to boost a firm's standing with stakeholders than the same action taken unilaterally.

In sum, the promise of effective green clubs is that they induce members to take progressive environmental action beyond what private motives compel them to take unilaterally. For club members, the benefit of membership over taking the same actions unilaterally is receiving the excludable branding certification that allows members to publicize their club membership, claim credit for their proenvironmental activities, and receive rewards from stakeholders who value the action that club membership signals. In such cases, green clubs create a win-all-around scenario: participating firms win stakeholders' rewards for their progressive environmental action, the general public enjoys the public goods, and club sponsors enjoy heightened prestige for producing the public good. The nature of this club benefit is likely to vary across programs, depending on how much positive reputation membership in the club conveys, and across companies within clubs, depending on how much members' stakeholders are willing and able to respond to the message club membership provides for each firm, and across policy and economic contexts.

Club attributes

Having outlined the basic features of clubs and how voluntary environmental programs can be conceptualized as clubs, we can now turn to showing how our theoretical perspective sheds light on important design features for making clubs effective. Like markets and governments, green clubs are vulnerable to institutional failures if they do not solve their collective action dilemmas.[22] For green clubs, two collective action dilemmas are analytically most salient. Failing to solve these dilemmas jeopardizes the success of the program. First, the Olsonian dilemma centers on clubs' capacity to attract sufficiently large membership rosters, and therefore their ability to capture the economies of scale and network effects for building their reputations. After all, joining a green club is voluntarily and membership can be costly. The second dilemma, the shirking dilemma, pertains to the green clubs' ability to compel members to adhere to club standards once they have joined the club. Firms may have incentives to join the program and enjoy the benefits of the club's reputation for environmental progressivism, but shirk their responsibility to adhere to club standards. Widespread shirking would undermine a green club's credibility and viability. If the green club strictly monitors rules and sanctions non-compliers, shirking can be mitigated. This would contribute to the club's reputation as a policy instrument that produces public goods, while enhancing its attractiveness to new members.

Below we examine how green club attributes affect programs' ability to address these two collective action dilemmas. High levels of excludable reputational benefits make clubs attractive and mitigate the Olsonian dilemma by inducing members to join the green club. Enforcement rules mitigate shirking, the second-order collective action dilemma, by monitoring and enforcing members' adherence to club standards. When firms join the green club and adhere to its standards, the club produces desirable public goods. Curbing the shirking dilemma indirectly helps mitigate the Olsonian dilemma by strengthening the club's reputation and therefore making it more attractive for potential members.

Club standards

Club standards specify what firms need to do to join the club and remain members in good standing. There are several different types of club standards. They might specify performance expectations (sometimes called outcome standards), such as requiring members to meet pollution- and waste-reduction targets or recycle a percentage of their waste stream. Other standards are more process oriented, such as

---

[22] For a detailed discussion on market and government failures, see chapters 5–9 of Weimer and Wining (1999).

requirements that members adopt an environmental management system (EMS), or that members regularly consult with community and environmental groups. Finally, some club standards can limit membership eligibility by descriptive preconditions, such as whether firms operate in a specific industry or have already established high standards of environmental performance.

As we noted briefly above, some programs have adopted another type of club standard: some industry associations have mandated their member firms to join a particular green club. Firms that do not join industry-sponsored green clubs may be expelled from the industry association – though in practice this is seldom carried out (Prakash, 2000b). Such industry-clubs are still voluntary; they are different from mandatory governmental regulations where non-compliance can trigger civil and criminal penalties and the only way for firms to escape governmental regulations is to migrate to another jurisdiction.[23] In contrast, firms can leave an industry association and continue to operate profitably in the industry and the association cannot imprison or fine them. Having said this, cases where members have been expelled from an industry association for refusing to join the association's clubs, such as Responsible Care (chemical industry's green club) or Sustainable Forestry Initiative (forestry industry's green club), are very rare.

Lenient club standards require marginal effort for firms to join the program. Of course, even lenient club standards must mandate at least some non-trivial membership costs, or else the club would be an empty gesture. While many firms might easily join a lenient green club, the club's reputation is not likely to be stellar because word would spread among stakeholders that the club requires little progressive environmental action by its members. Such clubs might face adverse selection problems because environmentally progressive firms would not want to subsidize or identify with environmental laggards, and therefore opt out of the club.[24] In the long term, this would

---

[23] Industry-level clubs may institutionalize norms for environmental stewardship. Rees (1997) makes this argument in the context of Responsible Care. While we view credible monitoring and sanctioning as the key to curb shirking, Rees (1997) suggests that normative or sociological influences via club membership may work as well.

[24] Clubs might offer selective incentives to induce high-profile firms with stellar environmental reputations to join the programs. A few such "trophy" firms

further lower a club's legitimacy and make it unattractive even for laggards.

Stringent club standards require members to take substantial and costly action that leads to a high level of environmental performance. These are high-cost clubs. A green club with stringent club standards may admit only firms who have already achieved superior environmental performance, as in the EPA's Performance Track Programs (EPA, 2004b), or those that are willing to incur the substantial costs that high environmental performance requires. The advantage of stringent standards is that the club brand would be very credible and serve as a low-cost tool for signaling club members' commitment to protect the natural environment. Stakeholders would easily differentiate environmental leaders (members) from laggards (non-members). Armed with this information, these stakeholders could reward and punish firms accordingly. And this would insulate the club from the criticism that it is a greenwash, a smokescreen for polluters.

While stringent club standards carry obvious advantages for producing public goods and improving the club's reputation, such green clubs may price themselves out of the reach of many firms, leading to a smaller membership roster that does not fully exploit the scale economies and network effects for building and advertising the club's reputation. Further, if the preconditions for joining the green club are very high, members may have little room for further improvement in their environmental performance, in which case, club membership may do little to improve members' performance beyond their pre-membership levels. While not a greenwash, the stringent green club may still be deemed as being ineffective because it may then be viewed as adding little value *over and above* that created by command and control regulations and other incentives facing the firms.

Designing voluntary programs requires balancing competing imperatives. On the one hand, to enhance the club's credibility with external stakeholders, sponsors may prefer strict standards. On the other hand, such standards may lead to low membership and therefore dampen network effects and scale economies. In all likelihood, moderate club standards may hold the most promise. Their rules are

might greatly boost a program's reputation. While theoretically interesting, we do not find evidence of such strategies in voluntary programs.

sufficiently stringent that they require members to take important additional environmentally progressive action. Yet at the same time, they are accessible to a wide range of firms. This means that many firms can join the green club, many of which are likely to improve their environmental performance beyond their pre-membership levels. While moderate club standards carry less standing with stakeholders than stringent standards, the broad eligibility of the club can boost the club's membership rosters and lead to enhanced scale economies and network effects that advertise the brand to a wide audience.

Monitoring and enforcement rules

Once firms have joined a green club, members may encounter powerful incentives to willfully shirk their responsibilities by not adhering to the club standards. After all, the reputational and goodwill benefits of club membership accrue to all members, including the laggards that do not incur the costs of adhering to the club's standards. Non-adherence to club standards could be rooted in members' ignorance or willful evasion of club requirements (Brehm and Hamilton, 1996; Winter and May, 2001). Unlike command and control regulations, non-adherence rooted in ignorance is unlikely because joining green clubs is voluntary and firms are likely to have a fair idea of the club standards. Arguably, there may be instances where a club changes its standards to impose new obligations after a firm has joined the club. A member might then end up failing to adhere to club standards out of ignorance. For example, the two major green clubs in the forestry sector, the Forest Stewardship Council and the Sustainable Forestry Initiative, have changed their rules and standards quite often. But changing club standards is often complex, resulting in debate and contention among the club's membership. These debates are likely to draw the attention of club members and dispel ignorance about new rules. In the case of voluntary programs, firms' willful evasion is the more likely cause of non-adherence to club standards.

As with non-compliance with governmental regulations, shirking in clubs can occur because of information asymmetries between club members and sponsors, club members and their external stakeholders, coupled with the non-trivial costs of monitoring members' adherence to club rules. Voluntary programs may not require members to provide unvarnished information to club sponsors or external stake-holders[25] regarding their environmental programs and adherence to club standards. The rule architecture of a club may not provide effective monitoring mechanisms, leading external stakeholders to rely on club sponsors to enforce club standards. Unlike command and control policies, where external stakeholders often have deliberately designed access to compliance information (such as the EPA's Inte-grated Database for Enforcement Analysis) or performance informa-tion (as in the EPA's Toxics Release Inventory), clubs often operate behind closed doors. This exacerbates stakeholders' difficulties in learning about the club and how well its members are adhering to its standards. The lack of public scrutiny and consequent information asymmetries have caused some environmentalists to question green clubs' accountability (Steinzor, 1998). Indeed, many environmental groups fear that clubs have too much incentive to provide lax monitoring as a strategy for boosting membership.

Clubs' enforcement rules can be designed to mitigate shirking prob-lems. Responsible Care, the chemical industry's green club, requires member firms to establish citizen advisory panels for each facility in order to share (at least some) information about the facilities' opera-tion and receive public input (Prakash, 2000b). While this provides some transparency, one can envision a system with even more unfet-tered public access to monitor firms' adherence to club standards. Along with requiring transparency and public disclosure, clubs can institute more formal monitoring policies. George Stiglitz noted in his Nobel Prize lecture that actions firms take convey information:

In some cases, the action will be designed to obfuscate, to limit information disclosure . . . In others, the action will be designed to convey information in a credible way, to alter beliefs. The fact that customers will treat a firm that issues a better guarantee as if its product is better – and therefore be willing to pay a higher price – may affect the guarantee that the firm is willing to issue . . . A simple lesson emerges: some individuals wish to convey information; some individuals wish not to have information conveyed (either because such information might lead others to think less well of

---

[25] As demonstrated in the literature on the Toxics Release Inventory, if provided with access to information on firms' environmental performance and programs, external stakeholders can serve as watchdogs over firms' environmental perfor-mance (Hamilton, 1995; Konar and Cohen, 1997).

them, or because conveying information may interfere with their ability to appropriate rents). In either case, the fact that actions convey information leads people to alter their behavior, and changes how markets function. This is why information imperfections have such profound effects. Once one recognizes that actions convey information, two results follow. First, in making decisions about what to do, individuals will not only think about what they like (as in traditional economics) but how it will affect others' beliefs about them . . . Secondly, we noted earlier that individuals have an incentive to "lie" – the less able to say that they are more able. Similarly, if it becomes recognized that those who walk up to the fifth floor to apply for insurance are more healthy, then I might be willing to do so even if I am not so healthy, simply to fool the insurance company . . . Recognizing this, one needs to look for ways by which information is conveyed *in equilibrium*. (2001: 495)

As a mechanism for conveying information about firms' environmental actions and adherence to club standards, formal monitoring can vary in its level of stringency: first party (self-certification), second party (certified by a manager from a different unit of the same company or a different firm within the same industry), third party (certification by an external auditor but paid for by the company), and fourth party (certification by an external auditor who is not paid by the company) (Gereffi *et al.*, 2001). First party is the least stringent while fourth party is the most credible. In practice, very few clubs have fourth-party oversight; third party is currently considered the "best practice" on the assumption that external auditors monitor with due diligence.[26]

---

[26] Skepticism about audits as instruments for enforcement and monitoring is perhaps best articulated by Michael Power in his books, *The Audit Society* (1997) and *The Audit Explosion* (1994). Powers argues that the term audit is ill defined and not analytically differentiated from inspection or other forms of social control. He traces the rise of auditing as a tool of compliance to the rise of new public management and liberalism where the traditional tools of social control are increasingly being discarded in favor of some type of inspection. In some ways, the increased reliance on audits represents a general decline in trust in organization but increased trust in "experts" who monitor them. For Power, audits are tools to legitimize organizations and practices even when audits may uncover serious problems. However, given the relative lack of public access to audit findings and the relative absence of independent parties to verify the quality of audits, the reliance on audits as tools of social control seems problematic. For a recent discussion on these subjects, see the special issue of *Law & Policy*, July 2003.

Although third-party auditing has several merits, it may not be perfect. If firms hire auditors and they can choose from several auditing service vendors, auditors may have incentives to provide favorable reviews of their clients. One might argue that auditors who fail to monitor with due diligence will eventually undermine their own reputation, and in the long term make themselves less attractive to firms seeking validation through third-party audits (Milgrom *et al.*, 1990). After all, firms need auditors to attest to their adherence to club rules; an auditor with a shaky reputation adds little to the firms' claims about its environmental performance and adherence to club rules. While there is some merit to this argument, external auditors are not immune to shirking their own responsibilities as verifiers of firms' adherence to club standards. There is a broader issue of agency conflict and corporate governance here. The recent scandals in the accounting industry suggest that external auditors have overlooked instances where firms have abused regulations and standards, and in some cases they have even overlooked regulatory violations, all to curry favor with firms. The accounting industry has attributed this agency conflict to the merger of accounting and consulting roles within the major accounting companies and has therefore undertaken institutional responses to separate the two businesses. Some have further suggested that financial auditing should be publicly funded in order to minimize conflicts between auditors' roles as verifier of information and compliance with rules and clients of the very company whose information and compliance the auditing firm is verifying (Cleary, 2002; Verdonik, 2005). In any case, as this discussion suggests, the efficacy of monitoring through third-party auditing remains a contested issue.

This discussion raises an important point about how third party audits might influence firm behavior. In this book we are not claiming that third-party audits mitigate shirking only because they serve as a signaling device to external stakeholders. From our perspective, third-party audits are likely also to mitigate shirking by creating incentives for managers within the firm to adhere to program obligations. We agree that the efficacy of external audits is likely to increase if the voluntary programs require that audit information be shared with outside stakeholders. But outside stakeholders will play a role in reducing shirking via audits *only if* they have access to audit information and can then differentiate shirkers from non-shirkers.

Although clubs that do not require audit information to be shared with outside stakeholders may less effectively mitigate shirking compared to clubs with disclosure requirements, they may still be more effective than programs without any credible monitoring and enforcement mechanisms. For perspective, third-party audits as rule-enforcing instruments are widely employed (Juran, 1962) in accounting, food-processing, apparel, and forestry industries (Bartley, 2003). There is a broader literature on information asymmetries (Akerlof, 1970; Nelson, 1970) that provides a theoretical rationale for the use of third-party audits as institutional devices to mitigate shirking.[27] Specifically, third-party audits are useful for signaling quality for experience and post-experience goods. In addition to their "post-experience features," firms' environmental programs have "Potemkin attributes" (Schaltegger *et al.*, 2003) because stakeholders want to know about firms' production processes but are not in a position to observe them. Third-party audits (even without disclosure of audit information) can provide such assurance. While we do not have direct quantitative evidence about how audits actually reduce shirking, anecdotal evidence suggests that third-party audits play a significant role in mitigating shirking, primarily by influencing intra-firm politics (Prakash, 2000a). We also have strong theoretical grounds for this argument. A well-developed body of literature in organizational behavior suggests that the presence of outside observers improves team members' performance; dynamics similar to the "Hawthorne effect" (Mayo, 1945) may be taking place in the case of green clubs that employ third-party auditing.[28] A Hawthorne effect refers to an improvement

---

[27] Based on increasing levels of information asymmetries between the producers and buyers/stakeholders, the literature identifies three types of goods: search goods (buyers can assess quality prior to purchase; minimum asymmetry), experience goods (buyer can assess quality after consumption), and post-experience goods (buyers cannot assess quality even after consumption; maximum asymmetry) (Weimer and Vining, 1999).

[28] The Hawthorne effect refers to an improvement in the performance of the research target (individual or group) because of being singled out for observation and study by an outside observer. These studies marked the beginning of the human relations movement in organizational research. The studies derive their name from the location of the manufacturing plant of Western Electric (Hawthorne, IL, near Chicago) where the data were collected in the 1920s. In one of the segments of this research, the lighting conditions were manipulated for one group of workers (the treatment group) and the lighting conditions remained fixed for the control group. The researchers found that as the lighting

in the performance of the research target (individual or group) that results from being singled out for observation by an outside observer.

Mitigating shirking requires not just detecting members' non-compliance with club standards but sanctioning it as well. Developing an appropriate sanctioning mechanism is complicated: effective sanctions need to be graduated to correspond with the level of violation and the intent of the violator (Ostrom, 1990). Lax sanctioning would insufficiently prevent shirking, while the fear of excessive sanctioning could create disincentives to join a voluntary club. Because the purpose of sanctioning is both to punish and to educate, club sponsors need to strike a balance between these objectives. Clubs could sanction in various ways, ranging from naming and shaming (such as listing violators in the newsletter) to expulsion from the club. Clubs such as Responsible Care typically have been reticent about severe sanctioning; many claim that the purpose of the club is to educate and improve performance through positive reinforcement. This reticence could be problematic from a public policy perspective because it is not clear what "swords" are being employed to enforce the agreement among members that they will take progressive environmental action. And, as Thomas Hobbes (1651) noted, covenants without swords are mere words.

Towards a typology of green clubs

We have sketched how club standards and enforcement rules influence the Olsonian and the shirking dilemmas in green clubs. In this section, we further develop the typology of clubs, first introduced in chapter 1, as a joint product of these rules, and illustrate them with examples. We identify four ideal club types – stringent club standards with enforcement rules (Type 1: Mandarins), stringent club standards without enforcement rules (Type 2: Country Clubs), lenient club standards

---

increased in the treatment group, the productivity went up in both groups. To their further surprise, the researchers found that when the lighting decreased for the treatment group, the productivity continued to increase for both groups. The conclusion was that introducing outside observers made the workers feel important and resulted in improved productivity, although the physical environmental was not changed. The core theoretical insight that we employ is that the introduction of external observers (third-party auditors) may lead environmental managers to curb shirking. We owe this point to Abhishek Srivastava.

Table 2.2. Club design: an institutionalist approach

Club standards Enforcement rules	Stringent	Lenient
Credible	**Type 1: Mandarins** Low membership levels and low shirking; High entry barriers may attract only the top performers that have little organizational slack; Club appears successful because it differentiates leaders from laggards; Club may not significantly improve members' performance, e.g. National Performance Track; Project XL.	**Type 3: Bootcamps** High membership levels, low shirking; The club is likely to attract significant number of members and force members to improve their performance; Although entry barriers are low, stringent club standards may deter laggards from joining the club. Over the long run, the club may successfully differentiate laggards from leaders/ potential leaders, e.g. 1SO 14001.
Not-credible	**Type 2: Country Clubs** Low membership levels, high shirking; Attracting leaders and imposing few new requirements will not translate into improved performance. But high entry barriers will help to differentiate members from non-members, e.g. Responsible Care.	**Type 4: Greenwashes** High membership levels, high shirking; Club may attract members but not enforce club rules. Club will have low credibility, fail to distinguish leaders from laggards, and will face adverse selection problems.

with enforcement rules (Type 3: Bootcamps), and lenient club standards without credible enforcement rules (Type 4: Greenwashes) – and
provide examples of these types in practice today, thus showing how
our theory can account for why some programs have been shown to be
effective while others have not.

From a policy perspective, Type 1 Mandarin clubs have considerable merit. Their high club standards along with credible enforcement
mechanisms boost their reputation with external stakeholders. Mandarin clubs can therefore mitigate the Olsonian dilemma in the sense
that firms in large numbers would want to join in order to benefit
from the club's reputation. The presence of credible enforcement
mechanisms would also ensure low shirking levels, leading to an
effective production of public goods. A potential drawback of Type
1 green clubs is that the high standards tend to limit club membership
to only a small cadre of top performers that can afford the costs of
performing as the club standards require. This could diminish opportunities to achieve the scale economies and network effects for broad-
casting the club brand that large membership provides. Further, if
higher-performing firms have little room to improve their performance, policy analysts may find that the clubs to which these firms
belong do not produce public goods beyond what members would
otherwise have produced unilaterally.

With limited scale economies and network effects hindering their
ability to build broadly recognized brand names, Mandarin clubs are
likely to evolve towards niche players where external actors use clubs
to identify and reward exceptionally high performance. A prime example of a Type 1 club is the EPA's Project XL.[29] Launched in 1995 by
the EPA and its state partners, Project XL has stringent club standards:
only facilities with good compliance histories are eligible for membership and the program requires a high level of environmental performance once firms have joined. To enhance transparency, the EPA
requires that the applicants consult local and national stakeholders
during the project negotiation phase. Yet even this Mandarin club has
come under criticism from environmentalists for being too lax on
industrial polluters. As a consequence, project negotiations have been

---

[29] Other examples include the EPA's Star Track and the National Environment
Performance Track programs (EPA, 2004; Crow, 2000).

long and arduous. Not surprisingly, instead of the 50 pilot projects targeted by the program, only fourteen were implemented by August 1999 (EPA, 1999a).

Type 2 Country Clubs have high entry barriers that limit club membership to top performers but at the same time have weak and perhaps even non-credible enforcement rules. While strong on initial promise, the fate of these green clubs may stem from their lack of effective enforcement mechanisms that can compel members to follow through on their program commitments. Consequently, many members can shirk their club responsibilities after joining the green club. In such cases, the club's reputation is likely to suffer, further undermining incentives for firms to join the club. With sporadic membership and faulty credibility, country clubs are unlikely to grow and if they are to endure they are likely to evolve to having stronger enforcement mechanisms.

The chemical industry's initial experience with Responsible Care is perhaps an example of the problems with country clubs. Following the Bhopal disaster in 1984, public trust in the chemical industry reached a low level and the industry feared new and stringent government regulations (Hoffman, 1997). To win back public trust, to demonstrate that the industry could self-regulate, and perhaps to preempt new government regulations, the Chemical Manufacturers Association (now known as the American Chemistry Council) launched the Responsible Care program in 1988 (Rees, 1997; Prakash, 2000b). The industry faced a collective reputation problem that it sought to address by launching a green club and *mandating* that its members join. The program's club standards were high: members had to adopt the club's Six Codes of Conduct containing more than 100 specific standards governing members' manufacturing, distribution, and transportation operations. However, Responsible Care's enforcement rules were generally quite weak. The program did not require member firms to implement all the six codes immediately; members could chart their own time-frame for implementation. Responsible Care members initially received second-party or peer audits from personnel working for other club members. This evaluation was to be shared with the CMA/ACC but neither the firm nor the CMA/ACC was obligated to share it with stakeholders. Finally, the CMA/ACC did not aggressively sanction violators or laggard firms. Thus, while Responsible Care had some impressive club standards, its monitoring and enforcement mechanisms were weak.

The efficacy of Responsible Care has been called into question, which is perhaps not surprising given the program's weak enforcement mechanism. In their thorough analysis of the program, King and Lennox (2000) find that participants did not improve their environmental performance beyond what they would had they not joined the program, concluding that shirking was the culprit behind the program's failure (but see Rees, 1997). In response to these shortcomings, the CMA/ACC looked to strengthen Responsible Care's credibility. Beginning in 2003, the CMA started requiring Responsible Care members to undergo third-party audits. It has also begun to harmonize its club standards with ISO 14001, the world's most established green club by offering its members the possibility of joint Responsible Care/ISO 14001 certification (ACC, 2004).

Type 3 Bootcamps hold considerable promise from a policy perspective. Moderately lenient club standards allow a wide array of firms to join the club, including mid-range firms and even laggards for whom the costs of club membership are offset by the benefits of affiliating with the green club's positive reputation. Credible enforcement rules compel firms to adhere to club standards over time, and thereby improve their environmental and regulatory performance. For these bootcamps, the potential for network effects is significant because wide membership creates a virtuous cycle with members advertising the club brand for the rest of the membership, providing a more powerful brand that attracts even more members. The key policy promise is that these clubs can potentially produce high levels of desirable public goods by encouraging small to moderate improvements in environmental performance across a large membership roster. The critical challenge for club sponsors is to ensure that the levels of excludable reputational benefits are sufficient to induce less-than-stellar performers (the ones which are likely to spend most on new programs) to join the green club.

A good example of a Type 3 bootcamp is ISO 14001, the subject of this book. As we discuss in chapter 3, ISO 14001 is a Type 3 green club because it carries moderate club standards (EMS) and relatively stringent enforcement mechanisms (external audits). As we show in chapter 4, ISO 14001 carries a widely recognized and positive reputation among external stakeholders, especially government regulators.

Moreover, as we demonstrate in chapter 5, ISO 14001 appears to improve facilities' environmental performance and their compliance with government regulations.

Type 4 clubs have weak club standards and non-credible enforcement rules, and are the greenwashes about which environmental groups worry. Their lenient club standards coupled with non-credible enforcement rules mean that firms are less likely to improve their environmental and regulatory performance. As a club's reputation falters, the above-average performers have incentives to quit the club. This adverse selection problem would further pull down club performance. Such clubs are unlikely to have a major policy impact.

Club design and firm performance

To better understand the dynamics of how clubs operate, we present here a simple framework for studying firms' reaction to different club standards, holding enforcement mechanisms constant. Our objective is to develop empirically tractable implications from our theory regarding how different firms respond to a green club and how different clubs achieve varying levels of success in improving firms' performance. We simplify our discussion to a few simple constructs about firms, club standards, government regulations, and the reputational benefits firms receive for taking progressive environmental action. The discussion illustrates how different firms respond to green clubs across varying economic and policy contexts, setting the groundwork for our empirical analyses in later chapters.

In the discussion below, we assume that producing a cleaner environment is costly to firms, though these costs are heterogeneous across firms. We distil government regulations and club standards to a simple single dimension measuring environmental performance, and we assume governments and club sponsors can perfectly enforce compliance with their standards. We thus assume that all the different types of club standards can be meaningfully mapped onto a single environmental performance dimension that reflects the different types of environmental performance, such as pollution reduction, recycling, regulatory compliance, biodiversity protection and so on.

The government and club standards reflect the environmental performance each wants firms to achieve, with the green club choosing cleaner environmental standards than the government. We assume

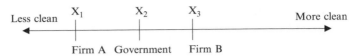

Figure 2.1. Governments' and firms' choices of environmental protection.

that a club's reputational benefit is based on the fact that at least some stakeholders demand a cleaner environment than that which is codified in the government's regulations and these stakeholders are able to reward firms accordingly. In our theoretical framework, firms first identify their desired environmental performance based on the private benefits they receive from their environmental actions; these unilateral choices may be higher or lower than the levels specified in the governmental rules and club standards. Firms then decide whether to join the green club by weighing the costs of their unilateral choice against the benefits to be gained from moving to the environmental performance specified in the club's standards.

Consider a first scenario in which a firm is choosing its level of environmental performance. Figure 2.1 shows the environmental performance preferences of two firms and the governmental regulations they face. The axis presents the level of environmental protection, with greater levels of environmental protection moving from left to right. In Figure 2.1, Firm A prefers a lower level of environmental protection than the one specified by governmental regulations perhaps because generating more negative pollution externalities reduces this firm's production costs. Firm A perceives regulatory compliance costs as the difference between its own internally chosen level of environmental performance (X_1) and the government's preferred level of environmental performance (X_2) as codified in its environmental regulations. Firm B prefers a higher level of environmental performance (X_3) than the governmental regulations require, perhaps because its environmentalist consumers are willing to pay a price premium for green products. Complying with governmental regulations will appear "costless" to Firm B in the sense that it will receive more private benefits for producing the environmental good by going "beyond compliance" with the government's regulations.

Figure 2.1 presents the case of how these firms might react to a green club. In Figure 2.1, the club sponsors specify a level of environmental

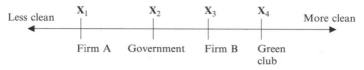

Figure 2.2. Governments', firms' and green clubs' choices of environmental protection.

protection members must achieve, as codified in club standards which are located in this case at X_4. The goal of the club is to induce Firms A and B to move from their preferred positions to a new, cleaner level of environmental performance. If we assume that cleaner environmental performance is more costly, Firm A has a great amount of improvement to make to achieve X_4 (from X_2 to X_4, if it is in compliance with government regulations) while the task for Firm B is less costly (from X_3 to X_4).

Whether Firms A and B join the green club depends on whether their costs of moving to the cleaner performance levels are lower than the benefits each firm receives for joining the green club. The greater the reputational benefit that comes from membership in the green club, the more the club can induce firms to incur larger membership costs leading to more improvements in their environmental practices. Since we assume the private benefits from progressive environmental action have already been exogenously set at X_1 and X_3 for firms A and B, and because we assume the public benefits are negligible for firms (independent of the private benefits they might receive for taking progressive action), the key incentive for improving firms' environmental performance is the club benefit that can induce firms to move to a higher level of environmental performance. In Figure 2.2, if the green club has a moderate reputational benefit, it might induce firm B (at X_3) to move from X_3 to X_4, but the club benefits may not be enough to induce Firm A to improve its environmental performance. If the club has a strong reputational benefit, it might induce Firm A to join the club and move to a level of environmental performance at X_4 from the X_2 that government regulations required it to adopt.

In this simple example, a green club with a reputation for environmental stewardship can claim credit for inducing firms to improve their environmental performance beyond what they would accomplish unilaterally. If the green club has little to no reputational benefit, some firms may still join the green club because they might choose the club's level of environmental performance for reasons of pure private gain. Such green clubs may provide some distinction between members and non-members in the sense that members may be better environmentalists than non-members, but the clubs would not induce members to take additional progressive environmental action beyond what members would have taken unilaterally.

The costs of joining a green club and the benefits accrued from affiliating with the club's brand name are likely to vary across firms and across economic and policy contexts. Some firms may receive more value from the club's positive brand identity, perhaps because their own corporate brand is not well known or perhaps because consumers in their industry or area have stronger demand for green products. Or, while enforcing governmental regulations, government regulators may reward firms that join a green club, an issue we address later. Because of this heterogeneity across firms, the roster of firms in any green club is likely to be diverse. Some members will have made a vast improvement in their environmental performance by joining the club; for these firms, the value of affiliating with the club's reputation was great, offsetting the significant cost of the environmental improvements. Other members are likely to have made little improvement in their performance beyond what they would have chosen unilaterally. These firms may have chosen a high level of environmental performance for purely private reasons; that is, they would have taken the same action without having joined the club. While such firms may take more progressive environmental action than non-members, the green club does not deserve credit for their achievements. In practice, distinguishing between progressive actions taken for private reasons and the same action taken to receive the club good is a daunting task, requiring knowledge of firms' environmental performances in the absence of the green club along with knowledge about how much value they receive from affiliation with the club. We can more easily observe the *average* effect of club participation by comparing the environmental performance of members and non-members, assuming other factors are properly controlled, as we do in chapter 5. If the club has a substantial positive reputation that is valuable to members, as we demonstrate in chapters 3 and 4, then we can attribute at least some of the members' environmental improvement to the existence of the club.

An implication of this discussion is that the marginal cost for firms to join a green club is lower in jurisdictions with more stringent government standards, assuming the government's standards are effectively enforced. Consider again Figure 2.2. Because the government compels Firm A to move from X_1 to X_3, the firm's marginal cost of joining the green club is the cost of moving from X_3 to X_4. Note that in this case, the marginal social benefit of joining the club (the amount of additional environmental good the green club creates) is the X_3 to X_4 increment, which is smaller than it would be if the government had lenient environmental standards (below X_1). This leads to the somewhat paradoxical conclusion that green clubs have the potential to change members' behavior the most where government regulations are least stringent. Even if every stakeholder recognized that all members have achieved the club's targeted level of performance (through effective compliance mechanisms), when the club standard is only somewhat stronger than governmental standards membership will do little to signal vastly superior environmental performance. At the same time, more stringent government standards lower the costs of joining the green club by reducing the *marginal* amount of environmental improvement firms below the government standards must achieve in order to join the green club. In such contexts, club sponsors may look to raise club standards to differentiate their club and its members from those merely complying with government regulations. The implication is that analysts evaluating green clubs need to be aware that clubs' efficacy may vary depending on characteristics of its member firms and the policy and economic context in which they operate.

By now it should be clear that the club benefits are a central analytic feature of voluntary environmental programs. Green clubs with stronger brand identities can attract more firms with greater room for environmental improvement. Assuming the club's enforcement standards are effective, these firms will on average generate greater *marginal* environmental gains from their participation in the club because the green club induces improvements in their environmental performance beyond what the firms would achieve unilaterally. The strength of a green club's reputation with firms' stakeholders depends on several factors. To a large degree, green clubs' reputations are stronger when they have effective enforcement mechanisms to prevent shirking and stringent club standards that require progressive environmental action from members. Also, building a strong brand reputation is where sponsorship can play an important role: stakeholders may be more likely to believe in a green club sponsored by an environmental group than one sponsored by an industry group, even if the two clubs have identical club standards and enforcement mechanisms. It can be difficult for stakeholders to verify whether club sponsors are implementing their standards and mechanisms effectively. Indeed, ISO 14001 enjoys a strong reputation in part because of ISO's standing as a management standards leader.

Green clubs, cooperation, and reputation

Club benefits accrue to members via how external stakeholders form perceptions about the club's reputation. The value of a club's reputation depends on how stakeholders use club membership as a criterion to reward or punish firms. We often think of brands in terms of a firm's corporate reputation or a product's reputation among consumers. But all types of stakeholders can potentially respond to such brand signals. Government officials, particularly those who enforce government regulations, are key stakeholders who influence firms' environmental policy choices. Faced with information asymmetries and non-trivial monitoring costs, regulators often look to distinguish firms who are trying to comply with regulations from those firms looking to duck their regulatory obligations for their own advantage.[30] While consumers and other stakeholders may certainly use environmental branding for their purchasing and investments, brands that signal firms' progressive environmental commitments may be of more value to government regulators who face high costs of enforcing governmental regulations. Government regulators significantly contribute to the institutional and policy contexts in which firms operate, and they are perhaps the most important factor influencing the levels of reputational benefits firms perceive if they were to join a green club. And yet government and firms are often at loggerheads regarding environmental regulations, a relationship that is frequently marked by distrust and conflict. In this section, we examine how green clubs that have credible reputations for improving members' environmental performance can help turn lose–lose conflict between firms and gov-

---

[30] This point was emphasized by several regulators during our interviews.

ernment regulators into win–win cooperation. As cooperation begets more cooperation and trust, green clubs become even more attractive as policy tools to generate public benefits.

As noted in chapter 1, command and control regulation coupled with deterrence-based enforcement is the central approach to environmental governance across the developed world, especially in the US. Regulators specify pollution-control technologies, such as the "best available technology" standards and/or how much pollution firms can emit or discharge into the atmosphere. Governments then enforce regulations by monitoring firms' behavior and punishing those that fail to achieve the regulatory standards.

Even if regulators enforce vigorously and impose severe penalties for discovered violations, deterrence may not be the optimal enforcement approach. If regulations could be enforced at low costs, policy objectives would perhaps be met. But enforcement costs are nontrivial and declining agency budgets relative to regulatory mandates have undermined enforcement frequency and efficacy (GAO, 1983; Fiorino, 2001). Moreover, rigid deterrence-based enforcement only feeds firms' complaints that high compliance costs hurt productivity and profits (Jaffe *et al.*, 1995; Walley and Whitehead, 1994), in turn raising firms' incentives to evade regulations (Majumdar and Marcus, 2001). Deterrence-based enforcement may contribute to the adversarial relationships among regulators, firms and environmental groups, risking more lawsuits and larger societal costs (Reilly, 1999; Scholz, 1991; Vogel, 1986; Kagan, 1991; for a critique, see Coglianese, 1996).

The cooperative approach to regulatory enforcement seeks to address many of the deterrence enforcement drawbacks by enlisting firms' assistance in solving environmental problems. Rather than generating conflict in the strict deterrence approach, a cooperative regulatory enforcement approach is based on a foundation of flexibility and mutual trust between firms and governments (Scholz, 1991). In this approach, regulators do not rigidly interpret the law and penalize every violation by firms that regulators believe are operating in good faith. Instead, regulators forgo punishing self-disclosed violations, particularly minor self-disclosed ones, reduce sanctioning levels for severe violations, and even provide positive incentives such as technical assistance to help firms comply with the law (Scholz, 1991). Flexible regulation requires granting regulators considerable discretion regarding monitoring, enforcement, and sanctioning firms, because they are looking to identify the well-intentioned firms from the purposively deceptive ones. If green clubs accurately signal that firms are going beyond compliance with government environmental regulations, then a flexible enforcement style may enable regulators to reward firms for joining the club. This, in turn, would enhance the value firms receive from their membership in the club. In other words, regulatory flexibility becomes an important component in firms' calculus of the reputational benefits that a green club may provide.

A win–win interaction occurs if government regulators choose a cooperative enforcement style and firms choose a self-policing compliance strategy. Regulators win because self-policing lightens their enforcement burdens while achieving superior environmental outcomes. Firms win because the incentives under cooperative enforcement (forgiveness for minor violations, flexibility with meeting standards) make compliance easier and may even improve their bottom-line profits.

The dilemma confronting firms and regulators is that although this cooperation promises superior outcomes, both firms and governments have powerful incentives to behave opportunistically; that is, to pursue their self-interest with guile (Williamson, 1986) and thus create lose–lose interactions. Unscrupulous firms can exploit governments' trust and regulatory flexibility by evading environmental regulations even more effectively under the more lax monitoring. Governments can exploit firms' self-policing by fully punishing regulatory violations that firms voluntarily disclosed in good faith. Governments may fear that firms will interpret regulatory flexibility as permission to circumvent regulations and a license to pollute. Moreover, many environmental groups suspect firms will inevitably abuse any goodwill or incentives the government offers. From the environmental groups' perspective, regulatory relief may mean little or no regulation and they consequently pressure regulators to adopt deterrence enforcement. Firms may fear that opportunistic regulators may interpret voluntarily disclosed violations as admissions of guilt worthy of substantial punishment, leaving those firms at a competitive disadvantage (through more expensive clean production processes as well as assessed fines) relative to their more evasive competitors. Firms also realize that environmental groups may make it politically and legally problematic for regulators to credibly commit to cooperation (Kollman and Prakash, 2001). Consequently, mutual suspicion about others' opportunism undermines cooperation, leading to costly and less effective regulatory interactions. As Ayres and Braithwaite note (1992: 3–4):

Good policy analysis is not about choosing between the free market and government regulation. Nor is it simply deciding what the law should proscribe. If we accept that sound policy analysis is about understanding private regulation – by industry associations, by firms, by peers, and by individual consciences – and how it is independent with state regulation, then interesting possibilities open to steer the mix of private and public regulation.

To illustrate these issues better, we recast the business–government regulatory dynamic into what we call the "regulation dilemma" (Scholz, 1991; Ayres and Braithwaite, 1992), a simple application of the well-known prisoner's dilemma (PD) game (Luce and Raiffa, 1957; Rapoport and Chammah, 1965). Table 2.3 shows the payoff schedule for a hypothetical government and firm in the regulation dilemma. Given interdependence, the outcomes for each player depend on her own and the other's choice, with both the government and the firm choosing a cooperative or a deterrence/evasion stance towards the other. The key point is that no matter what the government chooses, firms are better off evading (b > f, d > h) and no matter what the firm chooses, the government is better off choosing deterrence (a > c, e > g). This creates a vicious cycle of opportunism and a series of "lose–lose" outcomes. Unfortunately, this behavioral equilibrium is "pareto suboptimal"; each side would be better off if governments chose flexible enforcement and firms chose to self-police (cooperation: g, h).

Thus, both firms and regulators prefer cooperation (through self-policing and flexible enforcement, respectively) to conflict (through evasion and deterrence, respectively), but only if they are confident the other side will cooperate as well. If each fears the other will exploit cooperation, firms would attempt to evade regulations and governments would choose deterrence. In fact, both regulators and firms know that the other has good reason, at least in the short run, to promise cooperation but deliver deterrence or evasion. Thus, as in a prisoners' dilemma game, both sides end up willingly choosing conflict over cooperation (that is, "defection" is the dominant strategy), even though both would prefer cooperation to deterrence.

Table 2.3. The regulation dilemma

Firms regulator	Evasion	Self-policing
Deterrence	Conflict	5,1
	(2,2)	(e,f)
	a,b	
Flexible enforcement	1,5	Cooperation
	(c,d)	4,4
		(g,h)

To achieve win–win cooperation, both firms and regulators must find ways to credibly signal to the other that they have genuine cooperative intentions. Simultaneous signaling may be ideal but is not always practical; one side may need to signal its future cooperative intentions first to induce the other to move.[31] In a theoretical sense, two generic solutions prescribe how actors in PD games can turn defection into cooperation: building a reputation for cooperation and adopting binding institutional commitments. Fortunately, both of these solutions have real-world counterparts available to firms and regulators. The first is to have governments and firms build reputations for cooperation through their past performance. Incentives to cooperate increase when players engage in long-term, face-to-face, and repeated interactions that become informally institutionalized in players' reputations (Axelrod, 1984; Hardin, 1982). Thus, regulators can build a cooperative reputation over time by forgiving minor offenses, particularly by those firms that self-disclose. Firms can build a reputation for quickly disclosing and correcting their own violations. Because reputation-building takes time and is expensive, a short time horizon coupled with a desire to benefit from an existing "trustworthy" reputation may create incentives to shun opportunism. Yet on the positive side, as trust begets more trust over time and good reputations become solidified, a virtuous circle of cooperation may evolve. Indeed, there is considerable variation in

---

[31] Many different game forms (for example, tit-for-tat) could lead to cooperative outcomes. Further, the payoff matrix may change as actors continually update their perceptions based on previous iterations. For a review of this multidisciplinary literature, see R. Hardin (1982) and Ostrom (1990).

how much flexibility governments use in enforcing environmental regulations, or at least to what degree managers perceive flexibility in the governments' enforcement styles.

A second cooperative strategy, and perhaps a more durable and effective one, is to have each side commit to cooperation *in advance*. Because both participants have strong reasons to suspect the other will behave opportunistically, advance commitments can be made more credible by raising the cost of defection, for example by joining or establishing self-binding institutions that impose non-trivial costs on opportunistic behavior (Milgrom *et al.*, 1990; Ostrom, 1990).

Governments can credibly commit to cooperation in advance through flexibility programs and adopting environmental audit policies that grant significant immunity to firms' violations discovered through self-audits and voluntarily disclosed to regulators. For example, among US state governments, regulators have created a wide range of environmental leadership green clubs that offer participating firms benefits for superior environmental performance. Another way regulators can commitment to more cooperation is through policies and/or laws offering privilege and/or immunity protections for firms' environmental self-audits. The EPA (1986, 1995a, 1995b, 1997, 1999b) and about 25 states promise some form of regulatory relief to firms that promptly disclose and correct violations uncovered by audits (details in Table 2.2). Of course, these policies vary across states (Morandi, 1998): some have passed legislation while others have merely formulated non-binding agency-level policies. Also, some states grant both audit privilege (information gathered in audits is not disclosed to regulatory agencies or the public) and immunity (from fines and penalties) for self-disclosed information while others grant only immunity. The role of NGOs becomes important here. The credibility of government's signal depends not only on government's perceived intentions but also on the potential for environmental groups to challenge governmental policies, particularly in the judicial arena. Even if governments enact policies, the presence of a highly litigious climate and militant environmental groups can dampen firms' perception of the value of such policy initiatives. In chapters 4 and 5 we test whether such policy commitments from governments induce firms to join ISO 14001.

For their part, firms can signal their cooperative intentions by joining a strong green club that requires self-policing and has strong and credible external monitoring mechanisms. Many green clubs, including ISO 14001, do not impose rigid operational constraints on firms but rather encourage them to take environmentally progressive action beyond what the law requires. Such clubs require members to establish environmental management systems with procedures for regular self-policing and credible mechanism to monitor firms' environmental programs.

This is where green clubs may be able to promote win–win cooperation by offering firms a credible way to demonstrate their progressive environmental practices. ISO 14001 requires firms to establish environmental management systems and have them audited by external auditors, an expensive investment with no short-run quantifiable benefits (Kolk, 2000). Because audits may uncover self-incriminating evidence of regulatory violations, firms may want governments to promise significant regulatory relief for voluntarily disclosed violations (Kollman and Prakash, 2001). The reason is that such audits may create self-incriminatory evidence that opportunistic regulators and environmental groups may employ against them. ISO 14001 research suggests that firms are deeply concerned that third-party audits, a requirement for ISO 14001 certification, are not protected by attorney–client privileges in most states (Prakash, 2000a; Kollman and Prakash, 2001). Is this concern valid and, if so, has it influenced firms' response rates to ISO 14001? If governments assure firms that information uncovered during third-party audits will not be used against firms, will firms be more likely to join green clubs? Further, will governmental assurances be credible in the context of a litigious climate where NGOs often challenge governments and firms in the judicial arena? We investigate these questions in chapter 4.

Conclusions

In sum, green clubs are an institutional vehicle for inducing firms to take progressive environmental action beyond what they would have taken unilaterally. Green clubs also have the potential to build trust and cooperation between firms and their stakeholders, particularly for government officials enforcing regulations. For firms, the big payoff from joining a green club is the reputational benefits they receive from external stakeholders, including regulators, consumers, and environmental groups. To a large extent, firms' assessment of the reputational benefits is influenced by the policy and regulatory context in which they operate. If a green club fits well within the policy context, its reputational benefit is likely to be deemed higher, making it more attractive for firms to join.

While green clubs may not be a panacea for solving environmental problems, prematurely rejecting them might mean that an important opportunity to strengthen environmental governance is missed. We have provided the initial steps for a theoretical framework for evaluating voluntary programs on two crucial dimensions, club standards and enforcement rules, and provided a better sense of the promise and pitfalls of different categories of green clubs. Through the theoretical lenses of club theory, we seek to explain how club attributes can induce members to produce valuable public goods by mitigating the Olsonian dilemma of inducing members to join the club and the shirking dilemma of having members adhere to club standards.

Our theory suggests that Mandarin and Bootcamps clubs hold considerable promise. They are likely to have positive reputations that induce members to join the club, their club standards hold members to these higher performance standards, and their enforcement regimes mitigate shirking. Assuming credible enforcement, one can envision a continuum of clubs with increasingly stringent standards. At each level, firms at the margin would weigh the costs of joining the green club against the benefit of affiliation with the club's brand reputation. Clubs with standards towards the more lenient end of the spectrum (Bootcamps) may have an advantage over their more stringent cousins (Mandarins) because the former can attract more members and thus capture network and scale economies associated with producing reputational benefits. Towards the more stringent end, Mandarins are very useful if the policy objective is to identify the top performers and selectively reward them.

In chapter 3, we describe the green club examined in this book, ISO 14001, and place it in the context of our theoretical framework. In chapter 4, we examine variations in how firms have responded to ISO 14001 both across countries and within US states. In doing so we examine how varying policy and institutional contexts influence firms' perceptions of ISO 14001's reputational value and therefore their propensity to join the club. In addition to considering the role of the policy context, we also examine the role of firm- and facility-level characteristics in influencing ISO 14001's attractiveness. In chapter 5, we show that ISO 14001 improves facilities' compliance with governmental law and improves their environmental performance. In other words, we investigate whether ISO 14001 mitigates shirking.

3 | ISO 14001 and voluntary programs

HAPTER 2 laid out a framework for a theoretical analysis of voluntary environmental programs based on club theory. Indeed, we include "Green Clubs" in the title of this book to emphasize their prominence in environmental governance debates. Dating back to the late 1980s, there has been a steadily growing interest in voluntary environmental programs among businesses, industry associations, regulators and even some environmental groups (Gibson, 1999). Many of these newer programs seek to establish common management standards and/or outcome goals among companies within or across industries. However, voluntary regulatory programs that seek to influence firms' activities have been around for a long time and have not been confined to environmental issues.[1] Webb (2004: 2) notes the following:

For thousands of years, merchant behaviour has been controlled through non-governmental techniques. In the Middle Ages in Europe (and much earlier elsewhere), merchant guilds regulated virtually every aspect of a given commercial activity, from market access through means of production, product quality and price, enforcement of contracts, and even an element of welfare protection for guild members and their families. While guilds have faded in importance with the rise of the State, private regulatory techniques which use non-governmental intermediaries to ensure compliance have continued to flourish, against a backdrop of law: the Better Business Bureau, for example, had its origins in merchant "vigilance committees" first created in the late 1800s, the International Chamber of Commerce first published its Code of Advertising Practice in 1937, and many other forms of industry self-regulation were put in place throughout the twentieth century.

Voluntary regulatory programs tend to focus on three substantive areas: setting rates and prices among members of an industry;

---

[1] For one detailed listing, see www.codesofconduct.org

controlling market entry for new competition; and establishing common legal, technological or management standards across market participants (Gupta and Lad, 1983).

Although scholars employ different phrases to characterize such voluntary action, a key analytical feature these programs share is that each proffers a code of conduct or performance not mandated by government enacted law or regulations (Cutler *et al.*, 1999; Haufler, 2001; Kollman and Prakash, 2001; Hall and Biersteker, 2002; Cashore *et al.*, 2004). As institutions with some authoritative capacity to establish, monitor, and enforce rules, voluntary programs can have important influence. Even governments, the ultimate repository of rule-making authority, have sought validation through membership in voluntary programs, underscoring the role even nongovernmental voluntary programs can play as authoritative governance institutions. The states of Minnesota and Wisconsin have earned Forest Stewardship Council's certification for their state-owned forests (Meidinger, 2000). ISO 14001 certifications have been granted to local governments and military bases in the US and Europe.

In this chapter we begin with a brief history of the organization that developed and sponsored ISO 14001, the International Organization for Standardization, or, simply called, ISO. We then discuss ISO 14001's key features in the context of our green club theory. We describe ISO 14001's club standards, its enforcement rules and the standing of its brand identity among stakeholders. Our discussion will show that ISO 14001's club standards and enforcement rules suggest it is a Type 3 Bootcamp club in the context of the club typology presented in chapter 2. The ISO 14001 brand also has a strong positive standing among firms' stakeholders, especially government regulators. We conclude with a discussion of key issues surrounding ISO 14001's environmental and regulatory performance, setting the stage for our empirical analyses in chapters 4 and 5.

The International Organization for Standardization: a brief history

The International Organization for Standardization grew out of several early twentieth-century initiatives to standardize technical standards and processes in emerging industries. In 1906, the International

Electrotechnical Commission was founded to develop technological standards for the burgeoning electronics industry. In 1926, the International Federation of the National Standardizing Associations (IFNSA) was established to develop standards in the field of mechanical engineering. IFNSA was fairly active in Europe through the 1930s, although it became dormant with the onset of the Second World War. Nevertheless, issues requiring common international standards did not go away. The United Nations Standards Coordination Committee (UNSCC) was established in 1946 to aid allied war efforts and subsequent reconstruction. In 1946, delegates from 25 countries met to discuss merging the IFNSA and UNSCC, leading to the creation of the ISO in 1947. After much debate, the delegates decided to headquarter the ISO in Geneva, with Paris and Montreal being the other two contenders. ISO's central mission is to facilitate international trade and commerce by developing common international standards for products, materials, and processes. Varying standards across countries create transaction costs that undermine trade. Its acronym, ISO, is no accident: "*Iso*" is a Greek word meaning equal. As of 2004, the ISO had developed over 13,700 international standards.[2]

ISO's members are the national standards institutions from each country. For example, the British Standards Institution, the Deutsche Institut Normen and the American National Standards Institute are all member representatives for their countries. ISO offers three types of memberships:

- *Full members* each have one vote in the ISO General Assembly. Full members pay membership fees assessed in relation to their gross domestic products and trade flows. At the time of writing, there were 99 full ISO members.
- *Corresponding members* do not have voting rights in the ISO General Assembly and also pay a reduced membership fee. Although corresponding members do not directly participate in standard development, ISO keeps them fully informed about its activities. At the time of writing, there were 35 corresponding ISO members.
- *Subscriber members* do not have voting rights and pay nominal membership fees. This type of membership is appropriate for

[2] This paragraph draws on ISO (2004a).

countries with small economies and little exposure to world trade. At the time of writing, twelve countries had opted for this category of membership.

While the ISO is not an inter-governmental organization, it is not an NGO in the sense of being an activist group or a social movement agitating for a specific policy outcome. It is, however, without doubt, a non-governmental institution. In their recent article on international standardization, Mattli and Buthe (2003) note:

Membership in ISO is open to national bodies (one per country) "most broadly representative of standardization in their countries." For the vast majority of industrialized countries, the national SDOs that serve as the country's representative to ISO and IEC are private organizations . . . In these forums some forty thousand experts – selected as representatives by the national SDOs, mostly from industry but also from research institutes, public regulatory agencies, and noncommercial interest groups – gather to tackle standardization issues . . . Funding of ISO (and IEC) standardization is private.

The American National Standards Institute (ANSI) is a good example of a national standards institute. ANSI's website provides the following description of the organization:

The American National Standards Institute (ANSI) is a private, non-profit organization (501[c]3) that administers and coordinates the US voluntary standardization and conformity assessment system [ANSI, 2005a]. Comprised of nearly 1,000 businesses, professional societies and trade associations, standards developers, government agencies, and consumer and labor organizations, ANSI represents the diverse interests of more than 120,000 entities and 3.2 million professionals worldwide. (ANSI, 2005b)

ISO 14001 is a non-governmental regulation in several other ways, including the manner in which it was established. It was not subjected to open public scrutiny that is required in several countries for establishing governmental laws. For example, in the United States, any proposed law has to be published in the *Federal Register* so that the public can comment on it to designated authorities. Governmental regulation can also be challenged in administrative or in judicial settings. No such action is available for challenges to ISO's standards.

Having said this, this book recognizes that voluntary regulation operates in the shadow of public law. As a result, while designing voluntary systems, the program sponsors are likely to have the relevant governmental laws in mind. And, this cross-fertilization is also likely to occur when legislators write laws.[3]

Developing standards in ISO

ISO looks to develop its standards through democratic processes, although participation is limited to ISO's full members (once ISO issues a standard, anyone in any country can adopt it, regardless of membership status). Each year, ISO convenes a meeting of its General Assembly to vote on various proposed standards, with each full member receiving one vote. Proposals are submitted to the General Assembly by the ISO Council, which serves as the executive committee for the organization. Representation on the ISO Council rotates every three years among full members. The Council itself does not develop the proposed standards. Instead, it forms ad hoc technical committees to develop specific standards and then disbands them once the standards are in place. Technical committee members represent specific countries. Typically, committee members are technical experts on loan from industry, technical bodies, or governmental agencies. Although NGOs (or trade associations) do not have an independent standing in the ISO, they can serve on technical committees as a part of a national delegation. To retain voting rights in technical committees, the ISO requires that members regularly attend meetings. An absence from two consecutive meetings can trigger action by the ISO. To approve a new standard, the ISO requires a two-thirds majority approval in the technical committee and a three-quarters majority in the General Assembly. The ISO reviews and, if necessary, revises each standard at least every five years (ISO, 2002).

ISO's standards development processes have been criticized for being unjust and inequitable (Clapp, 1998). First, the ISO standard development process does not grant NGOs independent standing, often leaving them on the outside of the standards development

---

[3] Braithwaite and Drahos (2000: 3) note:

> [F]or years some of Australia's air safety standards have been written by the Boeing Corporation in Seattle and if not by that corporation, by the US Federal Aviation Administration in Washington . . . Many of Australia's pharmaceutical standards have been set by the joint collaboration of the Japanese, European, and US industries and their regulators, called the International Conference on Harmonization.

process. Second, the costs of participating in ISO meetings and the difficulty in supplying technical experts tend to exclude participation by national standards bodies and industry associations from developing countries (Clapp, 1998). Consequently, although developing countries account for about 75 per cent of the national standards bodies in the ISO, they contribute less than 5 per cent to the technical rule-making work. The United Nations Conference on Trade and Development (UNCTAD, 2000) has therefore recommended that the ISO provide financial support to developing countries to facilitate their participation in standards development. Despite these criticisms, the ISO is not generally viewed as a mouthpiece for big industry and developed countries. The ISO enjoys widespread credibility for its technical expertise and its relatively open and fair rule standards development processes.

The ISO's foray into management systems standards began in the 1980s. Codifying management standards was a somewhat unusual step because ISO had previously been known for developing complex technical standards and had stayed away from the political and sociological dimensions of international standardization. The rapid economic growth in Japan and East Asia in the 1970s and the 1980s suggested that industrial organizational and management practices play an important role in economic development even at national level. The experience in these countries revealed that the pursuit of quality in industrial production had not only technical dimensions, but also socio-political dimensions through the standardization of innovative management practices. The new East Asian model for economic growth was based on national-level political institutions encouraging firms to focus on export markets, adopt corporate governance institutions that emphasized long-term strategic positions over short-term profits, and implement unique management systems that emphasized group work and collaboration on the shop floor (World Bank, 1992). Because quality industrial processes stem not just from technical skills, an ISO quality standard would need to tackle sociological and organizational issues as well.

In the late 1980s, the ISO established ISO 9000, a voluntary program that connects quality management systems to firms' broader organizational and industrial processes. ISO 9000 requires firms to set measurable quality objectives across levels of their organizational hierarchy, establish quality processes, identify resources and personnel necessary for meeting these objectives, assess whether the objectives have been met, and if not, what process or system changes are required to achieve them (ISO, 2004b). Since its debut, ISO 9000 has been a tremendous success and has been widely adopted around the world. By the end of December 2002, more than half a million facilities spread across 161 countries had received ISO 9000 certificates (ISO, 2003).[4]

In the late 1980s, scholars began to argue, perhaps somewhat optimistically, that because pollution represents wasted resources, pollution control should fall under the aegis of quality assurance (Porter, 1991). Therefore, firm-level environmental governance should be approached with the same philosophy as quality control. If pollution reduction creates profits, then businesses can benefit greatly by adopting demanding management systems for their environmental operations. In this perspective, pollution reduction becomes a simple way to align private incentives to achieve public goals.[5] The success of ISO 9000 spurred the ISO to extend the quality control approach to environmental governance (Braithwaite and Drahos, 2000; Corbett and Russo, 2001). In 1991, the ISO established the Strategic Advisory Group on the Environment to examine opportunities for introducing environmental management standards. After some study, the group recommended that the ISO move ahead with developing management-based environmental standards. As a result, in 1992, the ISO established a technical committee, TC 207, and charged it with developing

---

[4] Certificates are given at the facility level, not the firm level. Technically, certificates are best described as ISO 9001/2/3: 1994 or ISO 9001: 2000 (ISO, 2002: 24). In this book, we term them simply as ISO 9000 certificates.

[5] At a broader level, part of the popularity of an international green club such as ISO 14001 can be linked to several processes taking place under what is currently labeled "globalization." Increased flows of goods, services, and capital across borders, and the expanding reach of MNCs has created a demand for international regimes designed to regulate the behavior of these firms as well as policies of governments. By (allegedly) encouraging races to the bottom, globalization undermines regulatory policies that seek to align private incentives with public objectives. This puts pressure on governments to enact new laws. Given that varying national regulations can become non-tariff trade barriers, MNCs have welcomed ISO 14001 as a credible preemption strategy. For similar reasons, the World Trade Organization, whose mandate is to foster international trade, has supported the ISO 14000 series. The Rio Summit of 1992 also echoed this theme.

environmental standards based on a management systems approach similar to ISO 9000.

After a few years of deliberation by 207 and the ISO General Assembly, in 1996 the ISO launched the ISO 14000 series of standards, based on principles similar to those inscribed in ISO 9000.[6] ISO 14000 consists of a certification standard (ISO 14001) and several guideline standards governing environmental labeling (14020 and 14021), environmental performance evaluations (14031), life-cycle assessment (14040–43, 14048–49), and forestry (14061). For the purpose of this book, only ISO 14001 is relevant because it is the only standard for which firms receive certification.

By the 1990s, the ISO was in a strong position to promulgate a credible green club, particularly one grounded in environmental management systems such as those that would become the heart of ISO 14001's standards. The ISO had an international reputation for developing commercial and industrial standards with high levels of technical expertise and relatively neutral competence, a reputation which, on the heels of the ISO 9000's considerable (and somewhat surprising) success, extended to management standards for industrial production. Through ISO 9000, ISO had access to a network of external auditors and accreditation bodies to establish a credible third-party auditing system for ISO 14001 quickly. The contribution of ISO's standing to ISO 14001's early success should not be underestimated; even before it could establish a history of success, members looking to join a voluntary program could see that ISO 14001 would have some credibility with their stakeholders.

ISO 14001 as a green club

Our discussion of green clubs presented in chapter 2 identifies two important analytic features for voluntary programs. First are the club standards, the programs and policies that green clubs require members to adopt. ISO 14001's key club standard is the environmental management system that codifies how members must organize their internal

---

[6] In the language of marketing, ISO 14001 can be viewed as a brand extension strategy on the part of the ISO. Combining corporate branding (ISO) with product branding (14001) enables companies to enjoy economies of scale in branding and yet distinguish individual products. The automobile industry is a good example of such a strategy on a large scale.

operations regarding the environment. Second is the enforcement rules, the means by which green clubs ensure members are adhering to the club standards once they have become club members. ISO 14001's enforcement rule is a system of external audits and certification (and re-audits and re-certifications) that identifies and excludes members who fail to adhere to the ISO 14001 conduct code.

An effective green club must carry a positive brand reputation among its members' stakeholders. Affiliating with the club's brand is the carrot that induces members to take on the cost of adhering to the club standards and producing the club's public good. Below we discuss in more detail ISO 14001's club standards, enforcement rules, and the standing of its brand identity.

ISO 14001's clubs standards: Environmental management system

The central feature of ISO 14001's club standards is the comprehensive environmental management system (EMS) members must implement. An ISO 14001 caliber EMS requires firms to establish programs, systems, and structures for their internal operation regarding the environment. ISO 14001's EMS standards mandate that firms strive to comply with government laws and regulations, and in some ways ISO 14001 even requires members to exceed them. In the language of the ISO:

"Management system" refers to the organization's structure for managing its processes – or activities – that transform inputs of resources into a product or service which meet the organization's objectives, such as satisfying the customer's quality requirements, complying with regulations, or meeting environmental objectives. (ISO, 2004c)

The EMS approach is a process-based or systems-based standard, rather than outcome-based or technology-based standards that characterize most governments' environmental laws and regulations. To provide an example of a technology-based regulation, consider the EPA's inspection guide for organic finishing of metals:

The national technology-based standards, or effluent limitations guidelines, establish a minimum level of treatment that is required for all dischargers in an industry category based upon the application of various control technologies. Over time, as technology to better treat wastewater is developed, the effluent guidelines may become stricter. Standards are different for both existing and new facilities, and for direct and indirect dischargers.

Existing facilities that are direct dischargers are required to comply with effluent limitations based on the best available technology economically achievable (BAT) for toxic and non-conventional pollutants. For conventional pollutants, the effluent limitations for existing facilities are based on best conventional pollutant control technology (BCT). New sources that are direct dischargers must comply with New Source Performance Standards (NSPS) which are based on the best available demonstrated control technology. (PCRC, 2005)

ISO 14001 does not establish performance standards nor does it stipulate the technological processes that firms must apply to their environmental operations. Instead, ISO 14001 codifies firms' organizational processes and management standards, predicated on the belief that if appropriate processes and management systems are in place, desired outcomes will follow. In practice, a fully developed EMS can be quite extensive. Sayre (1996) provides the following check-list for the various EMS components:

Policy
- Does the company have a documented environmental policy?
- Has the policy been approved by the top management? Is there a designated top manager in charge of overseeing its implementation?
- Is the success in meeting policy objectives periodically reviewed?
- Does the policy require employees to adopt best available technology and commit to continual improvement?
- Does the policy meet or exceed legal requirements?

Environmental impact
- Has the company assessed the environmental impact of its operations and products in terms of their likelihood and severity?
- Does the location of any facility require specific environmental consideration?
- Has the facility assessed the environmental impact if the production processes were to malfunction?

Environmental objectives
- Have specific and measurable environmental targets been established?

- Is there a system for documenting relevant EMS and the targets they intend to achieve?
- Is progress towards various targets periodically tracked? Is there a system to take corrective action in the event targets are not being met?
- Is there a process to assess resources required to meet these targets?
- Does the facility identify specific personnel at various levels and make them responsible for achieving environmental targets?
- Do they have adequate resources to fulfill their responsibilities?
- Is there a training plan for employees directly and indirectly involved in the EMS implementation?

Environmental plan
- Does the environmental planning process involve stakeholders within and outside the firm?
- Is the plan periodically reviewed?
- Are there identified personnel who maintain the list of all applicable laws and regulations that pertain to facility operations?
- Is there a system of tracking compliance with these laws?

Organizational alignment
- Is the EMS integrated with the organization's strategic plan and business plan?
- Is there a process to resolve conflicts between environmental and non-environmental objectives?
- Does the top management regularly communicate to organizational personnel about environmental issues?
- Does the organization recognize and reward contribution to establishing and implementing EMS?

As the above discussion suggests, ISO 14001 EMS are quite comprehensive, covering a wide array of corporate policy-making. If implemented properly, they create vast paper trials and require trained personnel to manage them. Unlike some other clubs such as Responsible Care, they also require third-party monitoring. However, they do not impose any performance requirements on firms. ISO 14001's standards encourage firms to reduce pollution; they do not mandate that members abate their pollution emissions. Arguably, ISO 14001's club standards impose moderate to lenient requirements on firms. We return to this issue in chapter 6.

ISO 14001's enforcement rules: external audits

ISO 14001's enforcement rules are based on external, third-party audits. To become an "ISO 14001 member," that is to receive ISO 14001 certification, the ISO requires that facilities subject their EMS to external third-party audits to verify credibly that facilities have met the ISO 14001 EMS standards.[7] In the language of ISO, certification means:

> [A] third party gives written assurance that a product, service, system, process or material conforms to specific requirements . . . It should be noted that ISO itself does not assess the conformity of quality or environmental management systems to . . . ISO 14000 standards . . . [This] is carried out independently of ISO by more than 720 "certification" or "registration" bodies active nationally or internationally.   (ISO, 2005a)

Estimates of the cost of ISO 14001 certification can range from $25,000 to $100,000 *per facility* (Kolk, 2000). For a firm with twenty facilities, these costs could add up to $2 million. In addition to certification costs, establishing and maintaining an ISO 14001 caliber EMS can be quite expensive. An ISO 14001 caliber EMS can impose substantial indirect costs, such as maintaining extensive paper-trails and documenting processes. In his analysis of firms' "beyond compliance" environmental decisions, Prakash (2000a) reports that both Baxter and Eli Lily hired additional staff to cope with the paperwork and managerial requirements of their ISO 14001 certified EMS. William Glasser of the US EPA estimates that "large facilities spend on average about $1M in sunk transaction costs to pursue [ISO 14001] certification."[8]

An ISO 14001 certification audit is an extensive process. Facilities seeking ISO 14001 certification receive an external audit from a review team usually made up of members of a private consulting company specializing in conducting such audits. The external auditors review the facilities' technical capabilities and personnel training for

---

[7] Firms can self-audit and declare themselves to be in compliance, though ISO strongly encourages firms to receive third-party audits and certification.
[8] Email response, 29 January 2004.

its environmental management system. External auditors also review the facility's management processes, such as its internal auditing procedures for environmental matters, to ensure that the facility complies with the relevant government regulations. Theoretically, auditors perform a systems audit and not a compliance audit, which means they do not check the facility's actual compliance status and record with government regulations, but rather focus only on the facility's management systems for its regulatory compliance. In practice, however, ISO 14001 external review audits invariably address regulatory compliance issues. This raises important questions for auditors and facility managers. Is the information collected during the audit protected by any legal audit privilege? Are auditors legally bound to report to government officials any regulatory violations they discover? Can citizens sue auditors to obtain the audit results? Clearly, governments' laws and regulations surrounding external audits can have an important bearing on facilities' decisions about undergoing an audit and the type of information they are willing to share with their ISO 14001 auditors. These issues are examined in greater detail in chapters 4 and 5.

In the process of an external audit, the team can interview anybody at the facility, from managers to line workers, to assess whether facility personnel understand ISO 14001's procedural and paper documentation requirements. The length of external audits can range from a few weeks to several months, depending on the size of the facility and the paperwork documentation requirements. Few will deny that certification audits disrupt a facility's normal business; after all "outsiders" are in to check on the facilities' performance. Because of the time demands and other non-trivial costs that audits impose on the facility, some facilities may opt for an exploratory pre-audit (with a no-fail option) to assess their readiness before undergoing a more drawn-out formal third-party audit (RAB, 2004a). The prospect of outsiders coming in and evaluating management systems makes managers pay special heed to their facilities' performance, thereby creating intra-firm dynamics akin to the Hawthorne effect we discussed in chapter 2.[9] Managers want to appear "good" to external auditors.

---

[9] We have conducted detailed interviews with several firms over the last seven years and have been repeatedly told by managers about the key role of third-party audits in influencing firm-level dynamics. For example, see Prakash (2000a).

We have observed managers shaping up their organizational structure, reporting relationships, and managerial systems in preparation for the auditors' visit (Prakash, 2000a).[10]

As in any audit, auditors may find that a facility is not conforming to ISO guidelines. In the most minimal case, a facility may not have adopted the best management practice to perform a given task, or there may be isolated instances of management system failures such as documents that are not catalogued or up to date. Auditors may also uncover major shortfalls and systemic non-compliance with ISO 14001 standards. The audited facility may not have implemented key elements of the EMS, such as not identifying personnel in charge of specific tasks, not establishing regular training programs, and not developing a mission statement (RAB, 2004b).

Once the audit is over, auditors record their findings and decide whether to certify the facility, flunk the facility outright, or to provide it with additional time before they return to the facility for a reassessment. If auditors are satisfied that the facility conforms to ISO 14001's standards, they provide a written document that the facility conforms with ISO 14001's requirements. In essence, this constitutes the ISO 14001 certification. The auditors are expected to perform surveillance audits of the facilities they have certified at least once a year, and a complete reassessment of certified facilities' EMS every three years.

The responsibility of performing an external audit suggests that the auditors' credentials are important. ISO requires that third-party auditors themselves receive accreditation before evaluating the facilities seeking ISO 14001 certification. ISO itself does not perform facility certification, nor does it authorize any firms to perform certification audits. Instead, ISO recognizes an accreditation authority in each country that then grants licenses to those who can perform ISO 14001 certification audits. ISO defines accreditation as:

[T]he procedure by which an authoritative body gives formal recognition that a body or person is competent to carry out specific tasks... of ISO 9000 or ISO 14000 certification in specific business sectors.   (ISO, 2005a)

The accreditation authority evaluates prospective auditors' policies, practices and credentials to determine if they are competent to provide

---

[10] Regulators also perceive similar dynamics taking place within firms (phone interviews with Jeffrey Smoller and Mark McDermid, 15 August 2003).

ISO 14001 certification audits. After reviewing the paper evidence about the auditors' competencies, the accreditation body performs an on-site audit of the auditors by witnessing how an auditor goes about auditing a client. The goal is to observe directly whether the auditors have the practical skills to assess the quality of management systems. To prevent a conflict of interest, the accreditation authorities typically prohibit auditors from performing other consulting work for facilities seeking certification. The accreditation authority also requires every auditor to establish a formal system to respond to client complaints. The accreditation organization reviews such complaints during its surveillance audits. These national accreditation authorities include the United Kingdom Accreditation Service, Comité français d'accréditation, Trägergemeinschaft für Akkreditierung GmbH, China National Accreditation Council for Registrars, and the American National Standards Institute – The Registrar Accreditation Board National Accreditation Program (ISO, 2005b).

While the accreditation authority grants the external auditors accreditation that is valid for four years, the accreditation authority is expected to conduct additional surveillance audits six months after accreditation has been granted, and then annually for each of the next three years. Because accreditation expires after four years, a complete reassessment of the auditor is required at the end of the accreditation period. All these steps are in place to make sure auditors are certifying in good faith that facilities are ISO 14001 compliant.

Figure 3.1 summarizes the entire ISO 14001 authorization and accreditation process. The ISO identifies the national accreditation authorities in each country. The national accreditation authorities identify the external auditors. The external auditors identify the facilities that are compliant with ISO 14001 standards.

These elaborate procedures by which accreditation bodies monitor auditors and auditors monitor facilities are an important source of ISO 14001's credibility. It is not easy for facilities to shirk their responsibilities under ISO 14001 certification nor can the external auditors easily rubber stamp facilities as ISO 14001 compliant when they fall short of the standards certification requires. This credibility is important because for a firm to see value in joining the program, it must have confidence that its stakeholders believe membership indicates the firm is complying with what the program requires. Stakeholders must believe that the third-party auditors are not lax in

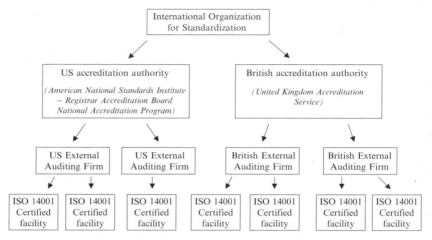

Figure 3.1. ISO 14001 accrediting and certifying authorities.

their audits and the external auditors continue to monitor facilities' compliance after their initial certification audit. In the long run, if external audits are not effective, many firms are likely to shirk their responsibilities under the program, and eventually ISO 14001 will have little effect on improving the environmental performance of its members.

With third-party monitoring, ISO 14001's enforcement mechanisms are quite credible – especially in relation to clubs such as Responsible Care that (until recently) did not require third-party monitoring. However, ISO 14001 does lag behind other clubs such as the European Union's Environmental Management and Audit System that require public disclosure of information on how well firms have adhered to club standards (Gunningham and Grabosky, 1998). Thus, public and environmental groups do not have full information to monitor firms' adherence to ISO 14001's standards. We discuss this issue in more detail in chapter 6.

ISO 14001's brand identity

From the perspective of our theory of green clubs, the primary benefit ISO 14001 members receive is enjoying the stakeholders' goodwill that comes from affiliating with the ISO 14001 brand. Our goal here is not to specify every mechanism by which ISO 14001 creates reputational value for its members, but rather to show that an important incentive for firms joining ISO 14001 is to affiliate with the positive ISO 14001 brand reputation. ISO 14001 is certainly well known among firms' stakeholders. The sponsoring organization the International Standards Organization, has for many years been the world leader in developing and promulgating management standards. ISO 14001 is the largest and most widely recognized green club in the world: there are nearly 50,000 certified facilities in about 118 countries (ISO, 2003). Examples of firms using ISO 14001 as a public relations tool are easy to find. For a prominent example, a quick scan of websites shows that virtually all the major auto manufacturers in the US are moving towards certifying all their facilities. The value of the ISO 14001 brand is evident on smaller scales as well: an economic development official in southeastern Iowa reported to us that several local farms recently formed an ISO 14001 certified cooperative. Their hope was that certification would signal sound management practices to attract biotech research investment. These anecdotal examples suggest that joining ISO 14001 offers important reputational value because it signals firms' commitment to adopting progressive environmental programs.

To understand ISO 14001's positive brand reputation further, we conducted semi-structured analytical interviews with government officials and facility environmental managers.[11] For our plant manager interviews, we began with general questions about the costs and benefits of ISO 14001, with more specific follow-up probes. From these interviews, we can clearly see that plant managers saw that ISO 14001 had a positive brand identity that could benefit their company, though only one manager noted that certification helped the companies' relations with consumers. This manager noted, "If I'm buying a vehicle and I'm somewhat environmentally conscious and Company A is [ISO 14001] certified and Company B is not, being certified gives a message that Company A is more environmentally sensitive."

---

[11] Plant manager interviews were conducted during the spring of 2003 and government regulator interviews during the fall of 2003 and winter of 2004. Most interviews were conducted over the phone; some in-person interviews also took place. A few days prior to the interview, we emailed a list of questions we wished to discuss (see Appendix 4.1). After the phone interview, to ensure we had noted the responses correctly, we emailed the summary of the conversation. For the email responses to our questions, such summaries were not required.

Another manager stated that ISO 14001 certification raised awareness among suppliers and vendors that the firm was attentive to environmental issues, though she was skeptical that most consumers were able to recognize ISO 14001. The third manager felt ISO 14001 held considerable value as a marketing tool and was disappointed that her parent corporation did not promote its ISO 14001 certification more aggressively. ISO 14001's positive brand name is evident in how these facilities advertised their certification locally: one manager reported that the local newspaper reported a favorable article when the facility received ISO 14001 certification, although the facility's earlier pollution prevention award received more prominent press coverage. A manager at another certified facility reported flying an ISO 14001 flag on the facility flagpole. Clearly, ISO 14001 offered a positive reputational benefit and these facilities were keen to advertise their membership in this club.

ISO 14001 has a positive brand image among government regulators in the US. In total, we spoke with nine state and federal environmental regulators, all of whom recognized ISO 14001 as an important voluntary program that indicated members were making a commitment to environmental action. According to Jeff Smoller and Mark McDermid of Wisconsin Department of Natural Resources, in evaluating any EMS-based club, regulators are likely to look for its functional equivalence with ISO 14001, in part because ISO 14001 is well known and regulators have a solid understanding of how it works. They went so far as to call ISO 14001 a "gold standard" among EMS-based voluntary regulation. This is because ISO 14001 reduces regulators' workload in terms of identifying paper-trails and elements of management systems within firms. This is not to say that regulators give ISO 14001 firms an "auto pass" for regulatory compliance. However, any EMS standard signals firms' intent to pursue environmental objectives in a disciplined manner. Externally verified EMS-based voluntary programs such as ISO 14001 can indicate that this objective is pursued with rigor. Smoller and McDermid add that regulators recognize that the quality of audits and auditors varies. Nevertheless third-party audits by trained and accredited auditors provide credible assurance about the quality of EMS-based clubs.[12]

---

[12] Phone interview with Jeff Smoller and Mark McDermid, 15 August 2003. While appreciating ISO 14001, several regulators noted that ISO 14001 could be stronger. David Ronald of the Multi-State Working Group on EMS notes:

William Glasser[13] of the EPA noted: "ISO certification does signal firms' commitment to better compliance as this is a commitment that is almost always memorialized in the Environmental Policy. ISO is not a compliance tool per se nor should it be construed or used as such. But it does support the emergence of systems thinking vis-à-vis environmental aspects/impacts and that, in turn, supports a greater awareness of and emphasis on compliance." Doug Smith of the EPA, Region 10, noted, "ISO 14001 signals firms' commitment to environmental excellence." Susan Roothaan of Texas DNR also noted that ISO 14001 signals firms' intent to better comply with the law.[14] Finally, David Ronald commented that "ISO [14001] requires a commitment to compliance [with government regulations]."[15]

ISO 14001's standing with regulators appears to stem from several factors. First, receiving certification requires firms to outlay substantial resource commitments. Doug Smith noted "[ISO 14001] requires a lot of work and resources to establish solid EMS and get it audited." Consequently, US firms often cannot simply receive certification with a few slight modifications to their existing practices. Second, several regulators saw considerable value in ISO 14001's third-party auditing. David Ronald, the Executive Director of the Multi-State Working Group, noted that third-party audits are useful to bring about cultural change within companies.[16] This is because no manager wants to look

> [ISO 14001] does not require that a company include legal compliance in its targets and objectives. That is left to the discretion of the company. An EMS should require that achieving legal compliance be among the specific targets and objectives of a company. An EMS cannot ensure or require legal compliance. It can only direct the management system to attempt to achieve legal compliance by including legal compliance in the companies' targets and objectives. The same is true for all targets and objectives set by a company in its EMS. Management attempts to achieve the targets and objectives by using the tools of the EMS. When it does not meet a target or objective, it makes corrections to do better.   (email response, 12 December 2003)

[13] Email, 30 January 2004.
[14] Interview with Jeff Smoller, 15 August 2003; interview with Doug Smith 24 January 2004, email response from Susan Roothaan, 16 December 2003.
[15] Some regulators do not view ISO 14001 favorably. Chuck Corell of Iowa Department of Natural Resources said that he does not treat ISO 14001 facilities any differently from non-ISO facilities. For him, the motivation for joining ISO 14001 is "the ability to show that the firm has had some documented level of environmental performance. In my opinion, all of these firms would be much better off developing a strong and honest relationship with their regulators." Email response, 15 March 2004.
[16] Interview with David Ronald, 11 December 2003.

bad to the top management that eventually gets the audit reports. Susan Roothaan also noted that "the largest driver from a psychological perspective is the desire not to fail.[17] If an organization knows it is being audited to a standard, top management will typically do what they can to pass." Third, ISO 14001 significantly eases regulators' tasks because the EMS produces the necessary paper to document members' environmental activities. As Douglas Smith explains, EPA Field inspectors get a list of facilities to inspect from EPA program managers. They spend two to three weeks studying the background information prior to visiting the facility. They typically spend two or three days at the facility and then another week writing their inspection report. A well-functioning EMS reduces inspectors' workload, both prior to and during the inspection. If EMS are in place, inspectors get information they need, and know whom to contact for specific pieces of information that are not readily available.[18]

As a branding device, ISO 14001 certification aims to signal that a firm has undertaken a degree of environmental commitment beyond what is required by government regulations. The value of this signal is apparent in how members advertise their affiliation with ISO 14001 to consumers, regulators, their supply chain, and so on. We will return to this issue in chapters 4 and 5 where we explore how ISO 14001's brand identity induces firms to take on the costs of joining the program.

ISO 14001: key policy issues

ISO 14001 has an impressive pedigree from its origins in the ISO's management approach to voluntary regulations. ISO 14001 is sponsored by the leading international standard-setting organization. The efficacy of management system approaches has been well documented through ISO 9000. It is widely recognized that establishing an ISO 14001 caliber EMS requires firms to make substantial investments in time, resources, and expertise. ISO has established demanding procedures to ensure that high-quality auditors conduct rigorous audits. Not surprisingly, many consider ISO 14001 to be preeminent among voluntary environmental programs.

---

[17] Email response from Susan Roothaan, 16 December 2003.
[18] Interview with Douglas Smith, 24 January 2004.

With all its virtues, there are important reservations about ISO 14001. ISO 14001 embodies a governance approach that is quite similar to that embodied in the financial accounting industry. In the pre-Enron meltdown era, governance in the accounting industry was considered the state of the art for non-governmental approaches to regulation, particularly for the efficacy of third-party auditing. Of course, after a series of US accounting scandals in the late 1990s, the view of the accounting industry's approach has dimmed considerably. More troubling is that in some ways ISO 14001's auditing procedures may be yet weaker than the financial industry's approach to accounting standards. In financial accounting systems, firms are required to publicly report their financial performance and the findings of external financial audits (NAPA, 2001). ISO 14001 stipulates no such requirements. This lack of verifiable commitment to complying with the law along with a lack of public access to audit reports has drawn criticism from environmental groups.

In sum, while ISO 14001 has been designed to ensure that firms adopt rigorous EMS and that external auditors ensure firms' adherence to them, it is not clear whether these practices and standards actually work. Firms may join ISO 14001, but membership in the program may not require of them anything beyond what they would have done on their own. Or, firms may join the program and not adhere to program standards, perhaps abetted by lax external auditors. Or, members join the program and adhere to its standards, perhaps taking on substantial additional costs, but not end up producing any tangible environmental gains beyond what they would otherwise have achieved. In the next two chapters, we investigate these questions. Chapters 4 examines why firms join ISO 14001 and presents some evidence, albeit somewhat indirect, that at least some firms join the program in part to enjoy the benefits of its reputation with stakeholders. Membership in ISO 14001 implies these firms are taking action beyond what they would take unilaterally. Chapter 5 examines whether joining ISO 14001 improves firms' environmental performance.

4 | Adopting ISO 14001

EFFECTIVELY reconciling private goals with public interest is the central challenge in designing environmental policies. Chapter 1 outlined how command and control regulations, market-based instruments, mandatory information-disclosure programs, and voluntary clubs are policy approaches to this end, each with its own strengths and weaknesses. Calls for government to enact tough regulations arose in the 1960s and 1970s primarily because firms were not adequately controlling pollution and safeguarding public health. After early successes, command and control regulations have struggled to make additional environmental gains, at least in the US, leading to calls for new approaches that harness the benefits of command and control while avoiding its pitfalls.

Green clubs' policy promise stems from their similarities with market-based and information-disclosure programs and from their potential to improve firms' environmental performance and strengthen their compliance with command and control regulations. Like command and control regulations, green clubs require firms to take concrete steps to protect the environment. Like market-based mechanisms, green clubs harness the power of market incentives to reward club members for their progressive environmental action. Like information-based policies, green clubs reduce transaction costs for stakeholders to differentiate the environmentally progressive firms from the laggards. In our perspective, command and control will continue to form the backbone of environmental governance, with green clubs and other policy instruments as complements to it in a multifaceted environmental governance system.

Green clubs' pitfalls stem from their potential failure to overcome the Olsonian and shirking dilemmas, in which cases they deserve the derisive criticisms they sometimes receive. All policy instruments carry some risk of institutional failure. Policy failures could stem from information asymmetries between firms and stakeholders, agency conflicts, shirking, or low rates of compliance with the policy's goals. Olsonian failures, due to low participation levels and shirking failures due to laggard firms not implementing club standards, can be particularly salient for green clubs. This chapter focuses on the Olsonian dilemma and the conditions under which firms join ISO 14001. Because joining a green club is voluntary it is important to investigate questions such as: what types of policy contexts improve firms' perceptions of reputational value of ISO 14001 membership; and what facility-level characteristics influence firms' decision calculus.

Green clubs such as ISO 14001 seek to solve the Olsonian dilemma by creating excludable benefits in the form of a positive reputation that accrues to members as a function of their membership in the club. In some ways, the value firms receive from affiliating with a green club is contingent on how the club's features fit with the legal, economic, and social contexts in which firms operate. These are the issues we explore in this chapter. Firms' institutional context is multifaceted: firms operate in different jurisdictions and with varying linkages with their stakeholders.

As noted in chapter 2, firms may unilaterally take progressive environmental action, perhaps even take action significantly more stringent than government regulations or any prominent green club requires. In joining ISO 14001, are firms performing action beyond what they would do in the absence of the program? Or are they just looking for some extra recognition for action they would have taken anyway in the absence of the program? On average, we should not expect profit-seeking firms to take significant "beyond-compliance" actions unilaterally unless there is a payoff for them to do so. To the extent that ISO 14001 reflects beyond unilateral action, we should observe some brand attraction to the program. Empirically sorting the effects of brand reputation from other factors influencing firms' decisions about joining a green club is challenging. To this end, we pursue several analytic approaches, including small and large N cross-national studies, interviews with government regulators in the US, and a large N empirical study of facilities regulated under air-pollution laws in the US. We look to identify whether more firms join ISO 14001 where regulatory and economic circumstances suggest certification carries more reputational value and in countries which are deeply embedded in cross-national economic and sociological networks.

This chapter is organized in four sections. In the first section, we examine how firms' perceptions of benefits of joining ISO 14001 in the US and the UK were shaped by the manner in which governments promoted the program (the supply side) and by patterns of business–government relations (the demand side). The logic of focusing on the US and the UK is as follows. Although offering firms broadly similar institutional environments, the US has been a laggard in ISO 14001 adoption while the UK is one of the leaders. Both the US and the UK represent an Anglo-Saxon type of capitalism and both are common-law countries, key factors that should influence ISO 14001 uptake among firms.[1] Hence, both countries have similar types of economic and regulatory contexts. Although the US economy is seven times the size of the UK's economy (with the size of the economy being a proxy for total number of certifiable firms), by the end of 2002, the US had 2,620 ISO 14001 registrants while the UK had 2,917 registrants. The divergence in the ISO 14001 uptake among firms is puzzling. In the second section, we turn to firms' response to ISO 14001 in a broader context by studying the adoption rates across 59 countries, including the US and the UK. These countries reflect more pronounced differences in political and economic contexts in which firms function and make decisions about joining ISO 14001. We expect firms' perceptions of the value of affiliating with ISO 14001's reputation to vary across countries, depending on domestic policy and economic circumstances. In the third section, we present a facility-level study of ISO 14001 across the US. Arguably, the policy environment shows less variability within a country than between countries. Further, because we have data on firm- and facility-level characteristics for the US, these provide an opportunity to understand how, after controlling for the policy and institutional contexts, firms and facility-level characteristics influence the value of joining ISO 14001. In the last section, we present our conclusions about conditions under which firms perceive ISO 14001's reputational benefits to be substantial enough for them to subscribe to it.

---

[1] More accurately, only England and not the UK as a whole has common law. The Scottish legal system is based on continental law. In the US, because of the French colonial ties, Louisiana's legal system is influenced by continental law (Hall, 2002).

Comparing ISO 14001 diffusion in the US and the UK

Club benefits accrue to members because external stakeholders such as consumers, investors and government regulators form perceptions about the club's reputation. The value of a club's reputation depends on how these stakeholders use club membership as a criterion to reward or punish firms. Because government regulators significantly contribute to the institutional and policy contexts in which firms operate, they are perhaps the most important determinant of the reputational value firms perceive in green club membership. To examine how the policy and regulatory contexts influence the reputational value of a green club, we begin by examining the US and British cases to place ISO 14001 in a wider environmental governance context: how do regulators and other stakeholders perceive green clubs and their sponsors? We show below that the benefits members receive from ISO 14001's reputation are influenced by how the club is "supplied" and promoted by national sponsoring organizations. We then discuss the demand side: how do conflictual business–government relations undermine or promote the reputational value associated with ISO 14001? We demonstrate how active sponsorship by the British Standards Institution and the cooperative relationship between businesses and governments boosted demand for joining ISO 14001 in the UK. In contrast, the absence of a legitimate sponsoring organization and adversarial business–government relations in the US suggest a weaker fit between ISO 14001 and the US policy context. The result is that US firms see less value in affiliating with the ISO 14001 brand, leading to fewer (per dollar of the gross national product) adoptions in the US.

Sponsors, regulators, and reputations

As described in chapter 3, ISO 14001 was crafted by an international non-governmental organization with a long and prolific history of producing high-quality international standards, including business management standards. The International Organization for Standardization's international prominence certainly boosts the visibility and credibility of ISO 14001 around the world. Within each country, national-level sponsoring bodies such as the British Standards Institution and the American National Standards Institute have opportunities to promote ISO programs by disseminating program information and developing common implementation procedures. Companies can find joining ISO 14001 quite costly because membership in the program requires maintaining extensive monitoring procedures, establishing paper-trails, and undertaking employee training. A proactive national sponsoring organization can reduce membership costs by providing detailed prescriptions for how firms can meet standards, tailored to local policy conditions. Though much of these promotional efforts are targeted towards firms, the primary audience for ISO 14001, the reputational value of ISO 14001 invariably spills over to other stakeholders who learn about this new environmental program.

In the UK, the BSI has considerable credibility and expertise for developing and promoting industrial management standards. Indeed, the BSI sees itself as an international leader in this area. The BSI website provides the following information:

BSI was the world's first national standards-making body (NSB) and is number one in the world today. Independent of government, BSI is globally recognized as an impartial body serving both the private and public sectors. BSI works with manufacturing and service industries, businesses, governments and consumers to facilitate the production of British, European and international standards. As the UK's National Standards Body (NSB), BSI represents UK interests across all of the European and international standards organizations and through their committees. BSI British Standards, part of BSI Group, has a close working relationship with the British government, primarily through the Department of Trade and Industry (DTI). The commitments and intentions of both are set out in the Memorandum of Understanding (MoU). The MoU provides a framework for BSI and the government to meet the challenges to the UK's standardization infrastructure. Together the Royal Charter and the MoU outline the BSI's role in the development of standards for public use, the promulgation of standards, the voluntary nature of standards and their relationship with legislation. BSI is a non-profit distributing organization, which means that any profits are reinvested into the products and services it provides.   (BSI, 2005a)

As the BSI website describes, the first attempt at standardization in Britain took place in 1901 at the meeting of the Engineering Standards Committee. This committee decided to standardize the various sizes of structural steel sections. As a result, the number of sizes in which steel section were available was reduced from 175 to 113, generating enormous savings in steel manufacturing and distribution. In 1902, the BSI created the British Standard Mark, also known as the kite mark. Over the next few years, and accelerated by World War I, the ambit of standardization greatly expanded to cover sectors such as railways, cement, steam engines, and telecoms. These standards were now being used by many government branches including the Admiralty, the War Office, the Board of Trade, Lloyd's Register, the Home Office, and several colonial governments. The standardization movement grew further in the inter-war years. In 1929, BSI was awarded the Royal Charter (BSI, 2005b).

In addition to being the oldest and largest national standards institute in the world, BSI also takes pride in having developed and published BS 5750, the world's first certifiable management standard. This voluntary program governs firms' quality management practices. BS 5750, which was released in the early 1980s, was the model for ISO 9000, the ISO's quality control management standard. In 1992, the BSI launched BS 7750, an environmental environment management standard which eventually became a model for ISO 14001, the ISO's environmental management standards.

BSI aggressively markets both its technical and management standards across the country and is continuously expanding the range of its services. Along with developing new standards and operating one of the world's largest certification bodies, BSI also operates many programs that disseminate information about EMS and other management systems to firms throughout the UK. Along these lines, BSI runs educational seminars, conferences, and even training courses for managers and auditors in firms interested in implementing ISO management systems. To educate the general public, BSI runs intensive publicity campaigns for various management standards and even for the companies who subscribe to them. The BSI website, for example, lists prominent companies who have been ISO 14001 certified and regularly issues press statements after a well-known company receives certification (BSI, 2005c). Such promotion generates the recognition that adds to ISO 14001's positive brand identity.

Business–government relations and green clubs

Firms' calculus regarding the value of joining ISO 14001 includes how certification may affect relations with key stakeholders (Gunningham *et al.*, 2003). As we explain below, firms' perceptions of ISO 14001's reputation depend on how their stakeholders – consumers, environmental groups, and regulators – respond to their membership in the program.[2] Thus firms' response to ISO 14001 is likely to be shaped by their policy context, especially the way in which governments enforce environmental regulations, because membership in the program may be a signal to government enforcement officials that the firm is working to comply with the regulations. The value firms perceive in joining ISO 14001 depends on factors such as the stringency of regulations, the flexibility with which regulators enforce them, and institutional constraints that deter regulators from behaving opportunistically when enforcing environmental regulations.

Firms in countries where regulators and firms are suspicious of one another and are locked in a conflictual relationship are likely to see less value in joining ISO 14001. After all, while green clubs are an institutional vehicle to signal firms' commitment to progressive environmental programs, regulators who are generally distrustful of firms may not find this signal sufficiently compelling to begin trusting the firms, and may not reward companies for taking on the costs of joining the program (Kollman and Prakash, 2001). Environmental groups often contributed to the creation of an adversarial relationship by viewing government–industry cooperation as evidence of governments' capitulation to economic interests at the expense of environmental protection. These groups are wary of businesses and often view green clubs as pro-business private regimes that lie beyond public accountability. Environmental groups tend to put more faith in open and transparent administrative rule-making processes of the command and control system, particularly where public groups have the right to provide their input and to monitor governments' decision-making processes. Consider the following press release, *Missouri Pushes "Polluter Protection" Law*, by State Environmental Resource Center

---

[2] Firms with certain characteristics (such as high levels of pollution intensity and rocky relationships with regulators) may be more susceptible to such demands, and stakeholders with some other characteristics (for example, high education levels) may be more aggressive in making demands for such "informal regulation" (World Bank, 2000). In this context, the literatures on Toxics Release Inventory and 33/50 programs offers useful insights (Arora and Cason, 1996; Konar and Cohen, 1997).

against Missouri's proposal to provide audit privilege to environmental audits:

Missouri SB 989 and its companion, HB 933, both of which have passed out of committee, are the most recent in a year-long effort to pass environmental audit privilege legislation in Missouri. Similar bills have been introduced every year since 1995. This bill would enable polluters to waive state penalties and keep their records sealed when they conduct "self-audits" and report their own violations of environmental laws. It would grant privilege and/or immunity to corporations who conduct self-audits, preventing such documents from being used against them in court or to assess fines . . . the bill includes unfair restrictions on the public's right-to-know about environmental dangers in their communities and their ability to take actions against the companies responsible for the damage. This bill puts the public's right-to-know about environmental, workplace, and industrial hazards far behind protecting the secrecy of polluters and other corporate wrongdoers. (Watchdog Alerts, 2004)

Or consider another example of environmental groups' stance towards environmental audits. In another press release, ALEC's Privileged Businesses, Public's "Right to Know Nothing" Act, the State Environmental Resource Council alleges:

For the past decade, the American Legislative Exchange Council (ALEC) has been promoting an "Environmental Audit Privilege and Qualified Disclosure Act" to state legislators. The bill's ignominious history belies its do-gooder rhetoric. Supporters of the Act say it's needed to ensure that well-meaning companies attempting to remedy environmental problems aren't prosecuted for their efforts, and to level the playing field between small and large businesses. But Coors Brewing Company drafted the legislation in response to a more than $1 million fine (later negotiated down to $237,000) that the Colorado Public Health and Environment Department levied against the company for releasing smog-forming volatile organic compounds in the late 1980s to early 1990s. ALEC's model legislation was revised in 1995 by its National Task Force on Energy, Environment, and Natural Resources, including Coors executive Allan E. Auger and Cindy Goldman, the wife of another Coors executive. (ALEC Watch, 2002)

As these quotes suggest, environmental groups are deeply suspicious of policies that provide legal protections for self-policing and are prepared to wage political battles to oppose them. In such contexts, the potential for green clubs to generate trust among various stakeholders and to mitigate the regulation dilemma is diminished.

Relations among business, environmental regulators and environmental groups in the US are quite rightly termed "adversarial." Alfred Chandler notes the following:

> Why is it that in the United States government and business have so often appeared as adversaries? Why has there not been more of the working relationships that characterize other advanced industrial nations? As one businessman, Crawford Greenwalt, the former chairman at DuPont, phrased the question: "Why is that my American colleagues are being constantly taken to court – made to stand trial – for activities that our counterparts in Britain and other parts of Europe are knighted, given peerages, or comparable honors?" The Lords McGowan and Melchett, the senior executives of Imperial Chemical Industries, asked the same question about the American scene, when much to their astonishment, the Attorney General of the United States hauled them into the New York District Court early in 1944 for violating the Sherman Antitrust Act, and at a time when they did almost no business in the United States. (1980: 1–2)

Chandler (1980) suggests that the source of this contentious stance stems from the manner in which industrialization occurred and the early emergence of manufacturing monopolies.[3] Unlike most European countries, the US government regulated big business early on during the Progressive era of the late 1800s, laying the foundation for confrontational and conflictual regulatory practices that remain part of the culture in many US federal regulatory agencies today. While the EPA is considerably younger than the Progressive era agencies, it was created with a similar regulatory mission: to curb the perceived widespread industry mistreatment of the environment. During its short existence, the EPA has learned that it needs to regulate industry aggressively if it is to maintain the support of its key constituencies.[4]

---

[3] Adversarial relationships coexist with instances of "capture" (Stigler, 1970). Some depression-era agencies (such as railroads) also served as cartel-enforcing vehicles for their industries.

[4] The Republican efforts to downsize the EPA in the 1980s during the Regan era, and again in the 1990s after the Republicans gained control of the US House of Representatives, were viewed as business inspired. The rationale offered for rolling back environmental regulations and reducing the EPA's headcount was that environmental regulations made American businesses uncompetitive, violated private property, and undermined federalism. Such rhetoric has reinforced environmental groups' deep distrust of business' commitment to environmental issues. And such rhetoric has made the EPA aware of the political necessity of carefully listening to its core political constituency: environmental groups.

Because of the fragmented nature of American government and its relatively weak bureaucracy, the EPA has come to rely on the public's right to challenge and prod official action through litigation. This type of "adversarial legalism" manifests itself in frequent court challenges of industry activity and strict environmental liability laws (Vogel, 1986; Kagan, 1991; Kagan and Axelrad, 2000). Former EPA Administrator William Reilly (1999) reports that more than 70 per cent of EPA's rulings have faced judicial challenges (but see Coglianeses, 1996).

The upshot of the historical trajectory of US regulatory policy is that relations among environmental groups, government regulators and industry are relatively hostile and mutually suspicious. In this context, the third-party audits that ISO 14001 certification requires may be particularly problematic because American firms hesitate to divulge compliance information to outsiders for fear that it could be used against them in future regulatory and legal proceedings. Although many US manufacturing firms have some sort of EMS in place for their internal operations, these EMSs have typically not been subjected to third-party auditing. Indeed, there have been several cases where regulators have penalized firms that have uncovered violations via self-initiated audits and reported them to the appropriate regulating authority. The Colorado–Coors case is often cited in this regard. In the course of a self-audit of its Golden, Colorado, brewing operations, the Coors Brewing Company discovered it was illegally emitting ethanol during one of its facility's beer manufacturing processes. Coors reported this violation to the Colorado Department of Public Health and Environment, and much to the company's dismay, state regulators responded with over $1 million in fines, even though it was very unlikely the state would have uncovered the violations had Coors not voluntarily disclosed them (Pfaff and Sanchirico, 2000).

To alleviate fears that regulators will respond to self-disclosures by opportunistically "throwing the book" at violations and to encourage self-audits among firms, several states have enacted laws and policies that grant some sort of audit and immunity privileges to self-incriminating evidence uncovered in third-party audits. The EPA has also formulated its own policies to encourage self-audits (EPA, 1986, 1995a, 1995b, 1997), but this policy neither grants immunity from criminal prosecution nor offers relief from fines that result from self-disclosed information. Instead, the EPA promises to waive the gravity component of the fine if the firm discovers the violation via self-audits, reports it to the EPA within 21 days of discovery, corrects the violation within 60 days, and takes steps to prevent its reoccurrence. Evidence suggests that firms have not been particularly enthused by the EPA's incentives. Under the EPA's policies, violations reported via self-audits have been relatively minor, and are more likely to pertain to omissions or mistakes in reporting requirements than more serious pollution emission or discharge violations (Pfaff and Sanchirico, 2000). Meanwhile, the impact of the states' more generous audit protection programs remains unclear.

Arguably, the EPA has undermined states' environmental audit programs by refusing to recognize the legal protections states offer for voluntarily disclosed, self-incriminating information. In fact, the EPA has even threatened to revoke regulatory authority granted to states that adopt audit protection policies. Environmental groups' hostility to self-audits coupled with EPA's tepid reaction have limited state regulators' flexibility in rewarding firms that have joined ISO 14001,[5] and thereby diminished the value firms might enjoy from affiliating with the ISO 14001 brand. It is hardly surprising that US firms have reacted to ISO 14001 with less than rounding enthusiasm.

In contrast to the US, the UK's regulatory approach is based on more voluntarism and cooperation between industry and government. Unlike in the US, the British government has historically been reluctant to resort to legally binding emissions limits or control technology standards to curb industrial pollution. Although national laws do stipulate non-binding, general guidelines for emissions limits, these laws have traditionally allowed regulators to excuse factories from complying with these limits if local environmental or economic conditions make compliance unnecessary or unrealistic. Given the discretion these laws grant to administrators, it is not surprising that in the past British environmental regulators have seldom taken violators to court and have built what is often referred to as a "cozy"

---

[5] In 1998, President Clinton issued Executive Order 13101 regarding greening of federal procurement. This required federal agencies to give preference in their purchasing to vendors that provide products that have "lesser" impact on the environment. Arguably, products manufactured in facilities with certified EMS such as ISO 14001 could fall in this category. However, the impact of this order either on greening of the vendors or on greening of the federal government is difficult to asses (Eisner, 2004).

relationship between themselves and the industries they regulate (Vogel, 1986).[6]

The historical development of the UK's environmental movement has also played an important role in shaping the British policy style. While British environmental groups are relatively strong in terms of their membership and finances, their ideology is considerably less anti-industry than their German or American counterparts (Lowe and Goyder, 1983; Boehmer-Christiansen and Skea, 1991). The relative moderation of British environmentalists can be attributed in part to the political influence of older, conservationist groups such as the National Trust and the Council for the Protection of Rural England, which tend to be politically conservative or moderate and more willing to take a cooperative stance towards industry. Of course, politically more aggressive groups such as Greenpeace and Friends of the Earth exist in Britain, but they do not dominate the environmental movement as they do in the US. As a result, the government has not been put under the same kind of pressure to take an aggressive approach to regulating industrial pollution.

ISO 14001 was in some ways tailored to fit the British voluntaristic and management system cultures of industrial regulation. During the 1980s, Great Britain was experimenting with environmental regulation via management systems, well before such an approach came under consideration in the US. BSI submitted BS 7750 to extensive pilot testing prior to the program's launch in 1992. Conducted with support from the UK Department of the Environment, the pilot program helped familiarize firms with EMS implementation while generating a great deal of publicity for the program.

As one might expect given their experience with a management systems approach to regulation, British regulators have reacted positively to the introduction of ISO 14001. The government has taken great pains to promote this program by linking it to other voluntary initiatives such as its high-profile environmental reporting initiatives (DEFR, 2003). In 2000, the British Prime Minister Tony Blair challenged the top British 350 companies to prepare corporate

---

[6] The willingness of environmental regulators to regulate polluting sites more aggressively has supposedly increased with the creation of the Environmental Agency in 1995. However, the extent to which the regulatory climate has really changed has been questioned by several scholars (Jordan, 1998).

environmental reports by the end of 2001: establishing EMS and submitting them to third-party audit were an integral part of this challenge. Additionally, the British DETR (Department for Environment, Transport and the Regions; now know as Department of Environment, Food and Rural Affairs, DEFR) has been very supportive of the BSI's efforts to develop EMS standards. Just recently, for example, DETR, along with a consortium of environmental groups, agreed to help BSI develop and promote a sustainability management system. Finally, the British government offers ISO 14001 certified firms limited regulatory relief by using EMS as a reducing factor in the risk assessment calculations it uses to determine site inspection frequencies. These positive governmental incentives have contributed to the enthusiastic response and high demand for ISO 14001 by UK firms.

British firms' enthusiastic response to ISO 14001 can be attributed to three important and interrelated factors. First, DETR and BSI's early experiments and promotion on EMS-based regulations created conditions where firms understood the issues for adapting their internal structures to conform to these approaches. Second, the BSI's heavy promotion and information dissemination efforts lowered costs for firms to learn how to fit their extant management practices with ISO 14001's EMS standards. Together, these two factors, coupled with the Department of the Environment's support for EMS regulations, created the third important condition for ISO 14001's success in Great Britain: firms recognized that ISO 14001 was well known and highly regarded among government regulators and other stakeholders. Not only would regulators look favorably on firms receiving ISO 14001 certification, but these regulators would also have resources, particularly policy discretion, to reward ISO 14001 certified firms.

The US case offers interesting insights into how the lack of a credible sponsoring organization and the lack of fit with the domestic regulatory culture impede ISO 14001 adoption by undermining the benefits firms receive for affiliating with this green club. Although the EPA has put some effort into promoting EMS-based programs (EPA, 1999), no US organization has promoted ISO 14001 as aggressively as did the BSI in the UK. The American National Standards Institute (ANSI), which represents the US at the International Organization for Standardization, certainly has not taken up this role aggressively.

ISO 14001 is a broad-based standard that virtually all firms may join. The US economy is quite fragmented across industries and US business associations tend to organize themselves along industry or even along sub-industry lines rather than across industrial sectors (Katzenstein, 1978). Because US industry organizations tend not to coordinate their efforts, they are not as effective at promoting cross-industry programs such as ISO 14001.[7] Perhaps for this reason, industry-level green clubs such as the chemical industry's Responsible Care program have been relatively more popular with US firms than ISO 14001 (Prakash, 2000b).

The absence of a strong and credible sponsoring organization in the US has hindered the take-up of ISO 14001 in two ways. First, the ISO 14001 brand name is less recognizable and less credible among firms and the general public. Less name recognition obviously means lower levels of reputational value to entice firms to join the program. Secondly, no regulatory body has stepped forward to help fit ISO 14001 into the US regulatory structure in a way that would enhance its appeal to firms.

To sum up our case studies, the presence of an active national sponsoring organization coupled with a supportive regulatory context provides firms with strong incentives for choosing to signal their progressive environmental action via ISO 14001. In the UK, the BSI's aggressive marketing of ISO 14001 and the positive response to EMS from both government regulators and environmental groups have generated considerable reputational value for ISO 14001 membership. In the US, the lack of a promotional vehicle for ISO 14001 coupled with the tepid response from key stakeholders (EPA, environmental groups) has resulted in an equally tepid response among US firms.

The value of ISO 14001 and firms' certification decisions

The previous section attributed the differences in ISO 14001 adoption rates between the US and the UK to variations in their domestic regulatory context. A key lesson from these comparative case studies is that the reputational value of joining a green club depends on how much stakeholders are willing and able to reward club members,

[7] In 2002, the American Chemistry Council began offering the option of joint certification of Responsible Care and ISO 14001. This is because, like ISO 14001, Responsible Care now requires third-party monitoring (Kusek, 2003). Second, Responsible Care has been revised to focus more on EMS-based approach.

which in turn depends on the fit of the club with regulatory institutions. These case studies help set the groundwork for a larger sample investigation of ISO 14001's reception in different countries around the world.

In chapter 2, we argued that the value of a voluntary program's reputation depends on its standing with various stakeholders and how these stakeholders use club membership in their decisions to reward or punish firms. Membership in ISO 14001 can be a signal of a firm's intention to take progressive environmental action. This signal may be more credible than unilateral action because joining ISO 14001 represents an institutionalized commitment, backed by external audits and the reputation of the ISO. ISO 14001 membership therefore can serve as a branding mechanism, that is, a device to reduce information asymmetries between a firm and its stakeholders regarding the firm's commitment to progressive environmental action. Ultimately, the extent to which firms in a country join this green club depends on the cumulative responses from various stakeholders about rewarding firms for the action they take as members of the green clubs. Table 4.1 shows ISO 14001 registrations in select countries around the world. Clearly, ISO 14001 has had more success in some countries than others, a variability which we examine to shed light on why firms join green clubs.

There is an established literature that suggests that national-level institutions influence adoption of organizational practices across issue areas (Cole, 1989; Baron *et al.*, 1988; Guillen, 1994). Our objective in this section is to understand how institutions and policy contexts across countries (which are highly variable) and within the US (which are less variable because local institutions are nested within national institutions) explain firms' perceptions of the value of affiliating with ISO 14001's brand identity and therefore their decisions about the program. The cross-national analysis has the advantage of exploiting the considerable variation in countries' approaches to environmental regulation and their economic context. The facility-level analysis which we present in the next section is a stringent test of our hypotheses because variation in states' economies and environmental regulations is more limited. However, for this analysis we can draw upon facility- and firm-level factors to explain facilities' ISO 14001 adoption decisions, data for which are not available for cross-national study. In doing such a domestic plus cross-national study, we bridge

Table 4.1. ISO 14001 certified facilities in selected countries, 2002

Country	ISO 14001 certificates
Japan	10,620
Germany	3,700
Spain	3,228
United Kingdom	2,917
China (excluding HK)	2,803
Sweden	2,730
United States	2,620
Italy	2,153
France	1,467
Australia	1,485
South Korea	1,065
Canada	1,064
Taiwan	1,024
Brazil	900
Thailand	671
Austria	429
Mexico	369
New Zealand	78
Russian Federation	23
Iceland	3
Guatemala	1

Source: ISO (2003).

the domestic–international divide that afflicts many social science disciplines. We study the phenomenon of the diffusion of the most important green club across countries and within a single country employing similar theoretical lenses. We first sketch the hypotheses drawn from chapter 2 and then present the data and results for the two analyses.

Hypotheses development

Policy context

Government regulators shape the institutional and policy contexts in which firms operate, and are perhaps the most important factor influencing the value firms receive from joining ISO 14001. Often facing massive enforcement shortfalls, particularly in the US, government regulators have much to gain by accurately distinguishing between firms that are trying to comply with regulations and firms looking to skirt regulatory obligations. Such distinctions would enable regulators to focus more effectively their meager enforcement resources. ISO 14001 branding, to the extent it reduces transaction costs by proving information about firms' overall commitment to environmental issues, is potentially of important value to regulators. Building on our analyses of the US and the UK cases, we identify three aspects of the domestic regulatory context that may shape the value firms receive from ISO 14001 certification: the stringency of environmental regulations, the flexibility with which governments enforce regulations (Scholz, 1991; Winter and May, 2000), and the litigiousness of the regulatory enforcement environment (Kagan and Axelrad, 2000).

Regulatory stringency entails how much government regulations require firms (in terms of reducing pollution or adopting certain prevention technologies) to protect the environment. Thus, more stringent regulations require more environmental protection and carry steeper compliance costs for firms. When government regulations are stringent, the relative cost of joining ISO 14001 is lower because firms are more likely to already have adopted stronger environmental practices, perhaps even put in place an EMS, in order to adhere to government regulations. ISO 14001 may also be of more value to government regulators enforcing stringent regulations because they may have stronger motives to ensure regulatory compliance. Because non-compliance with stringent regulations can lead to a greater loss of environmental protection than non-compliance with lenient regulations, regulatory officials may have a more pressing need to discriminate between environmental leaders who are more likely to comply with regulations and laggards who are more likely to be out of compliance. Government regulators enforcing stringent regulations may therefore reward firms that join ISO 14001. Taken together, we therefore propose:

H1:   Firms are more likely to join ISO 14001 where regulations are more stringent.

In the discussion of the regulation dilemma facing firms and government enforcement officials in chapter 2, we emphasized that firms may be more likely to take progressive environmental action if they trust that governments will reward them accordingly. Indeed, as we saw in the US and UK case studies, UK firms were more likely to join ISO 14001 because they saw that their regulatory officials had both the flexibility and the willingness to reward them for their actions. Regulatory flexibility refers to the degree to which governments refrain from fully sanctioning discovered violations, including those that firms voluntarily report (Scholz, 1991). While trust between firms and regulators is a two-way street, governments may need to be first-movers in signaling that they will reward firms for self-disclosing and correcting their regulatory violations. One way to win firms' confidence is to institutionally incorporate flexibility into the design of regulations and the administrative procedures governing regulatory enforcement. For example, government law may mandate that regulators take green club participation into account when assessing penalties for non-compliance. ISO 14001 may serve firms as a low-cost signal of firms' cooperative intent that allows regulators to differentiate the credible cooperative firms that deserve regulatory relief from evasive firms that do not. To encourage firms to join ISO 14001, regulators can offer deserving firms tangible incentives such as forgiving regulatory violations, including those discovered through the self-audits ISO 14001 certification requires along with other forms of regulatory assistance. Thus we propose:

H2: Firms are more likely to join ISO 14001 where regulators flexibly enforce environmental regulations.

In a regulatory culture steeped in litigation, firms may be wary of joining a green club such as ISO 14001 that requires external audits. Firms considering joining a green club may want assurances that any violations discovered in good faith through external audits are not punished to the full extent of the law. Rather, they may want regulators to treat such violations flexibly, allowing firms to correct them without imposing severe sanctions. In a litigious climate, regulators may have less of the discretion necessary to enforce flexibly environmental regulations; environmental groups might challenge in court any enforcement action that does not sufficiently punish violations, even if those firms have voluntarily self-disclosed. Despite whether regulators want to flexibly enforce regulations, firms operating in litigious climates may fear that legal challenges and judicial orders may eliminate the regulatory discretion that flexibility requires.

Therefore, regulators in litigious political environments may be less able to reward firms for their progressive environmental action, thus undermining the value of joining a voluntary program such as ISO 14001.

H3:   Firms are more likely to join ISO 14001 where environmental litigation is lower.

Economic context

As with the political context, the economic context may influence levels of the value of affiliating with the ISO 14001 brand. Along with government regulators, non-governmental actors, including citizens as both consumers and political actors, environmental groups, and other business firms, may use the ISO 14001 brand to identify and reward companies for taking progressive environmental action. This is especially important in our case because ISO 14001 is a green club whose adoption is not backed by legal sanction. Firms must find (and communicate to investors) reasons to justify the costs of adopting a voluntary regulation. Thus, in our analyses we look for factors that identify where these non-governmental actors have more willingness and ability to reward firms that join ISO 14001. One important factor in this area is wealth: if environmental amenities have positive income elasticity (Grossman and Kreuger, 1995),[8] wealthier citizens will demand more environmental protection (Ingelhart, 1977). Also, ISO 14001 is a complicated signal that may require citizens to hold some degree of formal education to interpret and act on. Therefore, citizens with a higher socioeconomic status have more resources and ability to reward environmentally progressive firms, leading to higher ISO 14001 adoption rates in contexts where citizens are wealthier and more highly educated.

H4:   Firms are more likely to adopt ISO 14001 where citizens have higher socioeconomic status.

In market economies, firms seek to develop and market products that consumers want. Competition creates the need for product differentiation. Previous research suggests that firms that are closer to the final

---

[8]   As per the Environmental Kuznet curve literature, we also examined GNP square as a covariate. This was not statistically significant and did not change the overall predictive power of our model.

consumer and spend a significant portion of their sales on advertising are more likely to join green clubs (Arora and Cason, 1996). Such firms want to take advantage of their superior environmental attributes. Branding can be interpreted as a signal from the firm to its stakeholders about its commitment to certain objectives while providing them a low-transaction cost tool to differentiate the firm from its competitors. Because many firms often invest a significant proportion of their revenues in supporting the brand image, they are unlikely to undertake policies that conflict with the brand image. For such brand-focused companies, ISO 14001 is less helpful because consumers seldom link facilities (which receive ISO 14001 certification) to products (Prakash, 2002). For companies that lack brand identities, ISO 14001 certification may provide a brand-like differentiation for their products. A firm can choose to brand at two levels: corporate and product. In corporate branding (as in Maytag, General Electric, Sony), the corporate image directly influences the marketing profile of a corporation's products. Because ISO 14001 certification is provided at the facility level, it may enhance corporate brands more than product brands. In short, ISO 14001 functions more as a support for corporate-level branding; when product-level branding is strong, corporate-level branding is less valuable. One can therefore expect that in countries where product branding levels are high, ISO 14001 adoption rates will be low. Therefore, we propose:

H5: Firms are more likely to adopt ISO 14001 in economic contexts where product branding is weak.

ISO 14001 can likewise be a marketing tool in competitive economic circumstances. Economic contexts in which it is easy to establish new firms, that is where entry barriers are low, tend to be more competitive. Low entry barriers increase competition and force incumbents as well as new firms to differentiate themselves on a variety of counts, including environmental stewardship (Porter and Linde, 1995). Therefore,

H6: ISO 14001 adoption rates are likely to be higher in markets with low entry barriers.

ISO 14001 has also become a tool for managing trade between companies and across countries. The influence of trading markets on firms' incentives to join ISO 14001 may stem from the policies of the dominant trading partner. At an international level, if country A absorbs a significant proportion of country B's exports, then country B can be expected to mimic or respond to the policies of country A. In other words, some type of Vogel's (1995) "California effect" can be expected to work for ISO 14001 through dyadic trade linkages. Governments may actively promote ISO 14001 if their economies rely on exporting to countries with high levels of ISO 14001 adoption rates (Roht-Arriaza, 1997). Further, many claim that adopting ISO 14001 will become a de facto condition of doing business in the global economy. Firms that outsource their operations sometimes require that their suppliers adopt ISO 14001. Ford and GM have announced that they will require their first-tier suppliers to receive ISO 14001 certification by 2004 (Coglianese and Nash, 2001).[9] Thus, we propose that:

H7:   ISO 14001 adoption rates will be higher for firms whose trading partners have adopted ISO 14001.

Cross-national study of ISO 14001 adoption

The discussion above highlights several ways that firms can respond to the ISO 14001 brand. To investigate these hypotheses, we present two analyses of firms' ISO 14001 adoption decisions. The first analysis exploits the rich variation in national economic and policy contexts by examining ISO 14001 adoption rates across countries. The second is a facility-level analysis of ISO 14001 adoption among US industrial facilities. This section presents the cross-national analysis; the following section presents the US facility analysis.

[9] There is an empirically limited (Jaffe *et al.*, 1995) but powerful argument that firms increase foreign investment to avoid stringent domestic environmental laws. The policy implication of such "industry flight" and "pollution haven" hypotheses is that to retain jobs, governments may come under pressure to create a "level playing field." Creating barriers to outward foreign investment and foreign trade could achieve this objective. Widespread adoption of ISO 14001 may preempt the proliferation of such non-tariff barriers under the guise of environmental protection. Such races to the bottom are rare because MNCs seldom base their foreign investment decisions on environmental costs alone. As Dunning's (1993) Organization–Location–Internalization framework demonstrates, foreign investment decisions are fairly complex. Firms consider costs of adopting different business models across countries and the liability issues stemming from industrial disasters in subsidiaries operating in developing countries (Bhopal being a case in point). Further, most of the foreign investment in the last decade is within the "triad" of developed countries (UNCTAD, 2002) that have comparable levels of environmental regulations.

Data and methods

To investigate these hypotheses about factors influencing country-specific ISO 14001 adoption rates, we compare ISO certification rates across 59 countries. Our sample is smaller than ideal because our test required culling data from many sources, not all of which had data for every country. We believe, however, that our sample is representative because it includes countries at different levels of development and from different continents. Our dependent variable is the number of ISO 14001 certified facilities in each country[10] as reported in the tenth cycle of the ISO 14001 census (ISO, 2001). Our independent variables measure countries' dependence on exports, their integration with networks of international governmental and non-governmental organizations, their domestic political and economic contexts, plus controls. These data are drawn from a variety of sources, as discussed below.

National policy context: variables and measures

Data on regulatory flexibility and stringency are drawn from 2001–2002 Global Competitiveness Report (GCR) (WEF, 2002). This report presents data from several prominent international institutions as well as original survey data gathered through the World Economic Forum's Annual Executive Opinion Survey. The survey was administered to 4,801 managers in 75 countries representing 90 per cent of the world's GDP and more than 80 per cent of its population. Appendix 4.1 lists the survey questions posed to these managers regarding their perceptions of *regulatory flexibility, regulatory stringency, entry barriers,* and *product branding.* We discuss these measures below.

---

[10] Arguably, our dependent variable might be the number of certified facilities as a proportion of total number of certifiable facilities. Data on total number of certifiable facilities are not available. Hence, we take GNP adjusted for purchasing power parity (PPP) as a proxy. PPP adjusted GNP is not a perfect proxy for total number of certifiable facilities because the number of facilities per dollar of GNP may vary across countries. Variations in value chain organization imply that the number of facilities per dollar of GNP varies. In response to this issue, we have taken PPP adjusted GNP, and not GNP per se, as a control variable. The reason is that a consumption basket that a dollar can purchase varies across countries. We are assuming that this variation in selling prices reflects variations in ways in which the value chains and the production systems are organized.

In their day-to-day operations, managers encounter several types of environmental laws. For most firms, three categories of environmental laws pertaining to the three media of air, water, and land are most important. Because managerial perceptions on these categories of laws are highly correlated, we constructed an index, *regulatory stringency* (H1), by pooling regulatory stringency measures for the stringency of air pollution, water pollution, and toxic waste disposal regulations, as reported in the GCR. The variable is scaled so that its mean is 0 and standard deviation is 1. More stringent government regulations may increase ISO 14001 certifications by lowering the marginal cost facing firms for joining the program. We measure flexible enforcement using managers' perceptions of how governments enforce environmental regulations as reported in the GCR survey. *Regulatory Flexibility* (H2) ranges from low perceived flexibility (scored 1) to high perceived flexibility (scored 7).

While one could argue that ISO 14001 adoption may reduce the risk of litigation, we expect the opposite: firms in litigious legal contexts should be less likely to join ISO 14001. Since we are not aware of any direct measure of levels of environmental litigation per country, we turn to a simple proxy: the number of environmental law firms in each country (H3-*environmental law firms*). Our logic here is that the propensity to litigate on environmental issues should be highly correlated with the number of litigation agents, that is, the number of environmental law firms. While recognizing that our measure is not perfect – a large number of law firms may well be associated with a smaller number of cases litigated per law firm; the average number of partners and associates in law firms may vary across countries; lawyers may perform different tasks in some countries – we believe that it adequately captures levels of environmental litigation. Data on a number of environmental law firms were taken from Martindale-Hubbell International Law Directory, which provides detailed profiles of more than 12,000 law firms and 124,000 lawyers in over 160 countries (Martindale-Hubbell, 2001).

National economic context: variables and measures

Domestic economic factors influence ISO 14001 adoption rates in several ways. Consumers in wealthier countries may demand that firms adopt more environmentally progressive policies. Our measure of national wealth, *GNP per capita* (H4), adjusted for purchasing power parity, is drawn from the 2002 World Development Report (World Bank, 2002). ISO 14001 certification provides firms in highly competitive markets with means to differentiate themselves. Because ISO 14001 can signal firms' commitment to progressive environmental policies, firms are more likely to join this code in countries where product branding is weak. *Product branding* (H5) measures the extent to which companies in each country have developed their own brands and is scored 1 for low branding and 7 for strong branding (see Appendix 4.1). *Entry barriers* (H5) measures the degree to which new firms can join markets and is scored 1 for difficult entry of new competitors into market and 7 for easy entry of new competitors, as reported by managers in the GCR survey (again see Appendix 4.1). To measure international supply chain effects, we develop a measure of *international trade* (H7), based on the export value of its foreign trade, weighted by the partners' level of ISO 14001 certification. If ISO 14001's reputational value is signaled and transmitted via trade networks, countries whose major export partners have higher ISO 14001 adoption rates should in turn have higher certification levels. Following Guler *et al.* (2002), we calculate each country's international trade context as:

$$\text{Internationaltrade}_{it} = \sum_{j} \text{ISO}_{jt-1} \times (\text{Exports}_{ij} / \text{Exports}_i)^2$$

Where ISO_{jt-1} is the number of ISO certifications in country *j* at time *t−1*, Exports_{ij} is country *i*'s exports to county *j*, Exports_i is country *i*'s total exports. Trade data are from Feenstra (2000).

National-level control variables

In examining country-level variations in the adoption of ISO 14001, we need to control for the total number of facilities that can potentially adopt this green club. We use gross national product adjusted for purchasing power parity, *GNP*, as a proxy for total number of certifiable facilities. Citizens' perceptions of environmental quality may be reflected in countries' pollution emissions. When pollution levels are high, citizens may demand that governments and firms adopt policies to curb pollution. Pollution levels in each country are measured via CO_2 *emissions,* which is the amount of CO_2 emissions (in tons) per unit of GDP (in dollars), as reported in the 2002 World Development Report (World Bank, 2002). Third, international organizations, governmental as well as non-governmental, are important vehicles for disseminating norms about business responsibility towards the environment, green clubs, regulatory reform, etc. Governments can join a range of inter-governmental organizations and regimes such as the European Union and the World Trade Organization. Citizens and citizen groups can likewise join international non-governmental organizations ranging from Greenpeace to the International Political Science Association. Networks of international organizations, governmental or non-governmental, can serve as the conduit through which countries and their citizens exchange ideas, develop common understanding, and perhaps even pressure each other to adopt common environmental programs (Boli and Thomas, 1999). Consequently, we propose that firms' perceptions about ISO 14001's reputational value are likely to be stronger in countries whose government and citizens join more international organizations. *Governmental international membership* measures the number of inter-governmental international organizations a country's government has joined, as recorded in the 1997 Yearbook of International Organizations (Union of International Associations 1997).[11] *Citizen international membership* measures the number of non-governmental international organizations a country's citizens have joined, as reported in the 1997 Yearbook of International Organizations (Union of International Associations, 1997). Finally, because ISO 14001 and ISO 9000 share the management system-based approach, learning costs in adoption of ISO 14001 could be lower for ISO 9000 certified firms (Christmann and Taylor, 2001). We therefore control for the number of ISO 9000 certified firms in each country. Data on ISO 9000 certification were taken from the twelfth cycle of the ISO (2003) survey.

---

[11] As another way of measuring political integration into global communities, we also examined whether or not a country is a member of the European Union. This measure was not statistically significant and did not change our results presented here.

Empirical model

To gauge the affects of countries' domestic and international contexts on ISO 14001 adoption, we estimate negative binomial event count models of the form $E[Y] = GNP^{\alpha}exp(X^{*}\beta)+\epsilon$ where Y is the number of ISO 14001 certifications; E[ ] denotes expectations; GNP is gross national product adjusted for purchasing power parity; X is a vector of independent and control variables affecting the number of certifications relative to GNP; α and β are (vectors of) parameters to be estimated; and ϵ is the residual. The independent variables include measures of countries' domestic and international contexts, and controls. Our choice of functional form is driven by the fact that we need to use an event-count model because the ISO 14001 certifications are discrete events with a non-normal distribution (King, 1989; Maddala, 1983). In the analysis below, the estimated value of the parameter α is greater than 0, indicating that negative binomial regression is preferred to Poisson regression (Long, 1997). Interpreting coefficients in count models is complicated somewhat by the models' non-linear functional form. Following Long (1997), we interpret each coefficient by calculating its "discrete change," where a discrete change is the difference in the number of predicted events associated with an increase in the independent variable from one standard deviation below its mean to one standard deviation above, holding all other independent variables constant at their means.

Cross-national results

ISO 14001 is a prominent green club based on a regulatory approach that firms often favor over more rigid command and control regulations based on emissions limits and control technologies. Yet firms' responses to ISO 14001 have varied across countries. Based on our theoretical discussion, our expectations are that countries' international contexts as well as domestic political and economic contexts influence national ISO 14001 adoption rates. Tables 4.2 and 4.3 present the results of the event-count analyses of the number of certified firms in 59 countries, including the discrete changes of statistically significant variables.

The nature of national policy contexts has an important influence on firms' decisions about joining ISO 14001. The results in Table 4.3

Table 4.2. Cross-national analysis of ISO 14001 certifications:
Descriptive statistics

Variable	Mean	Standard deviation	Minimum	Maximum
ISO 14001	337.68	821.08	0.00	5556.00
International context				
International trade	1.08	0.85	0.14	5.50
Governmental international membership	3.99	0.30	2.64	4.50
Citizen international membership	7.14	0.64	5.42	8.11
Political context				
Regulatory flexibility	3.96	0.61	2.60	5.40
Environmental law firms	33.20	76.51	0.00	400.00
Regulatory stringency	0.07	1.03	−1.66	1.81
Economic context				
GNP per capita	11945.21	8491.57	1406.72	29240.00
Entry barriers	5.23	0.44	3.90	6.10
Branding	4.29	1.10	2.50	6.40
Controls				
Log of GNP	25.74	1.64	22.65	29.71
ISO 9000	6166.66	11423.03	3.00	63725.00
CO_2 emissions	6.15	5.14	0.19	21.63

indicate that the value of ISO 14001's reputation, and therefore its adoption rates across countries, responds to the nature of regulatory enforcement as well as the stringency of environmental regulations. The coefficients for *regulatory flexibility, regulatory stringency,* and *environmental law firms* are statistically significant and in their hypothesized directions. A two-standard deviation increase in *regulatory flexibility* increases the number of ISO 14001 certified facilities by 73.3, holding the effects of other variables constant at their means. Firms are more likely to join ISO 14001 in countries where environmental regulations are enforced more flexibly. A two-standard deviation increase in *environmental law firms* decreases the number of ISO

14001 certified firms by 42.7, holding the effects of other variables constant at their mean.[12] Firms are less likely to join ISO 14001 in countries with more litigious legal climates. Likewise, a two-standard deviation increase in *regulatory stringency* increases the number of ISO 14001 certified firms by 142.2. Firms are more likely to join ISO 14001 in countries with more stringent environmental regulations. Thus, both the *stringency* of governments' environmental regulations and the nature of firms–regulators interactions influence ISO 14001's reputational benefits.[13] When governmental regulations are stringent, enforced flexibly and litigation threats are low, firms perceive more value in affiliating with ISO 14001, and hence its adoption rates are higher. These findings make sense in the context of our green clubs theory: the cost of ISO 14001 certification is not simply the initial certification costs coupled with the added management costs. As discussed earlier, certified firms risk higher compliance costs if governments fully punish violations that firms uncover during audits or if such violations risk lawsuits from environmental groups.

The results in Table 4.3 also show that economic and market factors offer important explanations for firms' ISO 14001 decisions. Citizens in wealthier countries may demand more environmental protection and thus influence ISO 14001 certification rates (H5). However, controlling for other factors, countries with wealthier citizens do not have more certified firms. This may be due to the fact that our control variable, CO_2 *emissions*, is strongly correlated with GNP per capita ($r = .73$). Countries with greater pollution emissions have fewer ISO 14001 certifications, perhaps an indication of lower pollution concerns among citizens in these countries. A two-standard deviation increase in CO_2 emissions reduces the number of ISO 14001 certifications by 40.5, holding constant the effects of other variables. Citizens,

---

[12] Arguably, in countries where there is a constant threat of lawsuits, regulators will be inclined to be less flexible and "go by the book" (Bardach and Kagan, 1982). However, *flexibility* and *environmental law firms* are only moderately correlated (0.30).

[13] The effects of flexibility and stringency on ISO 14001 certifications may be related; flexibility may have a stronger influence when regulations are stringent. In our analyses below, we ideally would include an interaction term between these two measures. However, this is not feasible, given the high correlation between them ($r = .75$).

Table 4.3. Countrywide 14001 registrations: negative
binomial analyses

Independent variables	Coefficient	Discrete change
International context		
International trade	.304** (.101)	28.5
Governmental international membership	−.703 (.250)	
Citizen international membership	.928** (.420)	71.0
Political context		
Regulatory flexibility	0.993** (0.303)	73.3
Environmental law firms	−0.005** (0.001)	−42.7
Regulatory stringency	0.976** (0.337)	142.2
Economic context		
GNP per capita	2.20E–05 (2.75E-05)	
Entry barriers	−0.225 (0.204)	
Branding	−0.923** (0.334)	−28.6
Controls		
Log of GNP	9.18** (0.102)	239.1
ISO 9000	1.36E-04** 6.87E-06	17.1
CO_2 emissions	−0.069** (0.034)	−40.5
Constant	−21.7** (3.63)	
Alpha	.702	
Chi^2	780.79**	
N	59	

Note:
standard errors in parentheses.
** $p < .05$, two tailed tests.

of course, can express preferences directly to firms through their
market behaviors or indirectly by pressuring their government.

Our results also suggest that firms' perceptions of ISO 14001's
reputational value depend more on the nature of domestic economic
branding. Countries with stronger and more developed product
brands have fewer ISO 14001 registered firms (H5). A two-standard
deviation increase in *product branding* decreases the number of ISO

14001 registrants by 43.7, holding the effects of other variables at their mean. This suggests that in countries with weak product brand identities, ISO 14001 may help firms distinguish themselves by signaling their commitment to environmental protection. Contrary to theoretical expectations (H6), access to local markets did not significantly affect numbers of ISO 14001 certified firms. Signals about business responsibility towards the environment and regulatory reform in general, and ISO 14001 in particular, can be transmitted via trade linkages as well as through networks of inter-governmental and non-governmental organizations. Countries whose export trading partners have higher levels of ISO 14001 certifications themselves have higher certification levels. A two-standard deviation increase in international trade (from one-standard deviation below its mean to one-standard deviation above) increases the number of ISO 14001 certified facilities by 28.5, holding the effects of other variables constant at their means. Along the lines of Vogel's (1995) "California effect," our analysis suggests that trade linkages create incentives for ISO 14001 adoption, if this green club has been widely adopted in important export destinations.

Overall, these results identify important factors influencing firms' perceptions of the value of affiliating with ISO 14001's reputation, and therefore in mitigating the club's Olsonian dilemma. Our analysis provides evidence that the regulatory context, as captured in the stringency, litigiousness, and enforcement flexibility of environmental regulations, affects ISO 14001 certification levels. Countries' domestic economic contexts influence the value of ISO 14001 branding. Unlike previous research that found that firms with highly developed brands are more likely to join green clubs (Arora and Cason, 1996), our analysis suggests that ISO 14001 itself functions as a brand, allowing firms lacking established brands to differentiate themselves from their competitors. In terms of the international context, firms are likely to find ISO 14001 membership useful in countries that are more heavily embedded in the international context via strong export ties with heavily ISO 14001 certified countries and membership in non-governmental international organizations. All in all, these analyses suggest that firms are joining ISO 14001 at least in part in response to the value of the program's brand among the firms' stakeholders. When government officials flexibly enforce regulations, more firms join ISO 14001, perhaps because they recognize that the officials have the discretion to reward firms for joining the program. The ISO 14001 brand also has more direct economic or market functions, whether by replacing weak domestic brands or by facilitating exports and international trade.

ISO 14001 adoption among US facilities

In this section we examine ISO 14001's adoption among facilities within the United States. Our motives for doing so are twofold. First, focusing on the US affords us the opportunity to investigate whether differences in states' policy context – which are nested in the national policy context – influence the value firms perceive in affiliating with the ISO 14001 brand. For example, environmental governance institutions in Virginia are likely to be different from those in New Jersey in ways that affect how regulators and other stakeholders can reward firms for joining ISO 14001. Yet differences among states in the US are less pronounced than the differences we observed between countries. States are nested in the US federal institutional context that limits how much states can deviate from the US EPA's environmental policy standards. For example, states are not able to adopt clean-air regulations that are less stringent than those the US EPA requires. Also, while some states have granted legal protection for self-incriminating evidence firms uncovered during environmental self-audits, the US EPA has stated it will not recognize such protection and privileges. In assessing ISO 14001's reputational value, firms are likely to be responding to institutional signals from state regulators well as federal regulators. Our second reason for choosing the US is pragmatic: data on facility-level characteristics and their regulatory and environmental performance are readily available from the US EPA and other sources. Such data allow us to investigate ISO 14001 at facility rather than national levels.

Our focus is on facilities regulated under US state and federal air-pollution regulations. Facilities in our sample meet air-pollution emissions thresholds in order to be tracked by the EPA's Toxics Release Inventory (TRI) program and are classified as "major sources" under federal clean-air laws. Information on facilities' regulatory compliance comes from the Aerometric Information Retrieval System (AIRS), a subsystem of the EPA's Integrated Data for Enforcement

Table 4.4. US facility ISO 14001 registrations: descriptive statistics

Variable	Mean	Std Dev	Min	Max
Facility				
Compliance$_{1995-96}$	2.25	6.21	0	24
Compliance$_{1995-96}{}^{2}$	43.57	137.59	0	576
Inspections	2.10	2.34	0	42
Enforcement actions	0.430	1.86	0	50
Penalty	6369.04	151982.9	0	9000000
Emissions$_{1995-96}$	3.92E + 08	1.33E + 09	5	2.24E + 10
Emissions$_{1995-96}{}^{2}$	2.04E + 18	1.82E + 19	25	5.04E + 20
Number of employees	406.56	830.84	1	17500
Branch	0.653	0.476	0	1
Single	0.196	0.397	0	1
ISO 14001	0.040	0.196	0	1
Policy context				
Litigiousness	0.133	0.294	0.0115	2.64
Hazardous-air regulations	0.619	0.486	0	1
Ambient-air regulations	0.110	0.313	0	1
State audit protections	0.522	0.500	0	1
State EMS programs	0.213	0.410	0	1
State non-EMS program	0.416	0.49	0	1
Regulatory flexibility	6.39	3.88	1.3333	24
Environmental groups	5.89	2.20	0.7778	14.16
Neighborhood context				
Education	81.26	6.73	58.1780	100
Income over $75,000	4.36	22.27	0	100
Minorities	21.87	4.08	0	100

Analysis (IDEA) system. Emissions data are from the TRI database. Other measures are drawn from Dunn and Bradstreet's Million Dollar Directory and other sources as discussed below. Our sample contains 3,709 facilities, 151 (4 per cent) of which were ISO 14001 certified as of December 2001. We use 1995–1996 though 2000–2001 because it straddles the ISO 14001's introduction and the publication of a recent roster of ISO 14001 certified facilities (Table 4.4).

Data and measures

In our sample of US facilities, we want to evaluate what factors distinguish facilities that have joined ISO 14001 from those that have not. We determine whether a facility joined ISO 14001 by 2001 by examining the list of ISO 14001 certified facilities published by the Center for Energy and Environmental Management (CEEM, 2000, 2001). The dependent variable, *ISO 14001 membership*, is scored 1 if the facility is certified in the program; if not, it was scored as 0.

Policy context

Unlike the cross-national analysis, in the facility-level analysis we can identify the government's enforcement actions directed at each facility as well as broader characteristics of the policy environment in which facilities operate. Beginning with the broader policy context measures, we focus on difference across US states. In the federalist system, the US EPA and the states share responsibility for regulating stationary source air pollution (Potoski, 2001). Stationary sources are factories and power plants such as those included in our sample (mobile sources of air pollution, including cars and trucks, constitute a different class of air-pollution policy). For each policy area, such as setting ambient air-quality and emissions standards and monitoring and enforcement facilities' performance, the US EPA sets minimum criteria for state programs. Each state's clean-air agency submits to the US EPA a State Implementation Plan (SIP) that details how the state will meet US EPA standards. If the US EPA determines that the SIP is inadequate, it can "preempt" all or part of the state's clean-air program and administer the failing portions in that state. Preemption has proven to be a powerful deterrent to states relaxing their clean air standards below US EPA criteria: nearly every state has received US EPA authority to administer all clean-air programs. However, in virtually all clean-air policy areas, states can choose to either match or exceed US EPA standards.

Thus, while all states meet the US EPA minimum standards for their clean-air regulations, some states have laws more stringent than federal requirements. To measure the stringency of environmental regulations, we measure both the stringency of regulations governing all facilities in a state and the regulatory enforcement measures a facility has received. We measure the stringency of state air-pollution regulations with the dummy variables *hazardous-air regulations* and *ambient-air regulations* each scored 1 if the state's regulations are more stringent than the corresponding EPA minimum criteria. Recall from our theoretical discussion that more stringent government standards lower the marginal cost of joining a voluntary regulation. Therefore,

H1: Facilities in states with more stringent air-pollution regulations are more likely to join ISO 14001.

Turning to the policy actions directed at individual facilities, we expect facilities' adoption decisions to be influenced by the stringency of regulatory enforcement. Facilities receiving more frequent regulatory enforcement, particularly regulatory inspections, may feel more pressure to demonstrate they are complying with government regulations. ISO 14001's EMS requirements, with their emphasis on recording, reporting and internal accountability, can signal to regulators a facility's positive intent to comply with government regulations. Hence,

H2: Facilities operating in regulatory contexts where regulations are stringently enforced are more likely to join ISO 14001.

We capture the stringency of the regulatory context via two measures. *Inspections*$_{95-96}$ is the number of state and EPA inspections each facility received in 1995 and 1996. *Enforcement actions*$_{95-96}$ is the number of enforcement actions, including notices of violation, levied by state and EPA officials against each facility in 1995 and 1996. Facilities that receive more inspections and enforcement actions may be more likely to join ISO 14001, perhaps in an effort to demonstrate they are looking to comply with government regulations.

As discussed earlier in this chapter, to encourage firms to conduct self-regulation, some states have moved to provide legal protection and immunity for self-incriminating evidence discovered during regulatory self-audits. Such legal protection may serve as signals of a state's cooperative intent towards firms that self-regulate and may encourage facilities to join ISO 14001. State audit protections may make it more attractive to join ISO 14001 because firms can enjoy some protection from regulatory violations that have been uncovered as a result of the external audits they receive through ISO 14001 certification.

H3:   Facilities operating in states that offer legal protection for
       environmental audits are more likely to join ISO 14001.

We measure states' legal environment with the variable *state audit
protection*, scored 1 if the state provides privilege or immunity protection for information uncovered in facilities' self-audits. When facilities
are less worried about lawsuits that would force them to reveal
information gathered during audits, they may be more likely to join
ISO 14001. Similarly, contentious legal environments may deter firms
from joining ISO 14001: a contested policy environment with an
active environmental movement may signal a higher possibility of
being sued over environmental issues.

H4:   Facilities operating in states that have high levels of environ-
       mental litigation are less likely to join ISO 14001.

We measure *state litigiousness* by using the ratio of environmental
court cases to TRI facilities in each state.[14] Similarly, the value of
affiliating with ISO 14001 is likely to be higher for facilities that are
out of compliance with governments' environmental regulations.
Non-compliant facilities are likely to be subjected to high levels of regulatory scrutiny. Joining ISO 14001 may be a way for non-compliant
facilities to earn goodwill with regulators by showing they are taking
additional efforts to improve compliance.

H5:   Facilities that have been out of compliance with governmental
       regulations in previous years are more likely to join ISO 14001.

We measure facilities' previous regulatory compliance (*Compli-
ance$_{95-96}$*) with the proportion of months that a facility is out of
compliance over a two-year period from 1995 through 1996. We also
include the measure *Compliance$_{95-96}^2$* since the effect of compliance
on joining ISO 14001 may vary across levels of compliance. The measures for inspections, enforcement actions, and compliance are all
drawn from the EPA's IDEA database.

---

[14] Data are from Lexis Nexus State Case database searches with the key words
     "air pollution," "water pollution" and "hazardous waste" for the entire 1990s.

Social contexts

Unlike cross-national comparison, the facilities' economic and social contexts do not vary significantly across US states. Hence, for our analysis of US facilities, we measure context in a much narrower sense. Residents in a facility's neighborhood can influence the facility's environmental activities (Hamilton, 1996). Residents are stakeholders in the sense that they can protest against a polluting facility, lobby government for more stringent policies and enforcement actions, and create positive and negative feedback for a facility.

H6: Facilities operating in areas inhabited by citizens of high socio-economic status are more likely to join ISO 14001.

Wealthier and more educated citizens may demand more environmental protection, may better recognize the value of the ISO 14001 brand, and may have the resources to influence the environmental decisions of facilities in their neighborhood. Thus, our analyses include measures of the socioeconomic status of the residents living in facilities' neighborhoods. From the EPA's IDEA database, *residents' education*[15] measures the percentage of residents living within a three-mile radius of a facility who have a high school education or greater. From the same database, we also include variables for the percentage of the area population who are *minorities* and the percentage of population making more than $75,000 per year (*income*). The analysis includes the natural log of these three neighborhood context variables.[16] Wealth, education and ethnicity may provide citizens with leverage for compelling facilities to join ISO 14001 (Pargal and Wheeler, 1996; Kahn, 2002). Finally, we further investigate the effects of citizens' demands for ISO 14001 with the variable *environmental groups*, the number of

---

[15] In their study of environmental complaints lodged in China during 1993–1997, Dasgupta and Wheeler (1996) find that complaints are associated with education levels.

[16] In a few cases, these measures recorded 0 residents making over $75,000 (64 cases) or 0 minority residents (26 cases), making natural logs problematic. One approach is to set the value for such cases at 0 and add a dummy variable to account for any intercept shift (see Cameron and Trivedi, 1998: 239–240). We experimented with this approach but were unable to get ML convergence; some standard errors were in question, although the reported coefficients were essentially identical to those presented here. In the analyses presented here we set the value at .05 for the 0 cases of these measures.

members in the Sierra Club and the National Wildlife Federation per 1,000 residents in 1998.

H7:   Facilities operating in states that have a high salience of environmental groups are more likely to join ISO 14001.

Controls

Several facility characteristics are likely to influence firms' perceptions of ISO 14001's reputational benefits in relation to the cost of joining this club. Larger facilities are more likely to join ISO 14001 because they are likely to reap higher levels of net benefits. In addition to having more resources to invest in costly EMS, larger facilities are more visible and more likely to be scrutinized by stakeholders (Arora and Cason, 1995; Chapple *et al.*, 2001). As a result, joining ISO 14001 is likely to be noticed and earn them reputational benefits. *Facility size* is the number of employees at the facility, as reported in the Dunn and Bradstreet database. We also include two dummy variables measuring whether the facility is a branch facility (branch), single-site company (single), or company headquarters (scored 0). Our model includes dummy variables reflecting each facility's two-digit SIC code.

Highly polluting facilities may have stronger incentive to join ISO 14001 because stakeholders are likely to focus their attention on them. We follow King and Lenox (2000: 175) to calculate each facility's total emissions, weighted by the emissions' toxicity. Toxicity is reflected in the "reportable quantity," the threshold amount for reporting an accidental release, according to the Comprehensive Environmental Response, Compensation, and Liability Act (CERCLA). Releases for a given facility are thus:

$$E_{it} = \sum w_c e_{cit}$$

Where E_{it} is the weighted total emissions for facility i in year t, w_c is the toxicity weight factor for chemical c in year t, and e_{cit} is the pounds of emissions of chemical. Time t is 1995 through 1996 and time $t + 1$ is 2000 through 2001. We use two-year time periods to smooth over any year-to-year fluctuations. *Emissions*$_{95-96}$ is the facility's air pollution in 1995 and 1996 as recorded in the TRI data, weighted by each pollutant's toxicity. The analysis for joining ISO 14001 also includes the variable *Emissions*$_{95-96}^2$ because the effect of emissions on joining ISO 14001 may vary across emission levels.

Empirical model

Because our dependent variable (joining ISO 14001) is dichotomous, our empirical model employs a probit specification. Interpreting the coefficients in our model is complicated by probit's non-linear functional form and by the fact that an occurrence of our dependent variable (an ISO 14001 certified facility) is quite rare. Following Long (1997), we calculate the discrete change in probability of our dependent variable occurring (a facility joins ISO 14001) given changes in our independent variables, holding all other variables at their mean. Note that these changes may seem quite small, but they should be interpreted relative to a "baseline" probability, which in our case is the rather small proportion of facilities joining ISO 14001. Only about 4 per cent of the facilities in our sample joined ISO 14001; holding all independent variables at their mean, the predicted probability of joining ISO 14001 is only .022. Overall, our model discriminates well among firms subscribing to ISO 14001: the chi-square statistic for the model is 212.58, significant at $p < .001$.

Results

Table 4.5 reports results of our probit analysis examining the diffusion of ISO 14001 across facilities. The dependent variable is whether or not a facility joined ISO 14001 by December 2001 and the independent variables gauge facilities' policy and other context, plus controls.

The policy context in which facilities operate influences whether they choose to join ISO 14001. Examining the measures of state-level policies, two features stand out. First, facilities in states with more stringent hazardous-air-pollution regulations are more likely to join ISO 14001 (H1). Joining ISO 14001 and adopting its stringent EMS requirements may help facilities meet higher regulatory standards. Second, our results indicate that most other government programs, laws, and regulations appear to have little influence on a facility's calculus about joining ISO 14001 (H3). None of the coefficients for *enforcement actions, state audit protection, state EMS program, state non-EMS program, ambient air regulations, litigiousness* and *regulatory flexibility* achieved statistical significance in the analysis of why facilities join ISO 14001. Facilities that receive more *regulatory*

Table 4.5. ISO 14001 registrations: US facility analysis

	Coefficients	Standard errors
Facility		
Compliance$_{1995-96}$	1.491**	0.693
Compliance$_{1995-96}^2$	−1.602**	0.76
Inspections	0.029**	0.015
Enforcement actions	−0.002	0.015
Emissions$_{1995-96}$	2.07E-10***	6.88E-11
Emissions$_{1995-96}^2$	−1.36E-20*	7.74E-21
Number of employees	7.76E-05**	3.31E-05
Branch	0.12	0.113
Single	−0.023	0.145
SIC code dummies		Yes
Policy context		
Litigiousness	0.101	0.065
Hazardous air regulations	0.233**	0.096
Ambient air regulations	0.048	0.152
State audit protections	−0.001	0.091
State programs	0.031	0.1
Regulatory flexibility	−0.004	0.011
Environmental groups	−0.035*	0.02
Neighborhood context		
Education	1.484**	0.63
Income over $75,000	0.025	0.026
Minorities	−0.008	0.03
Constant	−9.224	2.837
N	3709	
Rho	0.119	
Wald (independent eq.)	10.71**	
Wald (overall)	705.84**	

Note:
* $p < .10$, ** $p < .05$, *** $p < .10$, two tailed tests (same as Table 5.4).

inspections are significantly more likely to join ISO 14001, suggesting that facilities may be using ISO 14001 to signal their intent to comply with government regulations (H2). A two-standard deviation increase in the number of inspections, from one-standard deviation below the mean to one above, increases the probability of becoming ISO 14001 certified from .019 to .026.

The relationship between the amount of time a facility was out of compliance in 1995 and 1996 and its probability of ISO 14001 registration follows an inverted U-shaped curve (H5). The *Compliance$_{1995-96}$* coefficient is statistically significant and positive while the *Compliance$_{1995-96}^2$* coefficient is statistically significant and negative. Facilities that are always in compliance or always out of compliance are the least likely to join ISO 14001. The predicted probability of joining ISO 14001 for facilities in compliance for the entire two-year period, .01, is essentially the same as for those that are not in compliance for the same time period (.01). For those that are out of compliance for about half the time, the predicted probability of joining ISO 14001 is about .018. The statistically significant coefficients for *emissions* and *emissions^2* results suggest that low-pollution facilities are least likely to join ISO 14001, while moderate- and high-polluting facilities are roughly equally more likely to join ISO 14001.

Facilities in neighborhoods with a higher number of educated residents are more likely to join ISO 14001 (H6). A two-standard deviation increase in the logged percentage of educated residents (from one-standard deviation below the mean to one-standard deviation above), increases the probability that a facility will join ISO 14001 from .016 to .030, holding the effects of other variables constant at their mean. This may be because ISO 14001's reputation is more valuable to facilities when local residents are better able to detect, interpret, and use the information, or perhaps because more educated residents have a higher demand for environmental performance. Finally, larger facilities, those with more employees, are significantly more likely to join ISO 14001. This may be because such facilities are more likely to have the personnel to devote to establishing and maintaining expensive EMS.

Together, we can draw some tentative conclusions regarding factors that enhance the value of ISO 14001 branding and create incentives for facilities to join ISO 14001. As discussed in chapter 2, regulatory contexts play an important role in shaping firms' perceptions about costs and benefits of ISO 14001 membership. First, government inspections spur facilities to join ISO 14001 (H2), as do more stringent hazardous-air-pollution regulations (H1). Other governmental policies appear to have little influence on facilities' ISO 14001 decisions, at least for state-level policies in US air-pollution regulation. With the EPA setting its own policies in areas such as audit privilege and immunity protection (H3) while also holding preemption authority over states that do not meet its minimum requirements for air-pollution regulation, the variation in state policy contexts facing facilities may be too limited to influence their ISO 14001 certification decisions. Second, facilities with moderate compliance records are most likely to join ISO 14001. Third, facilities in neighborhoods with more educated residents are more likely to join ISO 14001 (H6). This suggests that because the ability of citizens to interpret ISO 14001's brand signal is greater in educated neighborhoods, facilities located in such locations will perceive ISO 14001 to be more valuable than ones located in less-educated areas.

Conclusions

Green clubs seek to encourage firms to adopt environmentally pro-gressive policies. If green clubs solve the Olsonian and shirking dilem-mas, their members produce public goods such as pollution reduction. As potentially useful instruments of environmental governance, one challenge is to popularize these clubs to gain an optimally broad membership roster. Understanding these dynamics is especially impor-tant in the context of ISO 14001 because adoption rates have varied across countries, and across states within the US. This is intriguing because firms have actively championed ISO 14001. The analytical issue then is to identify factors that make ISO 14001 membership desirable to firms. Our theoretical expectation is that international and domestic factors as well as facility-level characteristics can play an important role in this regard. This chapter offered an empirical ana-lysis of such factors, for understanding both cross-national diffusion and diffusion within the US.

Our comparative case studies demonstrate how domestic factors have influenced adoption rates in the UK and the US. In particular, we emphasized the role of business–government relations and the cred-ibility of the sponsoring organization in influencing firms' perceptions of ISO 14001. Drawing insights from our case studies, we conducted an econometric analysis of ISO 14001 diffusion across 59 countries. Domestic contexts in which firms operate have a crucial bearing on ISO 14001's attractiveness. Firms are more likely to join ISO 14001 where laws are stringent and flexibly enforced, and where affiliating with the ISO 14001 brand returns more value to firms. We demonstrated that firms are more likely to join ISO 14001 when they operate in countries that are more highly embedded in international trade networks and non-governmental organization networks. International trade creates incentives for firms to join green clubs as long as their key importers have done so. Vogel's (1995) "California effect" works in the case of ISO 14001. This important finding suggests that, in the context of green clubs, international trade by itself neither undermines nor promotes the spread of green clubs. The key issue is trade with whom. As long as the OECD countries with stringent environmental policies absorb the bulk of the world's imports,[17] firms in exporting countries, especially in the developing world, will have incentives to adopt green clubs such as ISO 14001.

In several ways, our analysis of ISO 14001 across US facilities reinforces the results of our cross-country analysis. We expected to find greater variations in policy contexts across countries than within a country. The critical finding is that stringent regulations and more regulatory inspections increase the rates of joining ISO 14001's. Other attributes of the policy context were not significant for within-country variations while they were significant for across-country variations in ISO 14001 adoption. With the EPA setting its own policies in areas such as audit privilege and immunity protection, while also holding preemption authority over states that do not meet its minimum requirements for air-pollution regulation, the variation in state policy contexts facing facilities may be too limited to influence their ISO 14001 certification decisions. This also holds for the role of the litigiousness variable: it is significant for cross-country variations but not for within-country variations. The second critical finding is that firms find ISO 14001 membership more valuable if they operate in wealthier and more educated social contexts. In some ways, the value of affiliating with ISO 14001's reputation is enhanced if stakeholders have the means and the willingness to scrutinize firms' environmental programs and to use ISO 14001 as a signal for structuring their interactions with firms. Our empirical analysis indicates that firms believe that wealthy stakeholders are indeed in a position to do so in the context of ISO 14001.

---

[17] For reference, OECD countries absorb over 70 per cent of world exports (OECD, 2001).

Having examined how various factors influence the value firms receive from affiliating with ISO 14001's brand reputation and hence the club's ability to mitigate the Olsonian dilemma, chapter 5 investigates conditions under which ISO 14001 is able to curb shirking and therefore mitigate the shirking dilemma. In some ways, successful mitigation of shirking feeds into the club's positive reputation, enhances the benefits members perceive from joining, and hence mitigates the Olsonian dilemma. Thus, results of chapter 5 have crucial bearing on understanding the dynamics of ISO 14001 adoption.

Appendix 4.1 Data from world competitiveness report

Flexibility of environmental regulations (Hypothesis 3)
Environmental regulations in your country: (1 = offer no option for achieving compliance, 7 = are flexible and offer many options for achieving compliance)
Air-pollution regulations (Hypothesis 4)
The stringency of air-pollution regulation in your country is: (1 = lax compared with most countries, 7 = among the world's most stringent)
Water-pollution regulations (Hypothesis 4)
The stringency of water-pollution regulations in your country is: (1 = lax compared with most countries, 7 = among the world's most stringent)
Toxic-waste disposal regulations (Hypothesis 4)
The stringency of regulations concerning toxic-waste disposal in your country is: (1 = lax compared with most countries, 7 = among the world's most stringent)
Entry into local markets (Hypothesis 6)
Entry of new competitors: (1 = almost never occurs in local markets, 7 = is common in local markets)
Extent of product branding (Hypothesis 7)
Companies that sell internationally: (1 = sell commodities or market under foreign brands, 7 = have developed their own international brands)

List of questions posed to US regulators

1. As a regulator, how do you assess the relative credibility of various voluntary programs? What program attributes signal that the program is credible and not a greenwash?
2. What role does third-party auditing play in influencing your perceptions about ISO 14001? Although the quality of auditors varies, on the whole, do you think third-party auditing makes ISO 14001 more rigorous? Why? In your opinion, how does third-party auditing influence operations within firms?
3. What sort of firms do you expect will join ISO 14001? Would ISO 14001 become more credible if it had membership requirements as in Performance Track? Do you think open membership of ISO 14001 undermines its credibility?
4. Do you think ISO 14001 "signals" firms' commitment to better comply with the law? Would ISO 14001 make firms comply better with the law?
5. In your opinion, what are the key motivators for firms to join ISO 14001? Do firms believe that ISO 14001 would improve their credibility with regulators?
6. As a regulator, would you treat ISO 14001 certified firms differently from non-ISO 14001 firms?

5 | ISO 14001 and firms' environmental and regulatory performance

THE ultimate test of a voluntary program, or any policy instrument for that matter, is whether the program induces participants to change their behavior in ways the program desires. An effective green club, one that induces participants to take progressive action beyond what they would take unilaterally, requires a few important conditions, as we discussed in chapter 2. First, the program must impose some non-trivial membership costs because the environmental protection the club looks to induce from its members is not free. Second, the program must provide some non-trivial excludable benefit to induce firms to take on the costs of joining the club. For green clubs, the excludable benefit is generally the goodwill that accrues to participants as a consequence of their membership in the program. The excludable benefit induces some firms that would otherwise have lower environmental performance than the club requires to take on the additional cost of membership and produce the program's targeted public goods. Finally, an effective voluntary environmental program must have a monitoring and enforcement mechanism that ensures members comply with the program standards once they have joined.

In chapter 3 we outlined how these features apply to ISO 14001. We showed that joining ISO 14001 carries important costs in terms of paying for the external audits, adopting and maintaining a stringent EMS, and so on. In chapters 3 and 4 we discussed how ISO 14001 offers an important brand name that carries value with government regulators and other important stakeholders. What remains, then, is to determine whether ISO 14001 improves members' environmental and regulatory performance beyond what they would have achieved unilaterally in the absence of the ISO 14001 program.

In this chapter we investigate the efficacy of the ISO 14001 program. As Alberini and Segerson (2002) correctly note, program efficacy can be evaluated along multiple dimensions, such as environmental performance (for example, pollution emissions), regulatory performance (for example, as compliance with government regulations), financial performance (on participants' profits), overall welfare impact, dynamic effects on innovation, etc. From the perspective of green club skeptics, environmental performance is perhaps the most important indicator of program efficacy. From the perspective of government officials, improvement in regulatory performance may be quite important. Hence, this book focuses on two dimensions of program efficacy: environmental performance and regulatory performance.

Alberini and Segerson also point out that the overall environmental impact of a policy instrument is a function of: (1) number of polluters that join the program; (2) pollution reduction per polluter; and (3) the impact the program has on the number of polluters in the industry overall. Chapter 4 investigated the first criterion. In this chapter we evaluate ISO 14001's performance along the second criterion. Future research may look to investigate whether ISO 14001 reduces the number of extant polluters, perhaps by becoming a de facto operating condition in a particular industry.

By environmental performance we mean facilities' emissions of toxic pollutants and by regulatory performance we mean facilities' compliance with mandatory government regulations. Analyzing the effectiveness of any program is notoriously complex and fraught with potential pitfalls. In the case of ISO 14001, perhaps the most obvious pitfall is that program participants may be different from non-participants in ways that obscure the program's true effect. If cleaner (or dirtier) firms are more likely to join the program, a naïve comparison between the performance of participants and non-participants is likely to overstate (or understate) the program's true effects. Or such naïve comparisons would be biased if some unobserved factors that influence firms' decisions to join ISO 14001 also influence their decisions about environmental performance. Experimental research designs, in which investigators randomly assign subjects to treatment (or program) and control groups, provide analytic power to overcome many of these pitfalls. This is because in such research designs we can assume with some degree of confidence that the two groups are identical except for their participation in the program. Unfortunately, experiments are often ethically problematic and too financially expensive to be practically applicable, particularly for large programs like ISO 14001.

Since we are unable to conduct an experiment for ISO 14001, we look instead to exploit a rich set of data using advanced empirical techniques to control statistically for differences between ISO 14001 certified and non-certified facilities so that the conclusions we draw are valid: US facilities regulated as "major sources" under US EPA air-pollution laws constitute the sample for this quasi-experimental design. We employ data drawn from a wide range of sources, including the US EPA, Dunn and Bradstreet's, CEEM, and others. Our strategy is to analyze the differences in environmental and regulatory performance between ISO 14001 certified and non-certified facilities using "treatment effects" analyses. This quasi-experimental statistical technique controls for differences between certified and non-certified facilities as well as observed and unobserved factors that may influence both facilities' decisions to join the program and their regulatory and environmental performance. This latter statistical adjustment complicates matters but is an important correction for the so-called "endogeneity problem": if we do not control for underlying factors (such as compliance or pollution histories) that influence facilities' decisions to join the program and their environmental and regulatory performance, we would mistakenly attribute performance improvement to facilities' participation in the program while in fact the improvement should have been attributed to the underlying factors. We present these data and empirical techniques in considerable detail so that readers may understand our study's strengths and weaknesses. Along the way, we also try to describe in more accessible terms the threats to the validity of our study and how we address them.

The results of our analyses suggest that as a group ISO 14001 certified facilities have better regulatory compliance records and lower pollution emissions than they likely would have achieved had they not joined the club. These conclusions persist even in analyses controlling for facilities' compliance and emission histories as well as addressing potential endogeneity issues between facilities' performance and their decision to join ISO 14001. In the next section of this chapter, we summarize the literature on the effectiveness of green clubs. We then present the methods and data for our evaluation of ISO 14001's effect on members' compliance with mandatory regulations and their pollution emissions. The following section presents the results of the study.

The efficacy of green clubs

Recent literature has examined the efficacy of green clubs in terms of participating firms' environmental and regulatory performance. As we noted in the introductory chapter, the evidence on environmental performance has been mixed. Khanna and Damon (1999) find that the releases of the chemicals targeted by the US EPA's 33/50 program declined significantly post-adoption. However, King and Lenox (2000) report that Responsible Care participants did not appear to reduce pollution emissions in relation to non-participants. Welch *et al.* (2000) find that electric utilities participating in EPA's Climate Change program did not reduce their CO_2 emissions any more than non-participants.

There is also literature examining the efficacy of ISO 14001 and similar EMS-based programs. Dasgupta *et al.* (2000), in their study of 236 firms in the food, chemical, non-metallic minerals and metal industry (which together generate 75 per cent to 95 per cent of Mexico's industrial pollution), find that ISO 14001 adopters better comply with government environmental regulations, which is an important finding given that many developing countries have difficulty enforcing government regulations. In his analysis of 316 US electronics facilities, Russo (2001) finds that ISO 14001 membership is associated with decreased toxic emissions. Anton *et al.* (2004) report that more comprehensive EMS (the core requirement for ISO 14001) lead to lower toxic emissions, particularly for firms that have higher pollution intensity.

However, some scholars have found that ISO 14001 in particular, and EMS-based programs in general, may not improve firms' performance. In their study of 83 US facilities, Andrews *et al.* (2003) suggest that joining ISO 14001 did not improve firms' environmental performance. In their study of 40 companies operating in Western Australia, Annandale *et al.* (2004) find that while EMS systems improved environmental practices, voluntary reporting of corporate environmental performance did not. In their study of 800 sites regulated under the United Kingdom's Integrated Pollution Control Regime, Dahlstrom *et al.* (2003) find that implementing an environmental management system improved certain procedural aspects of firms' environmental management but it was not associated with an improvement in firms' regulatory performance.

We present an empirical analysis of the effect of ISO 14001 certification on firms' environmental and regulatory performance using a sample of over 3,000 US facilities. Our analysis improves on existing studies of ISO 14001 by expanding the sample size and by controlling for potential endogeneity problems between facilities' decision to join ISO 14001 and their environmental performance. Our analysis suggests that ISO 14001 certified facilities have better regulatory performance and superior environmental performance compared to non-participants. How do we explain our findings? Our theory suggests that green clubs will be effective if they induce participating firms to adopt environmental programs that have non-trivial costs and establish an effective monitoring mechanism. For ISO 14001, the key club standard is to establish an EMS, and the key monitoring mechanism is third-party auditing. As the evidence presented in this chapter suggests, third-party monitoring seems to be succeeding in mitigating shirking and encouraging ISO 14001 certified firms to take up the non-trivial costs of establishing EMS. These EMS seem to be effective in influencing firms' behaviors because our results suggest that, on average, ISO 14001 participants show superior compliance with governmental air-pollution regulations and pollute less (in terms of toxicity-adjusted air emissions).

Evaluating ISO 14001 efficacy in the US

The analyses presented in this chapter compare the environmental and regulatory performance of ISO 14001 certified and non-certified facilities, controlling for non-random assignment between certification and non-certification along with other intervening factors. We return to the data on US facilities that we introduced in chapter 4 to focus again on facilities regulated under US state and federal air-pollution regulations. Facilities in the sample meet air-pollution emissions thresholds in order to be tracked by the EPA's Toxics Release Inventory (TRI) program and are classified as "major sources" under federal clean-air laws. Many of the variables in the current analyses were introduced in chapter 4 in our analysis of ISO 14001 adoption across US states. We start by describing how we measured our environmental and regulatory dependent variables and then describe the independent or control variables in the analyses.

Dependent variables: environmental and regulatory performance

The analyses include two dependent variables, one measuring environmental performance and the other measuring regulatory performance. For environmental performance, we use facilities' toxic air-pollutant emissions reported in the Toxics Release Inventory (TRI). Not all pollutants listed in the TRI are equally toxic. Some pollutants, such as mercury, harm human health even if ingested in small amounts. Other pollutants, while still harmful, can be ingested in larger amounts before causing significant health problems. Our procedures for weighting pollutants' toxicity attempts to take into account the fact that some pollutants are more toxic than others and facilities can change their emissions to replace high volumes of a low-toxic substance (therefore, high levels of TRI emissions) with a small amount of a highly toxic substance (therefore, lower levels of TRI emissions). As in chapter 4, we adjust the TRI toxic air-pollutant data for each facility as per King and Lenox's (2000: 175). A chemical's toxicity score is reflected in the "reportable quantity," the threshold amount for reporting an accidental release, with thresholds defined according to the Comprehensive Environmental Response, Compensation, and Liability Act (CERCLA).[1] The releases for each facility are calculated as:[2]

$$E_{it} = \sum w_c * e_{cit}$$

where E_{it} is the weighted total emissions for facility i in year t, w_c is the toxicity weight factor for chemical c in year t, and e_{cit} is the pounds of emissions of chemical.[3] Each dependent variable is the difference in

---

[1] We include only chemicals listed continuously from 1995 through 2001. There may be a substitution effect such that companies replace unlisted chemicals for listed ones in their production processes. For such substitution effects to confound our analyses, ISO certified facilities must be more likely to substitute chemicals than non-certified facilities, controlling for the other variables in the analyses.

[2] Ideally, this variable would be the ratio of emissions to quantities produced. Unfortunately, production quantities are not available in our data.

[3] The CERCLA pollution measures are weighted by 1/x, where x is the reportable quantity. The CHHI/RSEI weights are the air-stream measures.

pollution emissions between 1995–1996 and 2000–2001, where time t is 1995 through 1996 and time $t + 1$ is 2000 through 2001. Two-year time periods are used to smooth over any year-to-year fluctuations. We use the 1995–1996 though 2000–2001 interval because it straddles the ISO 14001's introduction and the publication of a recent roster of ISO 14001 certified facilities. *Environmental improvement* (EI_{it}) is calculated as:

$$EI_i = E_{it} - E_{i(t+1)}$$

The second dependent variable measures how facilities comply with government regulations. Our measure of regulatory compliance identifies whether a facility is out of compliance for at least one air pollutant or for the procedural requirements of its operating permit, as reported in the AIRS/AFS data system. *Compliance improvement* is the difference in the proportion of months that each facility spent out of compliance with a government clean-air regulation in 1995–1996 and 2000-2001. Regulatory *compliance improvement* (CI_{it}) is calculated as:

$$CI_i = C_{it} - C_{i(t+1)}$$

In the analyses below, a statistically significant and positive coefficient would indicate that a variable is associated with an improvement (a larger reduction) in environmental or regulatory performance. A facility in the sample can be found out of compliance for failing to adhere to the conditions of its permit, failing to record and report its pollution emissions, not adopting the appropriate pollution-control technology for its production processes, or exceeding emissions limits. Determining a facility to be out of compliance with government regulations is a fairly serious matter, usually the end of a process that began with a "notice of violation" warning and continuing through several more enforcement steps. Government regulators determine compliance status, with facilities having some access to appeal through administrative channels.

Independent variables

We are most interested in investigating whether ISO 14001 certification improves facilities' environmental and regulatory performance. Thus, the key hypotheses tested in this chapter are:

H1: Facilities with ISO 14001 certification will pollute less in relation to non-certified facilities.

H2: Facilities with ISO 14001 certification will show superior compliance with government regulations in relation to non-certified facilities.

The treatment effects statistical technique we employ to test the hypotheses requires us to adjust statistically for why firms join ISO 14001 in the first place. Therefore, we need independent variables to explain why facilities choose to join ISO 14001 as well as variables that control for why some firms have different environmental and regulatory performance from other facilities. A facility's environmental and regulatory performance and its decision to join ISO 14001 may be influenced by a variety of factors such as the size of the facility, the industry in which it operates, how it has complied with government regulations in the past, how much pollution it releases into the atmosphere and the regulatory and social contexts in which it operates.

As in chapter 4, we determine whether a facility joined ISO 14001 by 2001 by examining the list of ISO 14001 certified facilities published by the Center for Energy and Environmental Management (CEEM, 2000, 2001). *ISO 14001 membership* – the key variable of interest – is scored 1 if the facility is certified in the program while non-membership received a score of 0. As in chapter 4, we control for several factors in the facility, policy, and social contexts.

Facilities and their contexts

Facility size is the number of employees at the facility, as reported in the Dunn and Bradstreet database (*Employees*). We also include two dummy variables measuring whether the facility is a branch facility (*branch*), single-site company (*single*), or company headquarters (scored 0). *Emissions* is the facility's air pollution in time, t, as recorded in the TRI data, weighted by each pollutant's toxicity corresponding to the weighting approach used for the dependent variable. We measure facilities' previous regulatory compliance (*Compliance*) with the proportion of months that a facility is out of compliance over time, t. Facilities with higher initial emissions and non-compliance should have more significant emissions reductions and compliance improvements. Our model includes dummy variables reflecting each facility's two-digit SIC code. Facilities that receive more inspections and enforcement actions may be more likely to reduce their pollution emissions. *Inspections* is the number of state and EPA inspections and *enforcement actions* is the number of enforcement actions, including notices of violation levied by state and EPA officials that each facility received over time, *t*. *Penalty* is the dollar amount of any monetary penalty assessed against the facility in 1995–1996. The measures for compliance, inspections, enforcement actions, and penalties are drawn from the EPA's IDEA database.[4]

Policy context

The policy context in which facilities operate is expected to influence facilities' regulatory and pollution performance. Again, as in chapter 4, we measure states' legal environment with the variable *state audit protection*, scored 1 if the state provides privilege or immunity protection for information uncovered in facilities' self-audits.[5] We measure state litigiousness using the ratio of environmental court cases to TRI facilities in each state (*litigiousness*).

The nature of government mandatory regulations may affect how facilities view ISO 14001. Green clubs operate in the shadow of public law and public regulatory institutions. Governments may make such green clubs cohere better with existing institutions through the mix of regulations, enforcement practices, and other programs they offer. Many states have developed their own voluntary programs, including some that have explicit EMS requirements. Some programs stipulate membership criteria, such as superior compliance histories. We measure whether states offer voluntary programs with two dummy variables, *state EMS program*, scored 1 if the facility is located in a state that sponsors its own EMS-based voluntary program, and *state*

---

[4] Ideally, our analysis would control for facilities' EMS prior to their joining ISO 14001 because facilities with high-quality extant EMS would be more likely to join ISO 14001. We control for the "prior EMS" by treating 1995–1996 emissions as the baseline against which facilities' environmental improvements are assessed. We also control for 1995–1996 compliance which prior EMS should have influenced.

[5] ISO 14001 requires annual recertification audits. Firms may be more reluctant to conduct audits without attorney–client privilege protections (which only some states have granted) because regulators may punish self-disclosed violations (Kollman and Prakash, 2001; Pfaff and Sanchirico, 2000).

non-EMS program, scored 1 if the state sponsors a voluntary program that does not include an EMS component as reported in Crowe (2000). Our expectation is that the presence of voluntary programs, particularly EMS-based programs, encourages ISO 14001 adoption.[6]

Regulatory stringency and regulatory flexibility are expected to significantly influence firms' perceptions of the attractiveness of voluntary programs (Scholz, 1991; Scholz and Gray, 1997; Gormley, 1999; Winter and May 2001). *Regulatory flexibility* is the proportion of out-of-compliance facilities sanctioned through monetary penalties in the state where the facility is located. Enforcement flexibility may encourage ISO 14001 adoption because firms expect that self-reported violations will not always be severely punished. We also measure the extent to which regulators in each state severely punish violators (Scholz, 1991; Gormley, 1999; Winter and May, 2001). Stringent regulations may lower the relative cost of joining ISO 14001 because facilities would have adopted rigorous management systems to comply with regulations anyway. Following Potoski (2001), we measure the stringency of state hazardous air-pollutants regulations and ambient-air standards with the dummy variables *hazardous-air regulations* and *ambient-air regulations*, each scored 1 if the state's regulations are more stringent than the corresponding EPA minimum criteria. Our expectation is that facilities located in states with more stringent air-pollution regulations are more likely to become ISO 14001 certified. Finally, we control for states' political contexts with *environmental groups*, the number of members in the Sierra Club and the National Wildlife Federation per 1,000 residents in 1998. Facilities in states with stronger environmental groups may be more likely to join ISO 14001 and to reduce pollution emissions. Facilities in states with more litigious climates may be less willing to improve performance, while those in states with more stringent environmental regulations and stronger environmental groups may have greater performance improvements.

Social context

The analyses also include several controls for the facility's neighborhood context. *Residents' education* measures the percentage of

---

[6] These state programs are voluntary and do not cover all facilities in the state, only those that choose to join.

residents living within a three-mile radius of a facility who have a high school education or greater, as reported in the EPA's IDEA database (*education*). From the same database, we also include control variables for the percentage of the area population who are *minorities* and the percentage of population making more than $75,000 per year (*income*). The analysis includes the natural log of these three neighborhood context variables.[7] Wealth, education, and ethnicity may provide citizens with leverage for compelling facilities to improve their environmental performance (Kahn, 2002; Pargal and Wheeler, 1996).

Analytic method

A common goal in program evaluations is to determine whether receiving the program's "treatment" achieves desired outcomes or conditions among program participants. A "treatment" is the program feature that is thought to cause these improvements; our program treatment is the steps that facilities take to receive and maintain ISO 14001 certification. For other programs, a treatment might be a job training program for the unemployed, a new cancer drug therapy, and so on. In an ideal world, we would be able compare the environmental performance of a sample of ISO 14001 certified facilities against a sample of non-certified facilities that are otherwise identical to the certified facilities. This is because facilities have been randomly assigned to the certified and non-certified groups. However, conducting such an experiment is beyond our means for studying green clubs such as ISO 14001. Instead, we turn to the well-developed literature on quasi-experimental program evaluation techniques.

Our analyses must account for the fact that ISO 14001 certified facilities are systematically different to non-certified facilities. As we saw in chapter 4, in relation to non-certified facilities, ISO 14001 certified facilities are more likely to be larger, to have different

---

[7] In a few cases, these measures recorded 0 residents making over $75,000 (64 cases) or 0 minority residents (26 cases), making natural logs problematic. One approach is to set the value for such cases at 0 and add a dummy variable to account for any intercept shift (Cameron and Trivedi, 1998: 239–240). We experimented with this approach but were unable to get ML convergence; some standard errors were in question, although the reported coefficients were essentially identical to those presented here. In the analyses presented we set the value at .05 for the 0 cases of these measures.

pollution emissions and compliance histories, and to be located in different policy and neighborhood contexts. Consequently, our analyses will need to control for these factors to isolate the influence of ISO 14001 certification on environmental and regulatory performance. Our analyses therefore include control variables that measure facilities' policy and social contexts as well as the facility-level characteristics.

The most difficult problem our analyses must confront is: facilities' decisions about whether to participate in ISO14001 are likely to be endogenous to their environmental performance. That is, some of the observed and unobserved factors that influence whether a facility joins ISO 14001 are also likely to influence the amount of pollution this facility emits. Consequently, simply comparing the performance of certified and non-certified facilities would produce misleading results, and would be likely to *overstate* the effect of certification on performance; we might mistakenly attribute to ISO 14001 an improvement, when it was in fact caused by other factors correlated with both joining ISO 14001 and the environmental performance improvement. While the control variables address the endogeneity problem to some extent, there may still be unobserved factors that influence both whether a facility joins the program and its performance.

What we need, then, is an empirical technique that allows us to estimate the effect of ISO 14001 certification on performance, independent of the effects of the observed and unobserved factors that influence both whether facilities receive certification and their environmental performance. We use a treatment effects model to account for the effect of non-random assignment among ISO 14001 certified and non-certified facilities (Greene, 1999; Heckman and Robb, 1985; for applications, see Kane, 1994; Lubell *et al.*, 2002). The intuition behind this model is that if we can identify factors that influence joining ISO 14001 but do not influence firms' environmental/ regulatory performance, we can use that information to isolate the effect of ISO 14001 certification on environmental/regulatory performance, independent of the factors that influence both firms' decisions to join ISO 14001 and their environmental/regulatory performance.

In statistical terms, a treatment effects model simultaneously estimates a probit model for why facilities join ISO 14001 and a linear model of facilities' performance with independent variables including a measure of whether each facility joined ISO 14001, adjusted for potential endogeneity between facilities' decisions to join ISO 14001 and their environmental performance.[8] In a sense, the treatment effects model takes the "predicted values" of the likelihood each facility joins ISO 14001, calculated from the probit model, and then places them as an independent variable in the linear model of facilities' performance. By modeling the selection of facilities into ISO 14001, we seek to isolate the impact of facilities' ISO 14001 membership on their performance from other factors that induce facilities to join ISO 14001 and emit pollution or comply with regulations in the first place. If our treatment effects model is identified, that is, if it contains *some* information on why facilities join ISO 14001 that is devoid of information about why facilities improve their performance, the predicted ISO 14001 values will tell us the effect of ISO 14001 certification on facilities' performance, independent of the effects of factors that influence both facilities joining ISO 14001 and their performance.

Below we describe the treatment effects model in more technical detail. We are interested in modeling the outcome (or dependent) variables measuring facilities' environmental and regulatory performance. For each outcome variable, we employ the same treatment effects statistical technique. Thus, we begin with the outcome equation of the model:

$$Y_i = \beta_1 X_{1i} + \gamma Z_i + \varepsilon_{1i} \qquad \text{(Equation 1 : Outcome Equation)}$$

$$(5.1)$$

Where Y is the *i*th facility's environmental/regulatory performance improvement, X_1 is a vector of exogenous variables pertaining to facilities' contexts and characteristics, including their previous environmental performance, Z_i is the facility's participation in ISO 14001, β_1 and γ are (vectors of) parameters, and $\varepsilon_1 i$ is a random error

---

[8] This is a statistically more efficient procedure than similar non-nested models (Khanna and Damon, 1999; King and Lenox, 2000) that separately estimate the first-stage model using probit and then use predicted values (of joining the program) as an independent variable in the separate second-stage analysis, usually estimated via OLS. The nested and non-nested approaches are asymptotically equivalent; that is, they produce identical results as N approaches infinity. In smaller samples, nested approaches will produce somewhat smaller standard errors. We did experiment with a two-stage procedure, estimating first a log model for joining ISO 14001 and then submitting the predicted values into an OLS analysis of compliance. The results were essentially the same as those presented here.

term. Z_i is scored 1 if the facility is ISO 14001 certified, otherwise it is scored zero. The facility's ISO 14001 decision, Z_i, is likely to be influenced by some of the same observed and unobserved factors that influence Y_i. To correct for selection bias, the treatment effects analysis models a selection equation of facilities' decisions to join ISO 14001 (Z_i) along with the outcome equation of their environmental/regulatory performance (Y_i). For the selection equation, we assume that the ith facility's net benefit of joining ISO 14001 is $Z_\wedge^i = X_{2i}\beta_2 + \varepsilon_2 i$, where X_{2i} is an exogenous vector of independent variables, some of which are included in X_1, β_2 is a vector of coefficients, and $\varepsilon_2 it$ is an independent, normally distributed error term. $Z_\wedge^i$ is unobserved, but we observe $Z_i = 1$ if $Z_i{}^* = 0$, else $Z_i{}^* = 0$. The probability of a firm joining ISO 14001, $Z_i{}^*$, is thus:

$$Z_i^* = F(X_{2i}\beta_2) + \varepsilon_{2i} \qquad (\text{Equation 2 : Selection Equation})$$

(5.2)

where F is the cumulative normal distribution. The treatment effects analysis of Y_i includes the estimates of $Z_i{}^*$ from Equation 5.2 for Z_i in Equation 5.1.

To identify the treatment effects model, we need to include a variable in the selection equation of which facilities join ISO 14001 (Equation 5.2) that does not affect facilities' ultimate performance and thus can be excluded from the outcome equation (Equation 5.1). In other words, in the selection equation (Equation 5.2) we include variables that are correlated with the endogenous variable (ISO 14001), excluded in the outcome equation, and are not correlated with the error term of the outcome equation.[9] Our identification strategies are slightly different for the compliance and pollution emissions dependent variables, although the underlying logic is similar. For the most part, clean-air regulations in the US do not directly specify the pollution emission-levels that facilities are allowed (Fiorino,

---

[9] A single variable can identify the model so long as it is sufficiently correlated with the treatment variable and uncorrelated with the errors of the outcome equation. Instrumental variable(s) that are weakly correlated with the treatment variable can be problematic (Bound *et al.*, 1995). A "weak" correlation is problematic when the joint F-test of the instrumental variable(s) on the treatment (endogenous) variable is close to 1 (Bound *et al.*, 1995: 446). F-tests on the instrumental variable(s) in our analyses exceed 1 by healthy margins. For an example, see Acemoglu, Johnson and Robinson (2001).

1995). Rather, government regulations instead determine the emission control technologies (e.g., Best Available Control Technology) and the reporting and tracking procedures that facilities must follow. Higher or lower compliance levels do not therefore translate directly into more or less pollution emissions, nor does compliance necessarily translate into more or fewer emissions. Thus, in the equations with the emissions dependent variables, we use *compliance$_{95-96}$* as an instrumental variable on the assumption that a facility's compliance does not affect its emissions status except via compliance's influence on joining ISO 14001. Likewise, in the equations with the compliance dependent variables, we use *emissions$_{95-96}$* as an instrumental variable on the assumption that a facility's emissions do not affect its compliance status except through emissions' influence on joining ISO 14001.

The treatment model includes the predictor *rho* from the first-stage equation to adjust for the correlation between $\varepsilon_1 i$ and $\varepsilon_2 i$. Since this variable is a non-linear function of the variables in the selection equation, the second-stage model is identified even without instrumental variables by assuming the errors of the selection are normally distributed (Greene, 1999; Heckman and Robb, 1985). If we use an instrumental variable we do not need to rely on this assumption for our analyses. The results, however, did not change from what we present below when we included an instrumental variable in our analyses (*compliance$_{95-96}$* in the outcome equation of the emissions model and *emissions$_{95-96}$* in the outcome equations of the compliance model).

Below we focus on the outcome equation of facilities' performance. The selection equation (Equation 5.2) in the treatment effects analyses is essentially identical to the analysis of why US facilities join ISO 14001, reported in chapter 4 (see Table 4.5). The sets of independent variables for the selection (X_{1i}, Equation 5.2) and outcome equations (X_{2i}, Equation 5.1) contain considerable overlap. For example, facilities may be more likely to join ISO 14001 if they receive frequent government inspections and frequent government inspections may improve facilities' environmental performance. Since ISO 14001 was launched in late 1996, we control for such problems by using information from 1995 and 1996 where possible and by using the treatment effects model (Greene, 1999).

The independent variables in the outcome analyses for environmental and regulatory improvement (X_1) include facility context (*size,* *branch, single, emissions, inspections*$_{95-96}$, *enforcement actions*$_{95-96}$, *penalties*$_{95-96}$), policy context (*litigiousness, hazardous-air regulations, ambient-air regulations, state audit protection, state EMS programs, state non-EMS programs, regulatory flexibility,* and *environmental groups*), neighborhood context (*education, minorities, income*), and the measure for ISO 14001 membership, adjusted from the selection equation. Variables in the selection equation (Equation 5.2) for why facilities join ISO 14001 (X_2), include the same variables as X_1, along with *compliance*$_{95-96}$, or *emissions*$_{95-96}$ (excluded in X_1 for identification purposes) and *compliance*$_{95-96}^2$ and *emissions*$_{95-96}^2$ since the effect of compliance and emissions on joining ISO 14001 may vary across levels of compliance and emissions.[10] Tables 5.1 and 5.2 provide descriptive statistics for the variables in the treatment effects analysis.

While our selection equation (2) adjusts the estimates of the effect of ISO 14001 in the outcome equation (1) for the observable factors in X_2, unobserved factors that influence both facilities' decisions to join ISO 14001 and their environmental regulatory performance may still potentially confound our analyses. Heckman and Hotz (1989) suggest that a simple way to test for these unobserved effects is to estimate a model of the dependent variable prior to treatment (in this case *compliance*$_{95-96}$ and *emissions*$_{95-96}$) controlling for the factors that influence the treatment selection, the post-treatment outcome and the variable identifying whether the facility received the treatment (ISO 14001 certification). An insignificant coefficient for the treatment variable (certification) in this analysis suggests there are not significant unobservable factors that influence both facilities' certification decisions and the environmental outcome dependent variable. We performed this analysis and the coefficient for ISO 14001 certification did not approach statistical significance, suggesting that our treatment effects model is justified in this case.

Below we present the results of our treatment effects analyses of the effect of ISO 14001 membership on facilities' environmental and regulatory performance. These analyses are quite complex. Fortunately, for the present purposes, we can focus on one key coefficient in each of the models: the coefficient for the ISO 14001 variable in the outcome equation (Equation 5.1) shows the difference in the

---

[10] See chapter 4 for a more detailed discussion of the selection equations.

Table 5.1. Descriptive statistics for environmental performance

Variable	Mean	Std Dev	Min	Max
ISO membership	0.04	0.20	0	1
Pollution reduction	8.09	71.64	−1115.60	1067.23
Facility				
Compliance$_{1995-96}$	0.10	0.28	0	1
Compliance$_{1995-96}{}^2$	0.09	0.26	0	1
Inspections	2.14	2.46	0	42
Enforcement actions	0.43	1.92	0	50
Emissions$_{1995-96}$	4.03E + 08	1.34E + 09	35	2.24E + 10
Emissions$_{1995-96}{}^2$	2.03E + 18	1.78E + 19	1250	5.04E + 20
Emissions$_{1995-96}$(logged)	16.92	3.19	3.55	23.8
Employees	406.9	806.33	1	17500
Branch	0.66	0.47	0	1
Single	0.19	0.40	0	1
Policy context				
Litigiousness	0.14	0.30	0.01	2.64
Hazardous-air regulations	0.61	0.49	0	1
Ambient-air regulations	0.11	0.31	0	1
State audit protections	0.53	0.50	0	1
State EMS programs	0.41	0.49	0	1
State non-EMS program	0.22	0.42	0	1
Regulatory flexibility	6.39	3.87	1.33	24
Environmental groups	5.89	2.20	0.78	14.17
Neighborhood context				
Education	4.40	0.08	4.06	4.61
Income over $75,000	1.15	0.87	−2.99	4.61
Minorities	2.38	1.39	−2.99	4.61

improvement between certified and non-certified facilities. Recall that the dependent variables gauge the difference in facilities' environmental and regulatory performance between 1995–1996 and 2000–2001. This means that a statistically significant and positive coefficient for the ISO 14001 variable indicates how much *more* certified facilities improved over the time-span compared to non-certified facilities. To interpret the ISO 14001 coefficient, we use the outcome

Table 5.2. *Descriptive statistics for regulatory performance*

Variable	Mean	Std Dev	Min	Max
ISO membership	.040	.20	0	1
Compliance improvement	−0.01	.34	−1	1
Facility				
Compliance$_{1995-96}$	.10	.28	0	1
Compliance$_{1995-96}{}^2$	.09	.26	0	1
Inspections	2.09	2.34	0	42
Enforcement actions	.43	1.86	0	50
Emissions$_{1995-96}$	3.92 + E08	1.33E + 09	5	22.4E + 10
Emissions$_{1995-96}{}^2$	2.04E + 18	1.82E + 19	25	5.04E + 20
Employees	406.56	830.84	1	17500
Branch	.65	.48	0	1
Single	.20	.40	0	1
Policy context				
Litigiousness	.13	.30	.01	2.63
Hazardous-air regulations	.61	.49	0	1
Ambient-air regulations	.11	.31	0	1
State audit protections	.53	.50	0	1
State EMS programs	.41	.49	0	1
State non-EMS program	.21	.41	0	1
Regulatory flexibility	6.39	3.87	1.33	24
Environmental groups	5.89	2.20	.777	14.16
Neighborhood context				
Education	4.39	.08	4.06	4.60
Income over $75,000	1.15	.90	−3.00	4.60
Minorities	2.37	1.40	−3.00	4.61

equation (Equation 5.1) coefficients to compare the predicted values of the dependent variables for certified and non-certified facilities, holding constant the effects of other variables in the model, and adjusting for the unobserved factors affecting both the decision to join ISO 14001 and environmental and regulatory performance. To provide a sense of scale for the predicted differences between certified and non-certified facilities, we then compare them to the dependent variables' standard deviation. The full models are reported in Tables 5.3 and 5.4.

Table 5.3. Treatment-effects analysis of facilities joining ISO 14001 and their environmental performance

	Column 1: Joining ISO 14001		Column 2: Environmental Performance	
	Coefficients	Standard Errors	Coefficients	Standards Errors
ISO 14001 membership			23.328[**]	11.353
Facility				
Compliance$_{1995-96}$	1.215[§]	.799		
Compliance$_{1995-96}^2$	−1.32[§]	.858		
Inspections	.028[*]	.014	−.398	.549
Enforcement actions	−.001	.024	.158	.680
Emissions$_{1995-96}$	2.25e-10[***]	7.66e-11	4.642[***]	.428
Emissions$_{1995-96}^2$	−1.44e-20[*]	7.86e-21		
Employees	.000[**]	.000	−.001	.001
Branch	.110	.134	2.459	3.689
Single	.030	.166	2.865	4.508
SIC code dummies	Yes		Yes	
Policy context				
Litigiousness	.060	.148	−4.367	4.669
Hazardous-air regulations	.209[*]	.116	2.373	3.184
Ambient-air regulations	−.139	.173	−9.719[**]	4.63
State audit protections	−.044	.104	−4.289	2.93
State EMS programs	.042	.128	.187	3.526
State non-EMS program	−.007	.133	1.522	3.888
Regulatory flexibility	−.005	.012	−.509	.371
Environmental groups	.021	.023	−.439	.698

	Column 1: Joining ISO 14001		Column 2: Environmental Performance	
	Coefficients	Standard Errors	Coefficients	Standards Errors
Neighborhood context				
Education	1.357**	.678**	18.351	19.691
Income over $75,000	−.032	.058	−1.317	1.773
Minorities	.013	.037	.700	1.034
Constant	−9.218***	3.009	−127.509	87.450
N	3052			
Rho	−.108			
Wald (overall)	226.20***			

Notes:
* p < .10, ** p < .05, *** p < .01, two tailed tests.
§ jointly significant p < .05. The variable Emissions$_{1995-96}$ is logged in the outcome equation.

Results

Tables 5.3 and 5.4 report the results of the treatment effects analyses of the influence of ISO 14001 certification on facilities' environmental and regulatory improvement between 1995–1996 and 2000–2001. In Table 5.3, the second column reports the environmental performance results, while in Table 5.4, the second column presents the regulatory performance results. The environmental performance coefficients can be interpreted as the change in the size of the pollution emissions reduction between 1995–1996 and 2000–2001 associated with a one-unit increase in the independent variable. Likewise, in the regulatory performance model, outcome equation coefficients can be interpreted as the change in the proportion of time spent out of compliance between 1995–1996 and 2000–2001 associated with a one-unit increase in the corresponding independent variable.

Turning first to the environmental performance model, Table 5.3, column 2, reports the results of our outcome equation (Equation 5.1) analysis of the influence of ISO 14001 on environmental performance.

While the coefficient for ISO 14001 is difficult to interpret, it is statistically significant and positive. This implies that, compared to non-certified facilities, ISO 14001 certified facilities experienced significantly *larger* reductions in pollution emissions, controlling for other factors and the endogeneity between facilities' decisions to join ISO 14001 and their environmental performance. The predicted environmental improvement for certified facilities is 12.8 while it is 7.7 for non-certified facilities. Thus, ISO 14001 certified facilities improved their environmental performance by about 5.1 more than non-certified facilities. This is not a very large improvement difference, but it is important: the standard deviation of the *environmental improvement* dependent variable is 71.6.

Turning now to the regulatory performance model, the results in Table 5.4, column 2, indicate that ISO 14001 certified firms spend less time out of compliance with clean-air regulations than similarly situated non-certified facilities. The coefficient for ISO 14001 is .072; it is statistically significant and positive. This implies that joining ISO 14001 reduced facilities' time spent out of compliance with clean-air regulations controlling for other factors and the endogeneity between facilities' decisions to join ISO 14001. Predicted improvement in regulatory performance was −.01 for ISO 14001 certified facilities and −.02 for non-certified facilities. Note that the negative values indicate that, on average, facilities in the sample spent more time out of compliance in 2000–2001 than in 1995–1996. Thus, the ISO 14001 certified facilities improved their regulatory performance by .01 more than non-certified facilities. That is, controlling for other factors, certified facilities spent on average one week less time out of compliance with government regulations in 2000–2001 than in 1995–1996. While this is a somewhat modest improvement for ISO 14001 certified facilities, note that the standard deviation for the regulatory performance dependent variable is only .19.

All in all, our treatment effects analysis indicates that joining ISO 14001 significantly improves facilities' regulatory and environmental performance. The scale of these improvements is not large, though it is statistically significant. There are important grounds for tempering our conclusions about how ISO 14001 fits with extant regulatory structures. First, while our empirical evidence implies that ISO 14001 is effective at improving members' regulatory compliance, our analysis is observational and quasi-experimental, and consequently

Table 5.4. *Treatment-effects analysis of facilities joining ISO 14001 and their regulatory compliance*

	Column 1: Joining ISO 14001		Column 2: Regulatory compliance	
	Coefficients	Standard errors	Coefficients	Standards errors
ISO membership			$.072^{**}$	.034
Facility				
Compliance$_{1995-96}$	1.61^{**}	.686	$.717^{***}$	.026
Compliance$_{1995-96}^{2}$	-1.74^{**}	.754		
Inspections	$.030^{**}$	.0143	$-.009^{***}$	.003
Enforcement actions	$-.008$	.0162	$-.006$	.004
Emissions$_{1995-96}$	$2.06E-10^{**}$	$6.86E-11$		
Emissions$_{1995-96}^{2}$	$-1.35E-20^{*}$	$7.72E-21$		
Employees	$9.26E-05^{***}$	0.000032	$-5.95e-06$	$5.96e-06$
Branch	.112	.111	.007	.014
Single	$-.039$	.144	.025	.016
SIC code dummies	Yes		Yes	
Policy context				
Litigiousness	.081	.128	$-.0756^{***}$	.022
Hazardous-air regulations	$.281^{**}$	.111	.007	.012
Ambient-air regulations	.022	.154	$.036^{**}$	.016
State audit protections	.020	.099	$-.060^{***}$	.011
State EMS programs	.069	.124	.009	.014
State non-EMS program	$-.033$	.118	$.0609^{***}$	.014
Regulatory flexibility	$-.002$	.012	$.006^{***}$	.001
Environmental groups	.027	.022	$-.0011$	.002
Neighborhood context				
Education	1.44^{**}	.665	.093	.076
Income over $75,000	$-.011$	.056	$-.002$	.004
Minorities	.008	.031	$-.004$	.006
Constant	-9.694^{***}	2.958	$-.439$	.335

Table 5.4. *(continued)*

	Column 1: Joining ISO 14001		Column 2: Regulatory compliance	
	Coefficients	Standard errors	Coefficients	Standards errors
N	3709			
Rho	0.119			
Wald (overall)	1563.54***			

Notes:
* p <.10, ** p < .05, *** p < .001, two tailed tests.
§ jointly significant p < .05.

risks the imperfections of all such studies. For example, since we lack
data on which other voluntary programs facilities have joined, it is
possible that some of the credit we attribute to ISO 14001 should
accrue to other programs. Second, because our analyses were re-
stricted to facilities located in the US, we must be cautious about
generalizing our findings to other policy contexts. Finally, we should
point out that our analyses indicate the difference between certified
and non-certified facilities *on average.* In chapter 2 our theoretical
analysis suggested that ISO 14001 certification should induce bigger
improvement gains in some members than others. For example, affiliating with ISO 14001 may reward some facilities more than others,
perhaps because they have a weaker reputation among stakeholders.
With only about 150 certified facilities, our sample was too small to
investigate these issues, though this should no longer be a problem as
ISO 14001 continues to proliferate in the US and around the world.

Before moving on, it is worth looking at the results for some of the
other variables in the outcome equations presented in Tables 5.3 and
5.4. Results of our analysis of environmental performance suggest
facilities that had high levels of pollution emissions are more likely
to show an improvement in environmental performance (Table 5.3,
column 2). However, facilities located in states with ambient-air regulations more stringent than the EPA's regulations are associated with
a deterioration in environmental performance. Other facility, state

and social context variables are not significantly associated with improvements in environmental performance.

The results of our analysis of regulatory performance (Table 5.4) suggest that some state-level policies are associated with varying levels of facilities' performance, although we must be careful about interpreting these coefficients. Regulatory flexibility and stringent regulations on ambient-air quality are associated with improved compliance; facilities in states where regulators are less likely to fine for non-compliance and those with stringent ambient-air-quality standards are more likely to be in compliance with clean-air regulations. However, facilities in states with more litigious legal contexts and environmental audit privilege and immunity laws have worse compliance records.

We should note that our data do not indicate whether these state policies, practices and regulations are a cause or consequence of facilities' compliance performance. For example, states may adopt flexible regulatory enforcement in order to improve compliance or states may be more flexible *because* facilities in their state already have solid compliance records. Facilities' compliance histories influence their future compliance status. Facilities that were out of compliance in 1995 and 1996 experienced significantly larger improvements in their environmental performance in 2000 and 2001. Likewise, facilities that received more inspections and enforcement actions in 1995 and 1996 significantly improved their compliance in 2000 and 2001.

Conclusion

The finding that joining ISO 14001 appears to improve facilities' regulatory compliance and environmental performance has important implications. As we have noted before, the credibility of green clubs is not strong among environmental activists (Steinzor, 1998) and the academic literature on their performance is uneven (compare, for example, King and Lenox, 2000 with Khanna and Damon, 1999). While club theory suggests reasons why ISO 14001 can be effective, there are grounds for skepticism. First, ISO 14001 is sponsored by a non-profit, non-governmental organization and was developed with significant input from multinational corporations. Environmental groups are suspicious of self-regulation, particularly in light of recent scandals in the accounting industry. Second, ISO 14001 has loose boundary conditions: all firms are eligible for ISO 14001 membership, even those with poor compliance records, so long as they are willing to take on the costs of establishing and maintaining a certifiable EMS. Contrast this with some state and federal government voluntary programs (the so-called performance track programs) that are limited only to firms with established records of superior performance. Third, because membership does not require investment in assets specific to ISO 14001, firms may have incentives to behave opportunistically by joining ISO 14001 without following its mandate (Williamson, 1986). Fourth, ISO 14001 seems not to have mechanisms for sanctioning members who fail to comply with club standards, although it does require annual recertification audits. Fifth, ISO 14001 does not require members to demonstrate improvements in regulatory compliance to maintain membership; it only seeks their commitment to do so and views the establishment and maintenance of an EMS as evidence of such commitment.

Future research should compare participants' environmental and regulatory performance across voluntary programs. This book has looked at the ISO 14001 club whose rules require monitoring via third-party audits. Scholars should also examine the levels of environmental and regulatory improvement in programs that require public disclosure of audit information along with third-party audits. We return to this point in the concluding chapter.

6 | Conclusions and future directions

OMMAND and control regulations have been the linchpin of most environmental regulations around the world for over three decades. Notwithstanding some success in reducing pollution, there have been mounting criticisms of the command and control approach. Some question its effectiveness, particularly in light of the weak inspection and monitoring regimes that come with tightening regulatory budgets. Some suggest that command and control fosters a costly adversarial relationship between governments and regulated firms, a worrisome trend because environmental governance in future may require a more cooperative relationship between governments and businesses. Others blame command and control for undermining static and dynamic efficiencies, misallocating resources and hindering technological growth, all of which are important for combating pollution. An important fear is that command and control's deficiencies will accentuate as pollution challenges shift from the regulated visible and large sources to more diverse, smaller non-point sources.

While the particularly shrill criticisms are overstated, there does appear to be room for experimenting with novel regulatory approaches that can complement command and control. The idea is to empower environmental governance systems to respond better to environmental problems of today and of the future. The quest for new environmental governance tools looks to shift from an exclusive reliance on centralized rule design and enforcement to creating incentives that induce firms to take environmentally progressive action voluntarily. At the risk of being repetitive, we want to make it clear that we are not advocating the dismantling of command and control environmental regulations. The challenge is to make the system more effective by complementing it with new policy approaches that correct some of the deficiencies of command and control.

In chapter 1, we briefly surveyed three policy approaches in this regard: market-based permits, mandatory information disclosures, and voluntary programs. Market-based permits place an economic cost on pollution in order to harness profit incentives to serve environmentally progressive ends. However, markets are difficult to establish because unitizing environmental resources and harms can be quite vexing. Establishing markets creates "winners" and "losers," often without a politically viable mechanism for placating the losers. Mandatory information-disclosure policies seek to lower stakeholders' transaction costs for influencing firms' environmental behavior by requiring firms to disclose information about their environmental programs and performance systematically. However, mandatory disclosure programs do not work well if stakeholders find that the information is difficult to collect, disseminate, interpret, and exploit. Well-functioning information-disclosure policies are predicated on well-functioning institutions such as stock markets, free press, and well-organized environmental groups that provide venues for stakeholders to process information and reward and punish firms for their environmental performance.

This book focuses on a third type of policy approach: voluntary programs, or green clubs as we have called them. A green club is a system of rules specifying standards for its members' environmental behavior. Club rules can regulate any number of things, such as how members manage their own environmental operations, how much pollution can be released into the atmosphere, the scope of recycling programs, and so on. An effective green club induces members to produce some broader environmental public good, such as a cleaner environment, a more sustainable production process, or better protection for endangered species. As an incentive, green clubs offer some excludable benefits, usually in the form of goodwill members receive for affiliating with the club's positive brand reputation.

Green clubs' potential stems from their similarities with the market-based and information-disclosure approaches and their compatibility with command and control. Like command and control regulations, green clubs require firms to take positive steps to protect the environment. Like market-based mechanisms, green clubs harness the power of market incentives (along with non-market incentives) to reward club members for their progressive environmental action. Like information-based policies, green clubs reduce transaction costs for stakeholders to enable them to differentiate environmentally progressive firms from laggards. From this perspective, command and control can remain the backbone of environmental governance, complemented by green clubs and other policy approaches.

Contrary to what naïve or perhaps overly simplified theories might predict, a substantial body of research shows that firms sometimes adopt progressive environmental policies entirely of their own accord (Prakash, 2000a). That is, firms sometimes look to clean the environment or mitigate the damage they cause to the natural world without the coercive stick of government authority compelling them to do so. In studying such behavior, scholars have looked for the private, sometimes even hidden, rewards firms receive in return for taking progressive environmental action. Perhaps managers have their own preferences for a cleaner environment. Or perhaps reducing pollution saves on production costs and yields a "green dividend." We do not want to preclude the possibility that green clubs might simply codify progressive environmental action that some firms would perform anyway for their own private benefit.

While such scenarios are important for understanding the behavior of firms, and perhaps they show ways to further environmental gains, win–win scenarios rooted in firms' private motives are insufficient for understanding their responses to green clubs. One limitation is that a firm might unilaterally decide to follow some green club's membership standards, and thereby enjoy the private benefits that come with such action, without actually joining the club. Or a firm might join a green club because it has already taken all the progressive action required by the club's standards. In either of these cases, although club members may have better environmental performance than non-members, the club itself hardly deserves credit for inducing members to take progressive environmental action; we should not give clubs credit for behavior their members would have taken in the absence of the club. Instead, an effective club offers some excludable benefit that entices members to take progressive environmental action they would not otherwise have adopted. We want to be clear on this point. While green club membership may well generate private benefits for firms, club benefits are the key analytical construct to understanding why green clubs may induce firms to take additional progressive environmental action.

Like other policy instruments, green clubs risk institutional failures. For green clubs, there are two types of institutional failures. A club can fail if it does not attract members (the Olsonian dilemma). A green club must offer a package of (excludable) benefits that outweigh members' costs of joining the program. In the case of ISO 14001, we have seen that the value of joining the program varies across different policy and economic contexts (chapter 4). Green clubs' second institutional failure is rooted in the possibility that member firms may not behave as the club standards specify. Monitoring and enforcement can mitigate such shirking. ISO 14001 is designed to curb shirking through annual third-party certification audits (chapter 5).

Our purpose has been to present theoretical and empirical analyses of green clubs, using ISO 14001 as our central example. Our theory is broader and has more important implications than we empirically tested in this book. In this concluding chapter, we highlight important analytical and policy issues surrounding green clubs and outline ideas for future research. Perhaps the most obvious place to begin future research is by addressing the limitations in this study. Our theory posits that some firms will improve their environmental performance more than others when joining the same green club (see chapter 2). For example, we would expect bigger improvements from firms who start with a lower level of environmental performance and perceive a significant gain in affiliating with ISO 14001. Due to data limitations, our empirical test lacked data to distinguish across different ISO 14001 members, so we estimated only the average improvement of ISO 14001 members compared to non-members.

Likewise, much of our analysis investigates potential differences across green clubs, depending on how their institutional architectures induce members to join while preventing members from shirking. In our view, the most important step for scholars is to study systematically how different program attributes mitigate the Olsonian and shirking dilemmas. In other words, the key analytical challenge is to link clubs' institutional design to their efficacy. In chapter 2, we proposed a typology of clubs, based on two institutional attributes – club standards and enforcement rules. We then identified four ideal club types – Mandarin clubs (Type 1) with stringent club standards and credible enforcement rules; Country Clubs (Type 2), with stringent club standards but non-credible enforcement rules; Bootcamps (Type 3) with lenient club standards and credible enforcement rules;

and Greenwashes (Type 4) with lenient club standards and non-credible enforcement rules. Although we focused our discussion on ISO 14001, a Type 3 club, our theory has implications for other club types as well. Also, this typology need not be static: any particular green club need not remain in the category in which it originates. Green clubs can evolve from one type to another. For example, a club may be introduced with very low standards but, after receiving criticism, may improve its standards (as occurred with Responsible Care, which bolstered its monitoring mechanisms from self-reporting to relatively stringent third-party monitoring). Similarly, as Cashore *et al.* (2004) point out in relation to forestry, the industry-sponsored Sustainable Forestry Initiative program has made its requirements more stringent in response to NGO criticisms, while the NGO-sponsored Forest Stewardship Council club has correspondingly rationalized its club requirements in response to business and industry criticism.

The remainder of this chapter proceeds as follows. The first section discusses the theoretical implications of our work. The second section lays out the policy implications that follow. The final section discusses the limitations of our study and identifies issues for future research.

Theoretical implications

Institutional failure

This book adopts an institutionalist perspective to examine voluntary programs. While institutions may be designed to mitigate collective-action dilemmas, virtually every institution can and does fail. Governments fail, markets fail, and voluntary programs also fail. While dumping an institution because it may fail is not an ideal way to confront looming policy challenges, a careless advocacy in favor of the status quo is no more effective. The challenge is to identify the sources of institutional failures in order to help devise mechanisms to overcome them, and then evaluate empirically the extent to which such failures have been rectified. The theoretical analysis in this book has significant implications on this count. By identifying two key sources of institutional failures – the Olsonian dilemma and the shirking dilemma – we have focused the analytical scrutiny on green clubs' institutional vulnerabilities. We identified ISO 14001's mechanisms for addressing these failures and have begun the evaluation of their efficacy. Our goal is to help identify policies' vulnerabilities *ex ante*, before they are adopted.

Club reputation

This book has argued that affiliating with a club's excludable brand reputation is the central reason firms join voluntary programs. The value of a club's reputation depends on how well the club is regarded by its key stakeholders. In all likelihood, stakeholders' trust in a club will increase if club standards are more stringent. In other words, stakeholders are likely to believe that higher costs imposed on club members means that the club has imposed "real requirements," such as the establishment of new programs, hiring of new personnel, maintainance of paper-trails, third-party auditing, etc. Stringent club standards, if adhered to, are likely to translate into improved regulatory and environmental performance. We also noted that enforcement rules to mitigate shirking would also eventually influence a club's reputation: less shirking means clubs have a stronger reputation for being effective.

While we have focused on club standards and monitoring and enforcement mechanisms as the key factors influencing clubs' reputations, other factors may also be influential. To advance the discussion of these issues, we will briefly highlight two key factors. First, a club's reputation may vary depending not just on the stringency but also on the nature of the standards. For example, some clubs may mandate continual performance improvements (such as EMAS and the 33/50 program) while others may require members to implement management systems (as in ISO 14001 and Responsible Care). Second, a club's reputation is likely to reflect in no small measure the credibility of its sponsoring organization, an issue we touched upon in chapter 4 in our presentation of the British experience of developing voluntary environmental programs.

In chapter 2 we simplified our discussion of green club standards by assuming that the relevant analytic feature was the standards' stringency; that is, how much progressive environmental action did the club standards require? Our assumption was that club requirements could be easily mapped to some environmental outcomes standards. In practice, of course, such mapping is no simple matter. ISO 14001 requires participating firms to establish EMS, as discussed in chapter

3. Process or management system-based standards such as ISO 14001's EMS requirement do not impose performance targets on club members. They are based on the philosophy that if appropriate management systems are in place, desired outcomes or performance will follow. Other green clubs have standards that prescribe members' outcome targets. For example, the EPA's 33/50 program required participating firms to commit to reducing releases of specified chemicals by 33 per cent by 1992 and by 50 per cent by 1995, with 1990 as the base year. Outcome standards may do more to boost a club's credibility than process standards. Most environmental groups and regulators seem to favor performance standards. For them, this helps to benchmark firms' performance and simplifies enforcing accountability if members reveal their compliance with club standards. Thus, future research should explore how different club standards influence members' compliance costs and environmental performance and how club standards affect their clubs' reputations.

The value of affiliating with a green club may well depend on the standing of its sponsor among potential members' stakeholders. Green clubs have been sponsored by a variety of actors: governments, industry associations, non-government activist groups, non-governmental technical bodies. The question then is whether the identity of the sponsoring organization influences the strength of the reputation of the clubs they sponsor. Credible sponsoring organizations may help mitigate the Olsonian dilemma. Do clubs sponsored by actors known for their commitment to the environment attract more members?

As described in chapter 3, ISO 14001 is sponsored by Geneva-based International Organization for Standardization. This Geneva-based non-profit organization is internationally recognized as a leader in setting technical standards. The International Organization for Standardization launched a successful quality-control management standard, ISO 9000, based on a management-system approach. Thus, one can expect that an environmental standard based on the ISO 9000 approach will carry substantial credibility. However, given its mandate to promote international trade, some see the ISO as a tool of business (Clapp, 1997). Thus, the credibility of the club sponsor can vary across firms' stakeholders, and consequently, firms' perception of a club's reputational value will likely vary depending on the response to their membership from different stakeholders. Of course, business–stakeholder relations are not static:

stakeholders can employ tactics to make themselves more salient to a firm or industry while firms can adopt strategies to reduce their dependence on specific stakeholders (Oliver, 1990). Nevertheless, it is important to recognize that stakeholders are diverse and have varying levels of signifiance for firms.

By the same logic, industry-sponsored green clubs may invite skepticism. After all, industry-sponsored clubs may be founded on conflict of interest. For example, many environmentalists allege that the American Forestry and Paper Association's Sustainable Forestry Initiative (SFI) is a greenwash because it does not move forestry firms towards their substantive objectives. NGOs allege that under cover of SFI membership, forestry firms will continue to pursue practices they oppose, such as harvesting old-growth forests, using pesticides for tree farming, and clear cutting. In May 2005, these NGOs ran a full-page advertisement in *The New York Times* that blasted the SFI. Consider the copy of this advertisement:

How can you trust the timber industry to measure its own environmental sustainability? Isn't that like the fox guarding the henhouse? Simply stated, the Sustainable Forestry Initiative® program is a historic greenwashing effort to blur the public's trust in ecolabeling, helping loggers appear "sustainable" when it's really just the Same-old Forest Industry.

Exacerbating the credibility problem further, industry-sponsored clubs sometimes provide less than desirable levels of transparency in rule-making and rule enforcement. While industry-sponsored clubs may appeal to firms because they offer reasonably achievable club standards, the distrust of key stakeholders may dilute the goodwill firms hope to corner by joining them.

While industry-sponsored clubs may have weaker credibility, firms may be uncomfortable in subscribing to a environmental-group-sponsored green club, especially one sponsored by groups with a history of anti-business activism. The forestry case introduced above is particularly illuminating in this regard (Overdevest, 2005; Bartley, 2003; Cashore *et al.*, 2004). The forestry industry has witnessed an ongoing competition between the industry-sponsored Sustainable Forestry Initiative (SFI) and the NGO-sponsored Forest Stewardship Council (FSC). NGOs believe that the SFI club is not stringent and transparent while forestry firms believe that the FSC club imposes unrealistic demands and provides excessive power to the NGOs. In the US, forestry firms have chosen to join the SFI club (specifically, the one that requires third-party auditing) rather than the FSC because of the anti-business stance of many of the FSC sponsors coupled with the club's greater stringency (Sasser *et al.*, 2005).

On this count, government-sponsored green clubs may be in a strong position to build a credible reputation. Regulators are one of the key stakeholder groups that most firms consider when assessing the potential benefits of green club membership. If regulators themselves have proposed a voluntary program, then obviously they would very much appreciate firms that become members. Furthermore, in government-sponsored clubs, NGOs may well have a significant input in developing and enforcing club standards, particularly in countries with accessible rule-making procedures. In some cases, NGO participation may have slowed down the process of implementing a green club to the point that firms are dissuaded from becoming members. Project XL's low participation rate has been attributed to an excessive emphasis on stakeholder input on what the club should require of its members (Marucs *et al.*, 2002; but see High-Tech Production, 2001).

Monitoring and goodwill

Our book has implications for the broader issue of inducing cooperative behavior between firms and regulators by signaling cooperative intentions. Information asymmetries often impede cooperation because neither side has complete confidence that the other is behaving as promised. Reducing information asymmetries between firms and regulators can make their actions and assurances about cooperation more credible. In green clubs, sponsors can reduce information asymmetries about club attributes by publicizing the specific obligations placed on club members as well as how the club is mitigating shirking through monitoring and enforcement. When firms join an effective green club, they signal their intentions to stakeholders about their commitment to environmental issues.

While signaling firms' good intentions is laudable, how can stakeholders verify that signals will translate into promised action? To paraphrase former President Reagan, can stakeholders trust firms in the absence of verification? Arguably, some stakeholders might believe that shirking can be curbed through sociological mechanisms such as normative pressures to play honest and by the rules. We believe that exclusively relying on sociological pressures to curb shirking is probably not a sufficient foundation for policy design. Recall the Responsible Care example we reported earlier. The chemical industry's green club sought to curb shirking via sociological pressures on the assumption that Responsible Care participants were deeply embedded in the chemical industry community and therefore subjected to sociological pressures to "do the right thing," "adopt the best practices," and "mimic the leading firm" (Rees, 1997; Hoffman, 1997; Gunningham and Grabosky, 1998). Until very recently, Responsible Care did not require participants to undergo third-party audits, and instead required only first-party and periodic second-party audits (Kusek, 2003). As noted earlier, King and Lenox (2000) report that Responsible Care participants shirked on their program requirements and, as a result, this green club was not effective in inducing participants to improve their environmental behavior.

The contrast between Responsible Care (in its early incarnation) and ISO 14001 is illuminating. Both clubs impose broadly similar obligations on members, most notably adopting an EMS. While the CMA/ACC requires participants to submit compliance or audit reports, it does not share this information with the public. Thus, Responsible Care has features to reduce information asymmetries between the association and participating firms, but not between external stakeholders and program participants, nor between external stakeholders and the association. Because the ACC/CMA does not sanction non-compliance, its access to information on firms' compliance with program rules is not likely to mitigate shirking. In contrast, ISO 14001 has a monitoring and enforcement mechanism in the form of annual external recertification audits. Because ISO 14001 is not sponsored by an industry association, its participants are more heterogeneous and less susceptible to sociological pressures to conform to program standards through normative diffusion.[1] If ISO 14001 succeeds in improving members' regulatory and environmental

---

[1] Do institutional pressures lead companies within the same industry to adopt similar strategies? The literature provides varying answers. Compare, for example, Hoffman (1997) with Sharma and Vredenburg (1998). Few will contest that, on average, the effects of institutional pressures are less likely to work for a voluntary program that involves several industries (ISO 14001) compared to one involving firms in the same industry (Responsible Care).

performance, enforcement via third-party audits deserves much of the credit.

The cross-club comparison between Responsible Care (in its earlier incarnation) and ISO 14001 suggests that the message to stakeholders that firms hope to convey by joining a club may eventually lose credibility if an effective mechanism to curb shirking is not in place. Analytically, we can identify three ways to curb shirking:

- External, third-party verification. An external entity has the authority to determine whether the firm is in compliance with club standards. If firms pay for the audit expenses and have a choice over who conducts the audit, the credibility of the audit results is likely to be compromised. Notwithstanding this limitation, as suggested in chapters 2 and 3, anecdotal evidence suggests that external audits influence intra-firm dynamics because managers do not want to "look bad" to other colleagues, especially when outsiders are performing the evaluation (Prakash, 2000). With external audits, managers tend to take program requirements more seriously than they would without audits. We speculate that this causal chain leads ISO 14001 participants to adhere to program rules, and thereby improve their environmental and regulatory performance.
- Public disclosure of audit information. Justice Brandeis' astute observation that "sunlight is the best disinfectant" certainly holds true for voluntary programs. With public disclosures of audit results, stakeholders can monitor compliance with club standards and then accordingly reward and punish firms and the green clubs themselves. In this way, voluntary programs can draw upon some of the positive features of mandatory information-based policies.
- Sanctioning for non-compliance. The club sponsor may itself act upon the audit information and sanction the members that have been found to be shirking their club obligations. Such sanctioning mechanisms may mitigate shirking because members may fear damaging their reputation should they be expelled from the club. On the other hand, the threat of expulsion may sour relationships between firms and club sponsors, leading some firms to drop out of the club to avoid another layer of coercive regulation.

Some bootcamp green clubs already have monitoring and enforcement programs made up of these auditing, disclosure, and sanctioning features. The EPA's 33/50 program and the European Union's

Environmental Management and Audit System (EMAS) require third-party auditing and public disclosure.[2] Several regulators we interviewed noted that ISO 14001 could be strengthened by requiring participating firms to make publicly available the reports from the third-party audit. Dan Fiorino of the EPA emphasized the importance of transparency in fostering trust among stakeholders about the program and in inducing accountability. David Ronald, Executive Director of the Multi-State Working Group, echoed this point.[3] For these regulators, transparency is a tool for fostering member accountability in green clubs (Florini, 2005). Club members should be required to report audit information on policy-relevant variables, in an accessible format, and this should be available to any stakeholder.[4] Without appropriate club requirements, firms could unload high volumes of information, in inaccessible formats, only to selected stakeholders. Such partial, controlled disclosures may well be interpreted as greenwashing firms' true environmental performance. An important implication then is whether bootcamps with two or three of these features – third-party auditing, public disclosures, and sanctioning – can successfully mitigate shirking. Or, are there diminishing returns to increasing transparency?

Network effects

This book makes the argument that collective action taken via green clubs generates scale economies in the production of the clubs' reputation. This is because larger membership rosters generate network effects, thereby enhancing the program's visibility to external stakeholders. Network effects raise important questions for green clubs. Are there diminishing returns to increasing club size? When does crowding set in? Are all types of green clubs equally susceptible to crowding? What happens if the number of clubs increases, as opposed to a growing membership roster within a club? In other words, what factors influence the optimal club size?

---

[2] As Dan Fiorino observes, EPA inspectors can be viewed as third-party auditors. Then, 33/50 is a bootcamp where third-party inspections are conducted by governmental regulators. Phone interview, 11 December 2003.

[3] Phone interview, 11 December 2003.

[4] Phone interview, 12 December 2003.

While we cannot think of any voluntary environmental program that has overcrowding issues, arguably, as green clubs proliferate and firms join them in increasing numbers, overcrowding may become problematic. To explore this one would need to examine the motivations of the club sponsor and the preferences of the key stakeholders whose attention firms may be seeking by joining the club. If a governmental regulator is looking to identify firms that have superior environmental performance, a green club with universal membership would be of little help. However, if the sponsor wants all the possible firms in the industry to join the clubs, as in several industry-sponsored clubs, universal membership may become the desired objective.

Policy implications

Instrument mix

Around the world, different countries and states within countries use varied mixes of policies and programs to address environmental problems. A country's policy is a reflection of its political, economic, and environmental circumstances. While command and control remains the foundation of most environmental regulation, many countries have begun experimenting with new policy tools. As we have noted, environmental groups tend to be most comfortable with command and control regulations. These groups are often skeptical of the efficacy of new policy approaches; voluntary programs, in particular, are viewed with suspicion if not hostility.

While we agree that such skepticism can be healthy, we believe that a viable governance system must experiment with new ways of doing things. Command and control regulations have experienced problems, to say the least, and policy scholars should explore ways in which these problems can be addressed without undermining the basic underpinnings of command and control's efficacy. This book offers an analytic approach to thinking about voluntary programs as complements to command and control. Recognizing that voluntary programs are not all alike, we propose a theoretically driven typology that provides the beginnings of a prescriptive formula for program design. Most importantly, our theoretical analysis identifies the key sources of institutional failures and how club sponsors can design their programs in response to them. Because reputational value is the key inducement for firms to join a club, and the managerial perception of these benefits depends not only on firm-level characteristics but also on their firms' policy and economic context, stakeholders can adopt a variety of strategies to encourage or discourage firms from joining a club. Our empirical research suggests that ISO 14001 is more likely to be adopted when it fits better with the policy and economic contexts. And, given our finding that ISO 14001 encourages firms to better comply with the public law (chapter 5), there is reason to believe that ISO 14001 and command and control do not work at cross-purposes. We also suggest that green clubs can be made more credible by requiring members to disclose information on their compliance with club standards. On this count as well, ISO 14001 is likely to cohere with mandatory information-disclosure policies.

In sum, when thinking about a specific instrument, it is important to examine its effect on other instruments of governance. If ISO 14001 were to improve participants' environmental performance but diminish regulatory performance, then the net policy gains from this club would be less than ideal. However, ISO 14001 appears to improve both environmental and regulatory performance and therefore seems to strengthen the overall impact of environmental policies, at least in the US.

International trade

Environmental groups often argue that international trade creates structural conditions that lead to a race to the bottom among countries' environmental standards (Daly, 1993). The charge is that developing countries' exporters exploit their less-stringent domestic environmental standards to capture markets in developed countries with more stringent standards. As a result, developed countries come under pressure from their citizens to lower regulatory standards to prevent jobs from moving abroad to pollution havens in less-developed countries. Thus, increased international trade abets a race to the bottom. Results presented in chapter 4 suggest that trade can serve as a vehicle to disseminate ISO 14001 if the key export markets have widely adopted this green club. From this perspective, international trade has significant political implications beyond the obvious distributive ones. Market access can serve as an important instrument to encourage the diffusion of preferred governance models and organizational practices. And this works not only for product standards as in Vogel's "California effect," but also for process standards as in ISO 14001. In some ways, the WTO is not an enemy of the environment; because developed countries with stringent environmental standards absorb the bulk of developing-country exports, free trade can lead to a ratcheting-up of environmental product and process standards in developing countries. From this perspective, environmental NGOs should not always oppose green clubs that lower trade barriers. In addition to campaigning for stringent domestic regulations, environmental groups may be well served to craft green clubs, pressure their domestic firms to join them, and require firms' suppliers to do so as well. There are several examples of this happening already, such as in the forestry and apparel industries where northern NGOs have used market power at home to encourage suppliers in developing countries to adopt progressive policies (Gereffi *et al.*, 2001).

Limitations and future research

Club's reputational value

This book emphasizes the role of reputational value in inducing firms to join a green club. Like consumer product brands, green club brands are multi-faced and have different meanings and values to different stakeholders. We examined how the policy context and the firms' internal characteristics influence firms' perception of the value of affiliating with a club. But our study may not capture all effects of the ISO 14001 brand, and some of the effects we have attributed to the club's brand may be the product of other confounding dynamics. The salience of different stakeholders varies across firms (Mitchell *et al.*, 1997) and all stakeholders may not have similar perceptions about the green club. Hence, future research needs to examine the firm–stakeholder relations in greater detail to understand how key stakeholders' perceptions about green clubs influences firms' propensities to join them.

This book has tended to conceptualize firms as unitary actors and may not adequately relate firms' internal processes and politics to firms' decisions to join ISO 14001 (Prakash, 2000a). Thus, future research should investigate how firms' organizational structure, levels of integration of environmental issues into business plans, education levels of the workforce, and whether the firm is a subsidiary of a multinational corporation influence whether firms join green clubs and whether they shirk their responsibilities as club members.

Third-party auditing

Our book argues that third-party auditing has been a key factor in curbing shirking among ISO 14001 certified firms. A repeated theme emerging from our interviews with regulators and managers is that ISO 14001's external audit requirement helped safeguard against willful shirking. Preventing shirking through external audits may spur a virtuous cycle of trust begetting more trust, as members are more likely to contribute to maintaining the club's reputation because they believe other members will do so as well. Having said this, future research could provide more direct evidence on how third-party auditing influences members' shirking. While we have compared ISO 14001 with Responsible Care in this regard, another strategy would be to compare environmental performance of ISO 14001 certified facilities with facilities that are "ISO 14001 ready" in the sense that they have put an ISO 14001 caliber EMS in place but have decided not to undergo third-party auditing and apply for certification.[5] Comparing the environmental performance of "ISO 14001 ready" with those formally certified through third-party audits may shed light on the importance of external monitoring and enforcement programs in green clubs.

Environmental performance

This book demonstrates that, as a group, ISO 14001 certified facilities have better environmental performance (lower pollution emissions, adjusted for their toxicity) than they would have had if they had not joined the club. This result persists even while controlling for facilities' compliance histories as well as for potential endogeneity between facilities' environmental performance and their decisions to join ISO 14001. However, there are other important dimensions to environmental performance that deserve scrutiny as well. Environmental

---

[5] Environmental Protection Agency's Region 10 is an example of this approach (interview with Barbara Lither, 19 May 2005).

performance could mean the protection of endangered species, reductions in greenhouse gas emissions, recycling and sustainable production, and so on. While these evaluative criteria are likely to vary depending on the circumstances in which firms operate, it is also important to study them because firms may not improve their environmental performance equally across these dimensions. Firms may have a tendency to focus on reducing pollution in the most visible medium. Under the guise of a narrowly targeted green club, firms may be able to move pollutants from a visible medium to a not-so-visible medium. While we do not find systematic evidence that this has been occurring in ISO 14001, scholars nevertheless need to make sure ISO 14001 members' reductions in air emissions are not offset by increased water or toxic-waste pollution.

While our analysis suggests that ISO 14001 improves club members' environmental and regulatory performance, important questions about the overall policy impact of clubs remain to be explored. First, improved performance obviously does not necessarily mean adequate performance. We would certainly want to make sure that firms are adequately protecting the environment even with well-functioning green clubs. Second, green clubs obviously do not address the performance of non-members, whose performance may remain below socially optimal standards. Thus we return to our argument that green clubs should be viewed as complements to conventional regulation, rather its substitutes. Traditionally regulations, mostly rooted in command and control, set a necessary floor for minimum acceptable environmental performance. While the task for green clubs as policy instruments is to raise the performance for club members, non-members may be in more need of policy attention. Future research could study conditions under which superior environmental practices and performance of club members diffuses over time and space by institutional mechanisms even to non-members. This would enable a better assessment of green clubs' policy impact.

Economic performance

An enduring debate among environmental policy and management scholars focuses on the relationship between corporate environmental performance and corporate financial performance. We have alluded to this debate in chapters 1 and 2. The crux of the argument is that firms have a lot of slack in the environmental management area; slack in terms of unexplored opportunities for reducing pollution that at the same time will increase profits. However, without some external stimulus compelling them to identify these opportunities, this slack will go unexploited, the profits unrealized and the environment will remain polluted. Michael Porter (1991) has been a vocal proponent of the win–win, or the green dividend, hypothesis. Although Porter advocates the regulatory route to force firms to identify profit opportunities, this argument can be extended to non-governmental pressures via green clubs. Future research should establish whether improved environmental and regulatory performance – as we have established for ISO 14001 – is accompanied by improved financial performance. Increased profits from environmental improvements stemming from club membership would be a powerful argument for encouraging more firms to join the program.

References

Acemoglu, D., S. Johnson and J. A. Robinson. 2001. The Colonial Origins of Comparative Development: An Empirical Investigation. *American Economic Review.* 91: 1329–1349.

Akerlof, G. A. 1970. The Market for "Lemons": Quality Uncertainty and the Market Mechanism. *Quarterly Journal of Economics.* 84: 488–500.

Alberini, A. and K. Segerson. 2002. Assessing Voluntary Programs to Improve Environmental Quality. *Environmental and Resource Economics.* 22: 157–184.

ALEC Watch. 2002. *ALEC's Pivileged Businesses, Public's Right to Know Nothing Act.* State Environmental Resource Center. Retrieved on 18 September 2004 from http://www.serconline.org/alec/alec23.html.

Allison, G. 1971. *The Essence of Decision.* Boston: Little Brown.

American Chemistry Council/ACC. 2004. *Responsible Care Practitioners Site.* Retrieved on 2 March 2004 from http://www.americanchemistry. com/rc.nsf/unid/lgrs-5fur2a?opendocument.

Anderson, T. L. and D. R. Leal. 2001. *Free Market Environmentalism.* Revised edition, New York: Palgrave.

Andrews, R. N. L., D. Amaral, N. Darnall, D. R. Gallagher, D. Edwards, A. Huston, C. D. Amore, L. Sun and Y. Zhang. 2003. Environmental Management Systems: Do they Improve Performance? Final Report, 30 January 2003, Retrieved on 7 November 2004, from http://ndems.cas. unc.edu/.

American National Standards Institute (ANSI). 2005. *About ANSI Overview.* Retrieved on 22 March 2005 from http://www.ansi.org/about_ ansi/overview/overview.aspx?menuid=1.

American National Standards Institute (ANSI). 2005b. *Structure and Management.* Retrieved on 22 March 2005 from http://www.ansi.org/ about_ ansi/organization_chart/chart_text.aspx?menuid=1.

Annadale, D., A. Morrison-Saunders and G. Bouma. 2004. The Impact of Voluntary Environmental Protection Instruments on Company Environmental Performance. *Business Strategy and the Environment.* 13: 1–12.

Anton, W. R. Q., G. Deltas and M. Khanna. 2004. Incentives for Environmental Self-Regulation and Implications for Environmental Performance. *Journal of Environmental Economics and Management.* 48: 632–654.

Antweiler, W. and K. Harrison. 2003. Toxic Release Inventories and Green Consumerism. *Canadian Journal of Economics.* 36: 495–520.

Arora, S. and T. N. Casson. 1996. Why do Firms Volunteer to Exceed Environmental Regulations? Understanding Participation in EPA's 33/50 Program. *Land Economics.* 72: 413–432.

Axelrod, R. 1984. *The Evolution of Cooperation.* New York: Basic Books.

Ayres, I. and J. Braithwaite. 1992. *Responsive Regulation.* Oxford University Press.

Ball, A., D. Owen and R. Gray. 2000. External Transparency or Internal Capture: The Role of Third-Party Statements in Adding Value to Corporate Environmental Reports. *Business Strategy & the Environment.* 9: 1–23.

Baltimore, C. 2002. Senator Says Documents Show EPA Cutting Enforcement. *Reuters,* Retrieved on 18 August 2003 from http://www.mapcruzin.com/news/rtk040202c.htm.

Bardach, E. and R. A. Kagan. 1982. *Going by the Book: The Problem of Regulatory Unreasonableness.* Philadelphia: Temple University Press.

Baron, J. N., P. D. Jennings and F. R. Dobbin. 1988. Mission Control? *American Sociological Review.* 53: 497–514.

Bartley, T. 2003. Certifying Forests and Factories. *Politics & Society.* 31: 433–464.

Becker, G. 1968. Crime and Punishment: An Economic Approach. *Journal of Political Economy.* 76: 1169–1217.

Berle, A. A. and G. C. Means. 1932. *The Modern Corporation and Private Property.* New York: Harcourt, Brace & World.

Bessen, S. M. and G. Saloner. 1988. *Compatibility Standards and the Market for Telecommunication Services.* Santa Monica, CA: Rand.

Boehmer-Christiansen, S. and J. Skea. 1991. *Acid Politics: Environmental and Energy Policies in Britain and Germany.* London: Belhaven Press.

Boli, J. and G. M. Thomas (eds.). 1999. *Constructing World Culture: International Non-Governmental Organizations since 1875.* Stanford University Press.

Borky, P., M. Glachant and F. Leveque. 1998. *Voluntary Approaches for Environmental Policy in OECD Countries: An Assessment.* Revised version. Paris: CERNA. Retrieved on 14 July 2000 from http://www.ensmo.fr/Fr/CERNA/CERNA.

Bound J., D. A. Jaeger and R. M. Baker. 1995. Problems with Instrumental Variables Estimation when the Correlation between the Instruments and the Endogenous Explanatory Variable is Weak. *Journal of the American Statistical Association.* 90 (June): 443–451.

Braithwaite, J. and P. Drahos. 2000. *Global Business Regulation.* Cambridge University Press.

Brandeis, L. D. 1914. *Other People's Money.* Retrieved on 9 July 2004 from http://library.louisville.edu/law/brandeis/opm-ch5.html.

Brehm, J. and J. T. Hamilton. 1996. Noncompliance in Environmental Reporting: Are Violators Ignorant, or Evasive, of the Law? *American Journal of Political Science.* 40: 444–477.

Bringer, R. P. and D. M. Benforado. 1994. Pollution Prevention and Total Quality Environmental Management. In R. V. Kolluro (ed.), *Environmental Strategies Handbook,* pp. 165–188. New York: McGraw Hill.

Brown, R. Steven. 2001. State Environmental Agency to Enforcement and Compliance. Retrieved on 2 January 2003 from http://www.sso.org/ecos/publications/ECOS%20RTC%20f.pdf.

Bryson, C. 1998. The Donora Fluoride Fog: A Secret History of America's Worst Air Pollution Disaster. *The Earth Island Journal.* Retrieved on 25 February 2003 from http://www.earthisland.org/eijournal/fall98/fe_fall98donora.html.

BSI. 2005a. *Who is British Standards?* Retrieved on 25 May 2005 from http://www.bsi-global.com/British_Standards/About/index.xalter.

BSI. 2005b. *What is BSI's Royal Charter?* Retrieved on 25 May 2005 from http://www.bsi-global.com/News/FAQ/Charter.xalter.

BSI. 2005c. *ISO 14001 Case Studies.* Retrieved on 25 May 2005 from http://emea.bsi-global.com/Environment/CaseStudies/index.xalter.

Buchanan, J. M. 1965. An Economic Theory of Clubs. *Economica.* 32: 1–14.

Bullard, R. D. 1990. *Dumping in Dixie: Race, Class, and Environment Quality.* Boulder, CO: Westview.

Cameron, A. and K. P. Trivedi. 1998. *Regression Analysis of Count Data.* New York: Cambridge University Press.

Carmin, J., N. Darnall and J. Mil-Homens. 2003. Stakeholder Involvement in the Design of U.S. Voluntary Environmental Programs. *Policy Studies Journal.* 31: 527–543.

Carpenter, D. P. 2001. *The Forging of Bureaucratic Autonomy.* Princeton University Press.

Carson, R. 1962. *The Silent Spring.* First Mariners book edition 2002. New York: Houghton Mifflin Company.

Cashore, B., G. Auld and D. Newsom. 2004. *Governing Through Markets.* New Haven: Yale University Press.

CEEM. 2000. ISO 14001 Registrations – North America, *Update*, Extra Edition, September 2000.

CEEM. 2001. ISO 14001 Registrations – North America, *Update*, Extra Edition, September 2001.

Chandler, A. D. 1980. Government versus Business: An American Phenomenon. In John T. Dunlop (ed.), *Business and Public Policy*, pp. 1–11. Boston: Harvard University Graduate School of Business Administration.

Chapple, W., A. Cook, V. Galt and D. Paton. 2001. The Characteristics and Attributes of UK Firms Obtaining Accreditation to ISO 14001. *Business Strategy & the Environment*. 10: 238–244.

Charter, M. and M. J. Polonsky (eds.). 2000. *Greener Marketing*. Sheffield: Greenleaf.

Christmann, P. and G. Taylor. 2001. Globalization and the Environment: Determinants of Firm-Self-Regulation in China. *Journal of International Business Studies*. 32: 439–458.

Clapp, J. 1998. The Privatization of Global Environmental Governance. *Global Governance*. 4: 295–316.

Cleary, E. J. 2002. Lesson for Lawyers from the Enron Debacle. Retrieved on 2 August 2005 from http://www2.mnbar.org/benchandbar/2002/apr02/prof-resp.htm.

Coase, R. H. 1960. The Problem of Social Cost. *Journal of Law and Economics*. 3: 1–44.

Coase, R. H. 1991. *Nobel Prize Lecture*. Retrieved on August 15 2005 from http://www.nobel.se/economics/laureates/1991/coase-lecture.html.

Coglianese, C. 1996. Litigating within Relationships: Disputes and Disturbances in the Regulatory Process. *Law and Society Review*. 30 (4): 735–765.

Coglianese, C. and J. Nash (eds.). 2001. *Regulating from Within*. Washington, DC: Resources for the Future Press.

Cole, D. H. and P. Grossman. 1999. When is Command and Control Efficient? *Wisconsin Law Review*. 5: 887–939.

Cole, R. E. 1989. *Strategies for Learning*. Berkeley: University of California Press.

Commons, J. R. 1961. *Institutional Economics: Its Place in Political Economy*. Madison, WI: University of Wisconsin Press.

Corbett, Charles J. and Michael V. Russo. 2001. ISO 14001: Irrelevant or Invaluable? *ISO Management Systems*. December 23–29.

Cornes, R. and T. Sandler. [1986]1996. *The Theory of Externalities, Public Goods, and Club Goods*. 2nd edition. Cambridge University Press.

Coursey, D., M. Issac and V. Smith. 1984. Natural Monopoly and Contested Markets: Some Experimental Results. *Journal of Law and Economics*. 27: 91–113.

Crow, M. 2000. Beyond Experiments. *The Environmental Forum*. 17: 18–29.

Cutler, C. A., V. Haufler, and T. Porter (eds.). 1999. *Private Authority and International Affairs*. Albany, NY: SUNY Press.

Dahlstrom, K., C. Howes, O. Leinster and J. Skea. 2003. Environmental Management Systems and Company Performance. *European Environment*. 13: 187–203.

Daly, H. 1993. The Perils of Free Trade. *Scientific American*. November: 51–55.

Dasgupta, S. and D. Wheeler. 1996. *Citizen Complaints as Environmental Indicators: Evidence from China*. World Bank Policy Research Department Working Paper, December.

Dasgupta, S., H. Hettige and D. Wheeler. 2000. What Improves Environmental Compliance? Evidence from Mexican Industry. *Journal of Environmental Economics and Management*. 39: 39–66.

David, P. A. 1985. Clio and the Economics of QWERTY. *American Economic Review Papers and Proceedings*. 75: 332–337.

Department of Environment, Food, and Rural Affairs (DEFR). 2003. *Environmental Reporting*. Retrieved on 18 September 2004 from http://www.defra.gov.uk/environment/envrp/.

DiMaggio, P. J. and W. W. Powell. 1983. The Iron Cage Revisited: Institutional Isomorphism and Collective Rationality in Organizational Fields. *American Sociological Review*. 48: 147–160.

Dolsak, N. and E. Ostrom (eds.). 2003. *The Commons in the New Millennium*. Cambridge, MA: MIT Press.

Dunning, J. H. 1993. *The Globalization of Business*. London: Routledge.

Eisner, M. E. 2004. Corporate Environmentalism, Regulatory Reform, and Industry Self-Regulation. *Governance*. 17: 145–167.

Environment Canada. 2003. About NPRI, retrieved on 10 August from http://www.ec.gc.ca/pdb/npri/npri_about_e.cfm.

Environmental Council of the States. 2001. State Environmental Agency Contribution to Enforcement and Compliance. *Environmental Law Review*. 23: 441–469.

Environmental Protection Agency (EPA). 1986. Environmental Auditing Policy Statement. *Federal Register*. 51: 25004–25006.

Environmental Protection Agency (EPA). 1995a. Voluntary Environmental Self-policing and Self Disclosure Interim Policy Statement. *Federal Register*. 60: 16875–16878.

Environmental Protection Agency (EPA). 1995b. Incentives for Self-Policing and Self Disclosure Interim Policy Statement. *Federal Register*. 60: 66706–66709.

Environmental Protection Agency (EPA). 1997. *Audit Policy Interpretive Guidance*, January 1997. Retrieved on 7 January 2000 from http://es.epa.gov/oeca.audpolguid.pdf.

Environmental Protection Agency (EPA). 1999a. *Project XL: 1999 Comprehensive Report*, Retrieved on 6 September 2002 from http://www.epa.gov/projectxl/.

Environmental Protection Agency (EPA). 1999b. *Action Plan for Promoting the Use of Environmental Management Systems*. Retrieved on 7 January 2000 from http://www.epa.gov/ems/plan99.htm.

Environmental Protection Agency (EPA). 2004. Annual Performance Reporting. Retrieved on 17 November 2004, from http://www.epa.gov/performancetrack/program/report.htm.

EPER. 2003. *Welcome to EPER*. Retrieved on 28 September 2004 from http://www.eper.cec.eu.int/eper/default.asp.

Europa. 2003. *Freedom to Access Information*. Retrieved on 28 September 2004 from http://europa.eu.int/scadplus/leg/en/lvb/l28091.htm.

Farrell, J. and G. Shapiro. 1985. Standardization, Compatibility, and Innovation. *Rand Journal of Economics*. 16: 70–83.

Feenstra, R. C. 2000. *World Trade Flows*. CD-ROM. University of California, Davis, Institute of Governmental Affairs.

Fiorinio, D. J. 1995. *Making Environmental Policy*. Berkeley: University of California Press.

Fiorinio, D. J. 1999. Rethinking Environmental Regulation. *Harvard Environmental Law Review*. 23: 441–469.

Fiorinio, D. J. 2001. Environmental Policy as Learning. *Public Administration Review*. 61: 322–334.

Fischer, K. and J. Schot (eds.). 1993. *Environmental Strategies for Industry*. Washington, DC: Island Press.

Florini, A. 2005. *The Coming Democracy*. Washington, DC: The Brookings Institution Press.

Frankel, J. A. 2003. The Environment and Globalization. Working Paper 10090. Cambridge, MA: NBER. www.nber.org/papers/w10090.

Freeman, R. E. 1984. *Strategic Management: A Stakeholder Approach*. Boston: Pittman.

Garcia-Johnson, R. 2001. *Exporting Environmentalism*. Cambridge, MA: MIT Press.

General Accounting Office (GAO). 1983. *Waste Water Dischargers are not Complying with EPA Pollution Control Limits*, RECED 84–53: Washington, DC.

General Accounting Office (GAO). 1994. *Toxic Substances: EPA Needs More Reliable Source Reduction Data and Progress Measures*. GAO/RCED 94–93.

Gereffi, G., R. Garcia-Johnson and E. Sasser. 2001. NGO-Industrial Complex. *Foreign Policy*. 125: 56–65.

Gibson, R. B. (ed.). 1999. *Voluntary Initiatives: The New Politics of Corporate Greening*. Ontario: Broadview Press.

Gormley, W. T., Jr. 1999. Regulatory Enforcement Styles. *Political Research Quarterly*. 51: 363–383.

Granovetter, M. 1985. Economic Action, Social Structure, and Embeddedness. *American Journal of Sociology*. 91: 481–510.

Greene, W. H. 1999. *Econometric Analysis*, 4th edition. New York: Prentice-Hall.

Grossman, G. M. and A. B. Krueger. 1995. Economic Growth and the Environment. *Quarterly Journal of Economics*. 110: 353–375.

Guillen, M. F. 1994. *Models of Management*. University of Chicago Press.

Guler, I., M. Guillen and J. M. MacPherson. 2002. Global Competition, Institutions, and Organizational Change: The International Diffusion of the ISO 9000 Quality Standards. *Administrative Science Quarterly*. 47: 207–232.

Gunningham, N. and P. Grabosky. 1998. *Smart Regulation*. Oxford University Press.

Gunningham, N. and D. Sinclair. 2002. *Leaders and Laggards*. Sheffield: Greenleaf.

Gunningham, N., R. Kagan, and D. Thornton. 2003. *Shades of Green: Business, Regulation, and Environment*. Stanford University Press.

Gupta, A. K. and L. J. Lad. 1983. Industry Self-Regulation: An Economic, Organizational, and Political Analysis. *The Academy of Management Review*. 8: 416–425.

Hajer, M. 1995. *The Politics of Environmental Discourse*. Oxford: Clarendon Press.

Hale, R. 1998. *The National Expansion of Star Track*, Boston: Environmental Protection Agency, Region I.

Hall, K. (ed.). 2000. *Oxford Companion to American Law*. New York: Oxford University Press.

Hall, P. 1986. *Governing the Economy*. New York: Oxford University Press.

Hall, R. and T. Biersteker (eds.). 2002. *The Emergence of Private Authority in Global Governance*. NewYork: Cambridge University Press.

Hamilton, J. T. 1995. Pollution as News: Media and Stock Market Reactions to the Toxic Release Inventory Data. *Journal of Environmental Economics and Management*. 28: 98–113.

Hardin, R. 1982. *Collective Action*. Baltimore: The Johns Hopkins University Press.

Harrison, K. and W. Antweiler. 2002. Incentives for Pollution Abatement. *Journal of Policy Analysis and Management*. 22: 361–382.

Haufler, V. 2001. *A Public Role for the Private Sector*, Washington, DC: Carnegie Endowment for International Peace.

Heckman, J. J. and V. J. Hotz. 1989. Choosing Among Alternative Non-experimental Methods for Estimating the Impact of Social Programs. *Journal of the American Statistical Association.* 84: 862–880.

Heckman, J. J. and R. Robb. 1985. Alternative Methods for Evaluating the Impact of Interventions. In J. Heckman and B. Singer (eds.). *Longitudinal Analysis of Labor Market Data*, pp. 156–246. New York: Cambridge University Press.

Henriques, I. and P. Sadorsky. 1996. The Determinants of an Environmentally Responsive Firm: An Empirical Approach. *Journal of Environmental Economics and Management.* 30: 381–395.

High-Tech Production. 2001. *Project XL Translates to Extra Lenient Deregulation.* Retrieved on 6 September 2002 from http://www.svtc.org/hightech_prod/liaisons/xl/xlaction.htm.

Hobbes, Thomas. 1651. *The Leviathan.* Retrieved on 15 August 2005 from http://oregonstate.edu/instruct/phl302/texts/hobbes/leviathan-contents.html.

Hoffman, A. J. 1997. *From Heresy to Dogma.* San Francisco: New Lexington Press.

Hoffman, A. J. and M. J. Ventresca (eds.). 2002. *Organizations, Policy and the Natural Environment.* Stanford University Press.

Honda. 2005. *Environmental Leadership.* Retrieved on 6 May 2005 from http://corporate.honda.com/environment/awards.aspx.

Housman, V. A. 2001. *State Audit Privilege and Immunity Laws*, email, 16, November 2001. On file.

Hunt, C. B. and E. R. Auster. 1990. Proactive Environmental Management. *Sloan Management Review.* 31: 7–18.

Imbens, G. W. 2004. Nonparametric Estimation of Average Treatment Effects Under Exogeneity. *Review of Economics and Statistics.* 86: 4–29.

Inglehart, R. 1977. *The Silent Revolution.* Princeton University Press.

ISO. 2002. *Environmental Management: The ISO 14000 Family of International Standards.* Retrieved on 2 June 2003 from http://www.iso.ch/iso/en/prods-services/otherpubs/iso14000/index.html.

ISO. 2003. *The ISO Survey of ISO 9000 and ISO 14000 Certificates: Twelfth Cycle.* Retrieved on 9 February, 2003 from wysiwyg://10/http:/www.iso.ch/iso/en/iso9000-14000/iso14000/iso14000index.html.

ISO. 2004a. *ISO, The Founding of ISO.* Retrieved on 19 July 2004 from http://www.iso.org/iso/en/aboutiso/introduction/fifty/pdf/foundingen.pdf.

ISO. 2004b. *Frequently Asked Questions on ISO 14001.* Retrieved on 19 July 2004 from http://www.iso.org/iso/en/aboutiso/introduction/index.html.

ISO. 2004c. *ISO 9000 and ISO 14000 – In Brief*. Retrieved on 20 July 2004 from http://www.iso.org/iso/en/iso9000-14000/index.html.

ISO. 2005a. *Introduction*. Retrieved on 10 August 2005 from http://www.iso.org/iso/en/info/ISODirectory/intro.html#.

ISO. 2005b. *The ISO Directory of ISO 9000 and ISO 14000 Accreditation and Certification Bodies*. Retrieved on 10 August 2005 from http://www.iso.org/iso/en/info/ISODirectory/countries.html.

Jaffe, A., S. Peterson, P. Portney and R. Stavins. 1995. Environmental Regulation and Competitiveness of US Manufacturing. *Journal of Economic Literature*. 33: 132–163.

Jones, B. D. 2001. *Politics and the Architecture of Choice: Bounded Rationality and Governance*. University of Chicago Press.

Juran, J. M. 1962. The Economics of Quality. In J. M. Jurna (ed.). *Quality Control Handbook*. pp. 1–31. New York: McGraw Hill.

Kagan, R. A. 1991. Adversary Legalism and American Government. *Journal of Policy Analysis and Management*. 10: 369–406.

Kagan, R. A. and L. Axelrad (eds.). 2000. *Regulatory Encounters*. Berkeley: University of California Press.

Kahn, M. 2002. Demographic Change and the Demand for Environmental Regulation. *Journal of Policy Analysis and Management*. 21: 45–62.

Kane, T. J. 1994. College Entry by Blacks since 1970. *The Journal of Political Economy*. 102: 878–911.

Keohane, R. O. 1989. International Institutions: Two Approaches. *International Studies Quarterly*. 32: 379–396.

Kettl, D. F. (ed.). 2002. *Environmental Governance: A Report on the Next Generation of Environmental Policy*. Washington, DC: Brookings Institution.

Khanna, M. and L. A. Damon. 1999. EPA's Voluntary 33/50 Program: Impact on Toxic Releases and Economic Performance of Firms. *Journal of Environmental Economics and Management*. 37: 1–25.

Khanna, M., W. Quimio and D. Bojilova. 1998. Toxic Release Information: A Policy Tool for Environmental Protection. *Journal of Environmental Economics and Management*. 36: 243–266.

King, A. and M. Lenox. 2000. Industry Self-Regulation without Sanctions: The Chemical Industry's Responsible Care Program. *Academy of Management Journal*. 43: 698–716.

King, G. 1989. *Unifying Political Methodology: The Likelihood Theory of Statistical Inference*. New York: Cambridge University Press.

Knight, F. H. 1924. Some Fallacies in the Interpretation of Social Costs. *Quarterly Journal of Economics*. 38: 582–606.

Kolk, A. 2000. *The Economics of Environmental Management*, Harlow: Financial Times.

Kollman, K. and A. Prakash. 2001. Green by Choice? *World Politics*. 53: 399–430.

Konar, S. and M. A. Cohen. 1997. Information as Regulation. *Journal of Environmental Economics and Management*. 32: 109–124.

Kusek, L. 2003. *New Responsible Care Performance Requirements Adopted*. Retrieved on 7 July 2003 from http://www.americanchemistry.com/.

Levi, M. 1988. *Of Rule and Revenue*. Los Angeles and Berkeley: University of California Press.

Liebowitz, S. J. and S. E. Margolis. 1995. Are Network Externalities a New Source of Market Failure? *Research in Law and Economics*. 17: 1–22.

Long, J. S. 1997. *Regression Models for Categorical and Limited Dependent Variables*. Thousand Oaks: Sage Publications.

Lowe, P. and J. Goyder. 1983. *Environmental Groups in Politics*. London: Allen and Unwin.

Lubell, M., M. Schneider, J. Scholz and M. Mete. 2002. Watershed Partnerships and the Emergence of Collective Action Institutions. *American Journal of Political Science*. 46: 148–163.

Luce, R. and H. Raiffa. 1957. *Games and Decisions*. New York: Wiley.

Lyon, T. P. and J. W. Maxwell. 2004. *Corporate Environmentalism and Public Policy*. Cambridge University Press.

Maddala, G. S. 1983. *Limited-dependent and Qualitative Variables in Econometrics*. New York: Cambridge University Press.

Majumdar, S. and A. Marcus. 2001. Rules versus Discretion. *Academy of Management Journal*. 44: 170–179.

March, J. and J. Olsen. 1989. *Rediscovering Institutions*. New York: Free Press.

Marcus, A., D. A. Geffen and K. Sexton. 2002. *Reinventing Environmental Regulations: Lessons from Project XL*. Washington, DC: Resources for the Future.

Martindale-Hubbell. 2000. *Martindale-Hubbell International Law Directory – III*. New Providence, NJ: Martindale-Hubbell.

Mattli, W. 2001. Private Justice in a Global Economy. *International Organization*. 55: 919–947.

Mattli, W. and T. Büthe. 2003. Setting International Standards: Technological Rationality or Primacy of Power? *World Politics*. 56: 1–42.

Mayo, E. 1945. *The Social Problems of an Industrial Civilization*. Salem, NH: Ayer.

Mazurek, J. 1998. The Use of Voluntary Agreements in the United States. OECD, ENV/ EPOC/ GEEI(98)27/ FINAL, Retrieved on 31 July 2000 from http://www.oecd.org/env/docs/epocgeei9827.

McGuire, M. 1972. Private Goods Clubs and Public Goods Club. *Swedish Journal of Economics*. 74: 84–99.

Meidinger, E. E. 2000. *How Environmental Certification Systems are Likely to Affect the US Legal System*, Draft 1.2. Retrieved on 15 June 2000 from http://www.ublaw.buffalo.edu/fas/meidinger/certlaw.pdf.

Metzenbaum, S. H. 2002. Measurement that Matters: Cleaning up Charles River. In Donald F. Kettl (ed.). *Environmental Governance*, pp. 58–117. Washington, DC: Brookings Institutions Press.

Michels, S. 1995. *What's Next for the EPA?* 21 December 1995. Transcript. http://www.pbs.org/newshour/bb/environment/epa_12-21.html 08/ 05/ 2003.

Milgrom, P., D. C. North and B. Weingast. 1990. The Role of Institutions in the Revival of Trade. *Economics and Politics*. 2: 1–23.

Millstone. 2005. *Changing the World, Bean by Bean*. Retrieved on 16 August 2005 from http://www.millstone.com/pages/pressroom/display_article.jsp?id=13type=news.

Mitchell, R., B. Agle and D. Wood. 1997. Toward a Theory of Stakeholder Identification and Salience. *Academy of Management Review*. 22: 853–886.

Mol, A. and D. Sonnenfeld (eds.). 2000. *Ecological Modernisation Around the World*. Portland, OR: Frank Cass.

Morandi, Larry. 1998. *State Environmental Audit Laws and Policies*, Washington, DC: National Conference of State Legislatures.

National Academy of Public Administration/NAPA. 2001. *Third-Party Auditing of Environmental Management Systems*. Washington, DC: NAPA.

Natural Resource Defense Council (NRDC). 1997. *The Story of Silent Spring*. Retrieved on 25 February 2003 from http://www.nrdc.org/health/pesticides/hcarson.asp.

Nelson, P. 1970. Information and Consumer Behaviour. *Journal of Political Economy*. 78: 311–329.

New York Times. 2005. *Don't Buy SFI*. 20 May. Retrieved on 10 August 2005 from http://www.dontbuysfi.com/home/.

Ng, Y. K. 1973. The Economic Theory of Clubs. *Economica*. 41: 308–321.

North, D. C. 1990. *Institutions, Institutional Change and Economic Performance*. New York: Cambridge University Press.

Office of Management and Budget (OMB). 2002. *Report to Congress on the Costs and Benefits of Federal Regulations*. Retrieved on 26 July 2003 from http://www.whitehouse.gov/omb/inforeg/chap2.html.

Oliver, C. 1991. Strategic Responses to Institutional Processes. *Academy of Management Review*. 16: 145–179.

Olson, M., Jr. 1965. *The Logic of Collective Action*. Cambridge, MA: Harvard University Press.

Organization for Economic Cooperation and Development (OECD). 1989. *Economic Instruments for Environmental Protection*, Paris: OECD.

Organization for Economic Cooperation and Development (OECD). 2001. *Economic Outlook*, No. 70, December 2001. Retrieved on 28 August 2003 from http://www.oecdwash.org/NEWS/LOCAL/oecdwash-jun2002.pdf.

Osborne, D. and T. Gaebler. 1992. *Reinventing Government*. Boston: Addison Wesley.

Ostrom, E. 1990. *Governing the Commons*. New York: Cambridge University Press.

Ostrom, E. 1991. Rational Choice Theory and Institutional Analysis. *American Political Science Review*. 85: 237–243.

Ostrom, V. and E. Ostrom. 1977. Public Goods and Public Choice. In E. S. Savas (ed.). *Alternatives for Delivering Public Services*. pp. 7–49. Boulder, CO: Westview.

Overdevest, C. 2005. Treadmill Politics, Information Politics, and Public Policy. *Organization & Environment*. 18: 72–90.

Painting and Coating Resource Center (PCRC). 2000. *Air Pollution Control Equipment*. Retrieved on 27 July 2005 from http://www.paintcenter.org/ctc/Define2.cfm.

Palmer, K., W. E. Oates and P. R. Portney. 1995. Tightening Environmental Standards. *Journal of Economic Perspective*. 9: 119–132.

Pargal, S. and D. Wheeler. 1996. Informal Regulation of Industrial Pollution in Developing Countries: Evidence from Indonesia. *Journal of Political Economy*. 104: 1314–1327.

Pfaff, A. and C. Sanchirico. 2000. Environmental Self-Auditing: Setting the Proper Incentives for Discovery and Correction of Environmental Harm. *Journal of Law Economics and Organization*. 16: 189–208.

Pigou, A. C. 1960[1920]. *The Economics of Welfare*. 4th edition. London: MacMillan.

Porter, M. 1991. America's Green Strategy. *Scientific American*. April: 168.

Porter, M. and C. V. der Linde. 1995. Toward a New Conception of the Environment–Competitiveness Relationship. *Journal of Economic Perspectives*. 9: 97–118.

Potoski, M. 2001. Clean Air Federalism: Do States Race to the Bottom? *Public Administration Review*. 61: 335–342.

Power, M. 1994. *The Audit Explosion*. London: Demos.

Power, M. 1997. *The Audit Society*. Oxford University Press.

Prakash, A. 2000a. *Greening the Firm*. Cambridge University Press.

Prakash, Aseem. 2000b. Responsible Care: An Assessment. *Business & Society*. 39: 183–209.

Prakash, A. 2002. Green Marketing, Public Policy, and Managerial Strategies. *Business Strategy and the Environment*. 11: 285–297.

PricewaterhouseCoopers LLP. 2002. *2002 Sustainability Survey Report*, www.pwcglobal.com/eas.

Putnam, R. D. 1995. Bowling Alone. *Journal of Democracy.* 6: 65–78.

Rabe, B. G. 2002. Permitting, Prevention, and Integration. In Donald F. Kettl (ed.). *Environmental Governance*, pp. 14–57. Washington, DC: Brookings Institution Press.

Rapoport, A. and A. Chammah. 1965. *Prisoner's Dilemmas: A Study of Conflict and Cooperation.* Ann Arbor: University of Michigan Press.

Rees, J. 1997. The Development of Communitarian Regulation in the Chemical Industry. *Law and Policy.* 19: 477.

Regen, J. L., B. J. Seldon and E. Elliott. 1997. Modeling Compliance to Environmental Regulation. *Journal of Policy Modeling.* 19: 683–696.

Registrar Accreditation Board (RAB). 2004a. *Frequently Asked Questions.* Retrieved on 21 July 2004, from http://www.rabnet.com/er_faq.shtml.

Registrar Accreditation Board (RAB). 2004b. *Frequently Asked Questions About ISO 14001 EMS CRBs.* Retrieved on 21 July 2004 from http://www.rabnet.com/er_faq.shtml#q15.

Reilly, W. K. 1999. Foreword. In K. Sexton, A. Marcus, K. William and T. Burkhardt (eds.). *Better Environmental Decisions*, pp. xi–xv. Washington, DC: Island Press.

Ringquist, E. 1993. *Environmental Protection at the State Level: Politics, and Progress in Controlling Pollution.* Armonk, NY: Sharpe.

Roht-Arriaza, N. 1997. Environmental Management System and Environmental Protection. *Journal of Environment and Development.* 6: 292–316.

Rugman, A. and A. Verbeke. 1998. Corporate Strategies and Environmental Regulations. *Strategic Management Journal.* 19: 363–375.

Russo, M. V. 2001. *Institutional Change and Theories of Organizational Strategy.* Retrieved on 7 November 2004 from http://lcb1.uoregon.edu/mrusso/ISOstudy.htm.

Sablatura, B. 1995. With Superfund, Lawyers Clean Up. *Houston Chronicle.* Retrieved on 13 November 2003 from http://www.chron.com/content/chronicle/page1/95/10/23/txmain23.html.

Samuelson, P. A. 1954. A Pure Theory of Public Expenditure. *Review of Economic and Statistics.* 36: 387–389.

Sand, P. H. 2002. The Right to Know. Retrieved on 20 July 2004 from www.inece.org/forumspublicaccess_sand.pdf.

Sasser, E., A. Praaksh, B. Cashore and G. Auld. 2005. Direct Targeting as NGO Political Strategy: Examining Private Authority Regimes in the Forestry Sector. Unpublished manuscript.

Sayre, D. 1996. *Inside ISO 14000.* Delray Beach, FL: St. Lucie Press.

Schaltegger, S., R. Burritt and H. Petersen. 2003. *An Introduction to Corporate Environmental Management*. Sheffield: Greenleaf.

Schelling, T. 1969. Models of Segregation. *American Economic Review.* 59: 488–493.

Scholz, J. T. 1991. Cooperative Regulatory Enforcement and the Politics of Administrative Effectiveness, *American Political Science Review.* 85: 115–136.

Scholz, J. T. and W. B. Gray. 1997. Can Government Facilitate Cooperation? An Informational Model of OSHA Enforcement. *American Journal of Political Science.* 41: 693–717.

Sharma, S. and H. Vredenburg. 1998. Proactive Corporate Strategy and Development of Competitively Valuable Organizational Capabilities. *Strategic Management Journal.* 19: 729–753.

Simon, H. A. 1957. *Models of Man.* New York: John Wiley.

Smith, A. 1776. An Inquiry into the Nature and Causes of the Wealth of Nations, Book. IV, Chapter 2. Retrieved on 4 August 2003 from http://www.bartleby.com/66/99/54299.html.

Steinzor, R. I. 1998. Reinventing Environmental Regulation: The Dangerous Journey from Command to Self-Control. *Harvard Environmental Law Review.* 22: 103.

Stern, D. I. 2005. Global Sulfur Emissions from 1850 to 2000. *Chemosphere.* 58: 163–175.

Stigler, G. 1971. The Theory of Economic Regulation. *Bell Journal of Economics.* 2: 3–21.

Stiglitz, J. 2001. *Information and the Challenge in the Change in the Paradigm in Economics*, Prize Lecture. Retrieved on 15 May 2005 from 2001http://nobelprize.org/economics/laureates/2001/stiglitz-lecture.pdf.

Teubner, G. 1983. Substantive and Reflexive Law Elements in Modern Law. *Law and Society Review.* 17: 239–285.

Tiebout, C. M. 1956. A Pure Theory of Public Expenditure. *Journal of Political Economy.* 64: 416–424.

Tietenberg, T. 1974. The Design of Property Rights for Air Pollution Control. *Public Policy.* 27: 275–292.

Tietenberg, T. 2002. Tradable Permit Approach to Protecting the Commons. In E. Ostrom, T. Dietz, N. Dolsak, P. Stern, S. Stonich and E. Weber (eds.). *The Drama of the Commons*, pp. 197–232. Washington, DC: National Academy Press.

UNCTAD. 2000. *Trains for Trade*. Retrieved on 9 September 2004 from http://r0.unctad.org/trade_env/rene/mod6entext.doc.

UNCTAD. 2002. *World Investment Report*. Geneva: UNCTAD.

Union of International Associations. 1997. *Yearbook of International Organizations*. Munich: K. G. Saur.

Verdonik, J. 2005. *What Changes Enron Will Cause in the Accounting Industry*. Retrieved on 2 August 2005 from http://www.boardstrategies.com/stores_sol/boarddoctor/changesenroncause.html.

Videras, J. and A. Alberini. 2000. The Appeal of Voluntary Environmental Programs. *Contemporary Economic Policy*. 18: 449–461.

Vogel, D. 1986. *National Styles of Regulations*. Ithaca, NY: Cornell University Press.

Vogel, D. 1995. *Trading Up*. Cambridge, MA: Harvard University Press.

Walley, N. and B. Whitehead. 1994. It's Not Easy Being Green. *Harvard Business Review*. May–June: 46–51.

Watchdog Alert. 2004. *Missouri Pushes "Polluter Protection" Law*. State Environmental Resource Center. Retrieved on 18 September 2004 from http://www.serconline.org/watchdog/watchdog2004/watchdog5.html.

Webb, Kernaghan. 2004. Understanding the Voluntary Codes Phenomenon. In Kernaghan Webb (ed.). *Voluntary Codes: Private Governance, the Public Interest and Innovation*, pp. 1–30. Ottawa: Carleton Research Unit for Innovation, Science and Environment.

Weimer, D. and A. Vining. [1988]1999. *Policy Analysis: Concepts and Practice*. 3rd edition. Englewood Cliffs, NJ: Prentice Hall.

Welch, E., A. Mazur and S. Bretschneider. 2000. Voluntary Behavior by Electric Utilities. *Journal of Policy Analysis and Management*. 19: 407–425.

Weyerhauser. 2005. *Certification: Current Status*. Retrieved on 16 August 2005 from http://www.weyerhaeuser.com/environment/certification/currentstatus.asp.

Williams, R. L. 2000. A Note on Robust Variance Estimation for Cluster-Correlated Data. *Biometrics*. 56: 645–646.

Williamson, O. E. 1985. *Economic Institutions of Capitalism*. New York: Free Press.

Winter, S. C. and P. J. May. 2001. Motivation for Compliance with Environmental Regulations. *Journal of Policy Analysis and Management*. 20: 675–698.

Wiseman, J. 1957. The Theory of Public Utility – An Empty Box. *Oxford Economic Papers*. 9: 56–74.

Wolf, C. 1979. A Theory of Nonmarket Failure: Framework for Implementation Analysis. *Journal of Law and Economics*. 22: 107.

World Bank. 1992. *The East Asian Miracle*. New York: Oxford University Press.

World Bank. 2000. *Greening Industry*. New York: Oxford University Press.

World Bank. 2002. *World Development Report*. New York: Oxford
    University Press.
World Economic Forum/WEF. 2002. *Global Competitiveness Report 2001–
    2002*. New York: Oxford University Press.
Zywicki, T. 1999. Environmental Externalities and Political Externalities.
    Tulsa Law Review. 73: 845–921.

Name index

Subject index